SLAVE ANCESTRAL RESEARCH
It's Something Else

Supplement to
*The Jackson-Moore
Family History
and
Genealogy*

Mary L. Jackson Fears

Foreword by
Charles L. Blockson, Ph.D.

HERITAGE BOOKS
2019

HERITAGE BOOKS
AN IMPRINT OF HERITAGE BOOKS, INC.

Books, CDs, and more—Worldwide

For our listing of thousands of titles see our website
at
www.HeritageBooks.com

Published 2019 by
HERITAGE BOOKS, INC.
Publishing Division
5810 Ruatan Street
Berwyn Heights, Md. 20740

Copyright © 1995 Mary L. Jackson Fears

Heritage Books by the author:
*Civil War and Living History Reenacting: About "People of Color"
How to Begin, What to Wear, Why Reenact*
Slave Ancestral Research: It's Something Else

Parts of this book appear as Chapter Seven in a summarized version in
The Jackson-Moore Family History and Genealogy by the author. c1995

Please direct all correspondence to:
Mary L. Jackson Fears
722 Mercedes Avenue
Daytona Beach, Florida 32114

Library of Congress Catalog Card Number: 95-75312

All rights reserved. No part of this book may be reproduced or transmitted in any form or by any means, electronic or mechanical, including photocopying, recording or by any information storage and retrieval system without written permission from the author, except for the inclusion of brief quotations in a review.

International Standard Book Number: 978-0-7884-0200-5

DEDICATION

In loving memory of my daughter, Julie LaVera Anderson, whose life was a testimony of Christian love and kindness; with whom I shared many times the meaning of this verse:

> "All things work together for good to them that love God, to them who are the called according to his purpose." Romans 8:28

CONTENTS

List of Charts	vii
List of Illustrations	vii
Foreword	xi
Acknowledgements	xii
Introduction	xiii
List of Abbreviations	xv

1. My Discovery of Grandpa Simon and Grandma Tildy McCants — 1

2. Slave Ancestral Research — 7

3. Taylor County Court Records — 21

4. A Discovery — 33

5. Are These My Folks: Abram, Emily, and Mary on Catharine Daniel's Inventory and Sale of Perishable Property? — 39

6. He's the One, John McCrary — 51

7. Talbot County Returns — 55

8. A Light at the End of the Tunnel — 59
    Beneath Taylor County Sod — 60
     On to Talbot County — 61
    On to Atlanta and the Georgia Archives — 67
    A Rude Awakening — 69
    Questions, Questions, Questions — 73

9. From Pillar to Post — 75

10. Baldwin County Probate Records — 77
    RECORD GROUP No. 1 Bartley McCrary — 79
     Jenny Poindexter — 81
     "Oh Lord, How Come We Here?" — 83

    RECORD GROUP No. 2 John McCrary, Sr. — 89
     Warren County Records — 93

    RECORD GROUP No. 3 Jonathan McCrary — 97

    RECORD GROUP No. 4 Isaac McCrary — 105

    RECORD GROUP No. 5 Robert McCrary — 111

    RECORD GROUP No. 6 William McCrary — 115
    Hiring Day — 121
    Matthew McCrary — 123
    RECORD GROUP No. 7 John McCrary (d.1854) — 125

11.	A Name, A Name, What Name Shall I Take?	143
12.	Where to Go From Here	147
	July 7, 1993, A Day Remembered	148
13.	The Day I Found My Folks	153
14.	John McCrary, 1789-1854, Estate Records	155
	The Division and Whereabouts of "Old Visues"	189
15.	Revelations from Revolutionary War Records	209
16.	The Transfer Chart	215
17.	"All Things Work Together For Good"	219
	The Metamorphosis of a Name	222
18.	Missing Links, Divine Guidance and John McCrary	225
19.	So Little to Go On, Reflections	231
20.	The Descendants of Luveser McCrary	235
	Notes	253
	Glossary	258
	Selected Bibliography	259
	Index	264
	About the Author	269

ILLUSTRATIONS

Charts		Following Page
1.	Lineage Chart	xvi
2.	Transfer Chart	217
3.	Missing Links	224
4.	Descendants of Luveser McCrary	236

Figures

7-1.	1900 Taylor County Georgia Census	2
7-1A.	1900 Soundex	3
7-2.	1870 Taylor County Georgia Census	8
7-2A.	1870 Taylor County Georgia Census	8
7-2B.	1880 Taylor County Georgia Census	8
7-2C.	1880 Taylor County Georgia Census	9
7-2D.	Charley Ray and Dorcas Holton Marriage Record	10
	1900 Berrien County Georgia Census	11
7-3.	Simon McCants and Matilda McCants Marriage Record	12
7-4.	Abel Johnson and Missouri McCants Marriage Record	13
7-5.	Slave Owners in Talbot and Taylor Counties in 1850 and 1860	17
7-6.	1850 Talbot County Georgia Slave Schedule, John B. McCrary	19
7-7.	Inventories and Appraisements Form William R. Miller	20
	Forms for copying Estate Inventories and Returns	25-26
7-8.	Death Certificate of Emma Davis	27
7-8A.	Inventory and Appraisements, Esais Taylor	28
7-8B.	Inventory of Sam'l P. Corbin	29
7-9A.	1860 Taylor County Georgia Slave Schedule,	31
7-9B.	Inventory and Appraisements, James Duncan	32
7-10.	Inventory and Appraisements, Catharine Daniel	37
7-11A.	Advertising in Georgia Journal and Messenger	38
	Leave to Sell Negroes	
	Catharine Daniel, "Sale of Negroes"	41

7-12A.	1850 Upson County Georgia Slave Schedule Eve Ragland and Catharne Daniel	42
7-12B.	1860 Upson County Georgia Census	43
7-13.	Annual Return of Catharine Daniel	44
7-14A.	1910 Taylor County Georgia Census	45
7-14B.	1920 Soundex Bibb County Georgia	46
7-15.	Inventory and Appraisements, John McCrary, Deceased c.1854	49-50
7-15A.	1850 Talbot County Slave Schedule, John McCrary	53
7-15B.	Talbot County Georgia Census of John McCary	54
7-16.	Talbot County Returns	57
7-17.	Troup County Georgia Deed, Henry Long	63-64
7-17.	Troup County Slave Sale, Wm. Beasley	65-66
7-18.	Baldwin County Georgia Tax Digest, Excerpts	68
7-19.	1870 Taylor County Georgia Census	71
7-19A.	1880 Taylor County Manufactures Schedule	72

RECORD GROUP No. 1

7-20.	Hiring Record, Bartley McCrary, Baldwin County Ga.	76
7-21.	Inventory and Appraisements, Bartley McCrary	78
7-22.	Estate Division, Bartley McCrary	80
7-23.	Sale of Negroes, Jenny Poindexter Baldwin County Georgia	82
7-24.	Inventory and Appraisements, Jenny Poindexter	85
7-25.	Estate Sale, Jenny Poindexter	86

RECORD GROUP No. 2

7-26.	Appraisers, Property, John McCrary, Deceased c.1814 Baldwin County Georgia	87-88
7-27.	Estate Division, John McCrary, Deceased c.1814 Warren County Georgia Records	90
7-27A.	Sale of Property, Real and Personal, Estate of Lettice McCrary, Warren County Georgia	92
7-27B.	Inventory and Appraisements, Matthew McCrary, Deceased c.1816, Warren County Georgia	94
7-27C.	Estate Division, Matthew McCrary Warren County Georgia	95

RECORD GROUP No. 3

7-28.	Inventory and Appraisements, Jonathan McCrary Baldwin County Georgia	96
7-29.	Estate Division, Jonathan McCrary	98
7-30.	Returns, William Grigg, Guardian of Minors, Jonathan McCrary, Deceased c.1808	100
7-30.	Hiring Record, Jonathan McCrary Estate	101
7-31.	William Grigg, Guardian, Slave Transfer Record	102

RECORD GROUP No. 4

7-32.	Appraisement Record, Isaac McCrary Baldwin County Georgia	104
7-33.	Returns, Negro Hirings, Property Sale, Isaac McCrary	106
7-34.	Estate Division, Isaac McCrary	108

RECORD GROUP No. 5

7-35.	Sale of Negroes, Robert McCrary Baldwin County Georgia	110
7-36.	Estate Division, Robert McCrary	112

RECORD GROUP No. 6

7-37.	Inventory, William McCrary	114
7-38.	Guardianship Transfer, Hiring Records, William McCrary	116
7-38	Hiring Record, Slave Name Omitted	119
7-39.	Return, Matthew McCrary, Deceased c.1846 Talbot County Georgia	123
7-39A	Separating "Man" From "Mare"	124

RECORD GROUP No. 7

7-40.	Inventory and Appraisements, John McCrary, Deceased c.1854	125-128
7-41.	1850 Talbot County Georgia Slave Schedule, John McCrary	130
	1860 Talbot County Georgia Slave Schedule, Henry McCrary	132
7-42.	1870 Taylor County Georgia Census, Excerpts ("Freedmen")	134
7-43.	Sale of Perishable Property, John McCrary, Deceased c.1854	135-140

JOHN McCRARY ESTATE PAPERS

7-44.	Georgia Journal and Messenger, Nov. 22, 1854 Advertisement, Sale of Personal Property, John McCrary, Deceased c.1854	149-150 151
7-45.	Petition for Letters of Guardianship John McCrary, Deceased c.1854	156
7-46.	John McCrary, Deceased c.1854, Estate Papers 158-177	
7-47.	Estate Division, John McCrary, Deceased c.1854	178-184
7-47A.	1860 Taylor County Georgia Slave Schedules of Distributees, John McCrary's Estate	186-187
7-47B.	Inventory and Appraisements, Andrew McCants, Deceased c.1862	188
7-47C.	Transfer of Slaves, Andrew McCants, Administrator of George R. McCants	192
7-47D.	Appraisements, George R. McCants, Deceased c.1851	194

7-48.	Estate Division, Summary Statements, John McCrary, Deceased c.1854	196-200
7-49.	Pay Bill, Capt. James Dillard, Revolutionary War Record	203-206
7-49A.	1796 Hancock County Georgia Tax Digest, John McCrary	214
7-50A.	National Archives copy, 1870 Taylor County Georgia Census p. 311	223
7-50B.	Return, Bartley McCrary	226
MAPS		
Map 1	County Map of Georgia, TRACKS AND TRAILS	230
	Family Photographs	239-250
	Key to Photographs	251-252

FOREWORD

Slave Ancestral Research: It's Something Else continues the proud tradition of uncovering the roots of African people in the Diaspora that began in earnest with the appearance of works such as Alex Haley's Roots and my own Black Genealogy in 1977.

I had no idea at the time that Black Genealogy was published that African-Americans would begin in such large numbers to research their heritages. Alex Haley's Roots, a quasi-historical epic that was later turned into a television miniseries, sparked a popular interest in family lineage that transcended the African-American community. I am pleased to see the fruition of Ms. Fears's fourteen year labor of love and passion, the latest in a growing ownership of our powerful scattered past.

Different authors have taken different approaches to documenting their search for the African past. My friends, Norma Jean and Carole Darden, for example, traced their lineage through food in their text Spoonbread and Strawberry Wine. The proliferation in tracing African roots, in the United States, in the Carribbean, in South America and even on the continent of Africa itself, has seen a myriad of different approaches to the subject. African people have learned to utilize resources such as computer databases and genealogical records. They have also organized family reunions as never before and even started national and local African-American genealogical societies.

Ms. Fears is to be commended for blending the best of these new traditions and literary styles in Something Else. Through her diligence, she has navigated thousands of public documents to trace her family history, weaving her journey into a narrative of discovery. Her saga, which warms the heart and soothes the soul of a people thirsting for a broader sense of identity, is fact written in the prose style, surpassing even the Haley fictional account with regard to historical veracity and authenticity. Thanks to Ms. Fears, African-Americans will have a renewed sense of the possible with regard to their own search for roots.

In addition, people of other races, creeds and colors will be inspired to begin the search for self that is so richly rewarded when family genealogy is earnestly pursued. This is due in no small part to Ms. Fears's personalization of the figures in her family history, beginning with Luveser McCrary in 1814. It is also due to the warm story of her successes and her failures, which humanizes the search for roots and retrieves it from the realm of stuffy and often overvalued "professional searchers." With love and patience and a lot of hard work, anyone can find out something about their family past.

While being able to tell the youngest members of a family of African descent about the first of their lineage to be brought to this hemisphere does not excuse the terrible crime of the Holocaust of enslavement, it does go a long way in restoring the human dignity and personhood of those initially enslaved. Luveser McCrary lives thanks to a great, great, great, great granddaughter. In the African tradition, no ancestor dies until there is no one left to speak their name. Thanks to the work of Mary Jackson Fears and other cultural workers of her courage and concern, many of the thousands gone and crossed over are being brought back into the land of the living memory.

Charles L. Blockson

Charles L. Blockson, Curator
The Charles L. Blockson Afro-American Collection

ACKNOWLEDGEMENTS

I want to thank the very helpful ladies at the Family History Center, Lake Mary, Florida; Librarian, Mary DeCaria at Bethune-Cookman College, Daytona Beach, FL; librarians in the Genealogy Department of Orlando Public Library, Orlando, Florida, especially Eileen Willis; Jan McLendon at the Georgia Archives, Atlanta, GA and Jeannette Jones at the Daughters of the American Revolution Library, Washington, DC for research assistance. Sincere and deep appreciation to my hosts, cousin LaVerne Jackson Jones and her husband Bernard for ferreting me around in Washington, DC to the Library of Congress, National Archives and other research centers. Two persons now deceased, Thelma Singleton Hudson and Marcelee Jones Holton, laid the groundwork for the success of this roots search by giving key information about the Holton family at the very beginning of this project. I treasure their memory and contribution to this research.

Heartfelt love and appreciation is expressed to my husband, Joel Van Fears, Sr. who traveled to many cities taking me on "Roots" trips to research centers and visits with relatives. I especially thank him for assistance in the preparation of the manuscript. Without his love and support, this work could not have been done. Thanks to my son Joel, Jr., for patience at mealtimes as I worked on the manuscript. Thanks to son, John H. Anderson and grandson John, Jr. for research assistance. Special thanks to my long-time friends and genealogy pals Laura Raines Jones, Faye Ellison Council and Arlene Echols for timely research tips and inspiration. Thanks to John Kemper for making the computer ancestral chart. Thanks to Toni Prevost, Margaret Lawrence, Dolores Richardson and Sallie Shelton Culver for reading the manuscript and their comments.

Thanks to the best family history writing instructor ever, Jan Florence Godown, for editorial consulting. Thanks to Dr. Milbrew Davis for encouragement and suggestions. Special recognition and thanks to my college classmate and mentor, Dr. Jake C. Miller, for his steadfast interest, encouragement and most valuable assistance during the writing.

February, 1995   Mary L. Jackson Fears
Daytona Beach, Florida

INTRODUCTION

This is the story of the search for my great grandmother Emma's great grandmother, Luveser McCrary. Luveser McCrary was my Seventh Generation slave ancestor. This work began as Chapter Seven in my family history book, and is the Supplement to the publication, *THE JACKSON-MOORE FAMILY HISTORY AND GENEALOGY*. As I did the research, I narrated my progress as a story. Genealogists recommended a separate publication as my experience would make a valuable contribution to the literature on slave ancestral research.

This work is not considered a "how-to" guide in genealogy. There are other publications named in the bibliography which serve that purpose. My purpose is to narrate the details of my roots search in a manner to inspire others. The story is told in the exact sequence of my progress. It details the rationale used to identify the slaveholding families, which was the key to finding my slave ancestors.

To anyone interested in tracing their Afro-American roots, my story is an excellent resource. Copies of many documents are included to assure accuracy. However, genealogy is not an exact science. If there are errors in my interpretation of the documents, I apologize, especially to the descendants of the slave-holding families. They are no more responsible for the doings of their forebears as I had in the choice of my ancestors being slave or free.

I recall the words of my daughter Julie L. Anderson, in whose memory this book is lovingly dedicated, spoken after the death of my mother, Jewell Moore Jackson. I said to Julie, "Things will never be the same." Julie responded, "Yes, but they can be better."

The story of this search for my slave ancestors began with the finding of my great grandmother Emma's brother, Peter, in the 1900 Taylor Co. Census. It details in sequence my progress through countless hours of microfilm viewing; travel to numerous libraries and archives in several states and interviews with distant relatives.

My book names slave ancestry research guides important to identify the types of records I used for my roots search. However, readers are led to understand that one must follow the compass of his mind as a guide to corroborate his findings as slave ancestral research presents unusual problems. While examining records created by slave owners, information needed for positive identification of the slave ancestor is often missing. A study of the genealogy of the slaveholding families may be necessary. This book provides for readers my step-by-step, and sometimes, stumbling-through experiences for the successful discovery of my slave ancestors. Their footpaths through the McCrary family is illustrated in a Transfer Chart with notes.

After 14 years, the crowning achievement was reached during my visit to the Daughters of the American Revolution Library (DAR Library) in Washington, D.C. Information in the Data Files of four Revolutionary War soldiers: John, Robert, Bartley and Thomas McCrary, unraveled the mystery surrounding McCrary family relationships and the transfer of their Negro slaves, (my kinfolks among them) within the McCrary family. Discovery of the DAR Library records on the McCrary family enabled me to return to my story and write "Added" information to the documents already found. The "Added" information, presented in a different type further explained the documents already found.

Over eight dozen documents are placed within the text. They are introduced and explained to the reader in the exact sequence that I found them. This is in keeping with my objective to have readers see the documents as I saw them at specific points in my research. The text continually narrates my next steps answering the question: "Where do I go from here?"

Most documents were copied from microfilm. Many were misaligned and almost impossible to read. Some typed copies are included. Related documents have the same figure numbers. Slave schedules were reduced. In Fig. 7-47A, the slave lists of several owners in 1860 were placed on one sheet to save space.

Readers may find it necessary to re-read some documents and passages in order to distinguish individual names as they were the same in several generations of the McCrary family. The key to slave ancestral research is to discover the surname of the slave owner/s. This work illustrates how I identified the slaveholding families, and traced my ancestor, Luveser to freedom.

LIST OF ABBREVIATIONS

acct.	account
Adm'r.	Administrator
agt.	agent
b.	born
B	black (in reference to race)
c.	circa (about)
Co.	county or company
Col.	Colonel
Cr.	credit
d., dec'd.	daughter, died or deceased
DAR	Daughters of the American Revolution
Dr.	debit or doctor
Do	ditto (the same)
ed.	editor
F	female or father (In Federal Census Schedules)
Fig.	figure
G.mother	grandmother
GA. or Ga.	Georgia
ID# No.	Identification Number
Jr. or Sr.	Junior or Senior
LDS	Latter Day Saints (as pertains to the Morman Church)
M	In Federal Census Schedules, the "M" refers to "male" in the "sex" column, "mother" in the "relationship" column and "married," M or "Mu" was for "mulatto" in the "color" column.
M.L.	mother-in-law (In Federal Census Schedules)
p. or pp.	page or pages
SC	South Carolina
Si.	sister
S	son (In Federal Census Schedules)
W	wife or white (race)
wd.	widowed or widow

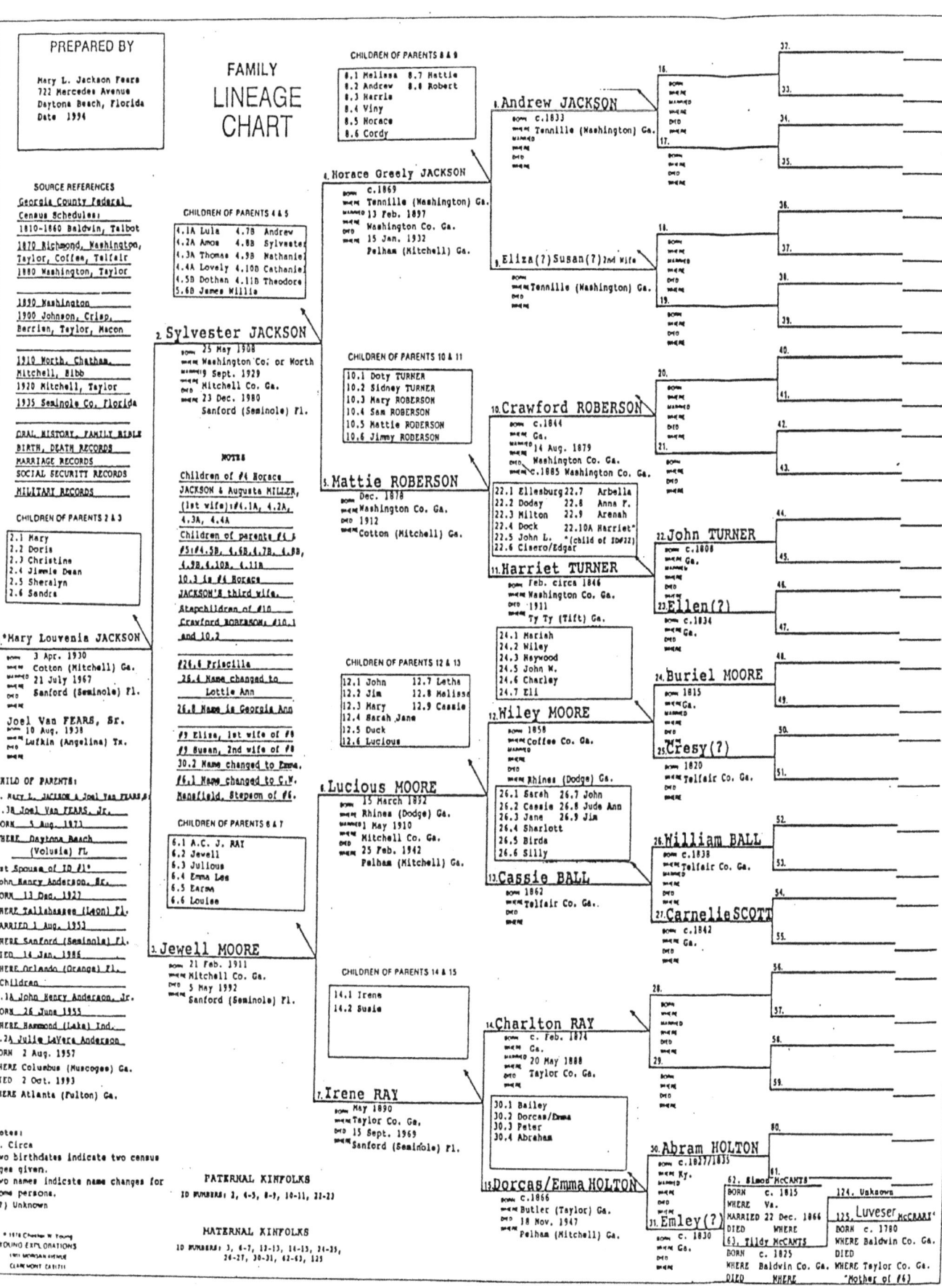

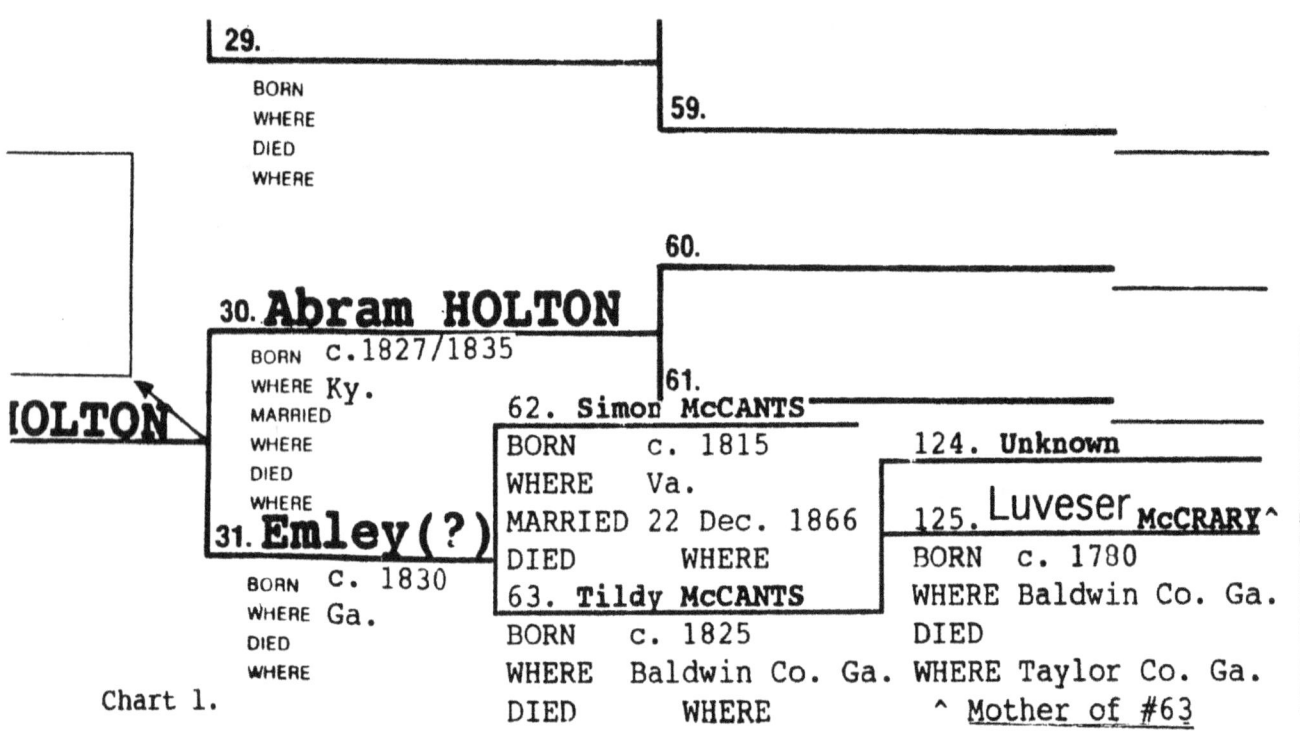

Chart 1.

FAMILY LINEAGE CHART

5th, 6th and 7th Generations of the Family Lineage Chart.
(Maternal Line)

Slave Ancestral Research

Chapter One

MY DISCOVERY OF GRANDPA SIMON AND GRANDMA TILDY McCANTS

I would have called them Grandma Tildy and Grandpa Simon. She was Mrs. Matilda McCants, wife of Mr. Simon McCants. They were never addressed that way in their day. I discovered Grandma Tildy, when I saw her name listed with her grandson, Peter Holton, in the Taylor County, Georgia 1900 Federal Census Schedule, Fig. 7-1. She was about 80 years old. Her birth date was c.1820. However, her birthplace was not Taylor County Georgia because the county was not created until 1852.

I discovered my Grandpa Simon when I found Matilda in the 1870 Taylor County, Georgia Census, Fig. 7-2. Simon and Matilda McCants are ID# 62 and 63 on Chart 1, my Family Lineage Chart. (Most counties named are in Georgia. Co. means county.)

Matilda and Simon's grandson, Peter Holton, was the brother of my great grandmother, Emma Holton (Ray Bay Davis). She married three times. (Emma Holton is ID#15 on my Family Lineage Chart.) Peter was my great granduncle. Since Matilda and Simon were Peter's grandparents and my great grandmother, Emma's grandparents, Matilda and Simon were my great, great, great grandparents! I had discovered in the 1900 Taylor County Census the names of my sixth generation ancestors! It stressed the importance of finding the name of every known relative in all available Federal Census Schedules.

Also in great uncle Peter Holton's household in 1900 was his mother-in-law, Missouri Johnson, and her daughter, Add Johnson. Peter and wife, Add had two children, Annie, age 11, and Peter Jr.,

HOW THE SEARCH BEGAN

1900 Taylor County Ga. Census

Page	Line	Name	Relation	Color	Sex	Birth Date	Age	Yrs. Married Single	Birth Place
131	100	+Holton, Pete	Head	B	M	1873	20	M 20	Ga.
		Add	Wife	B	F	1874	26	M 20	Ga.
		Annie	Daugh	B	F	1888	11		
		Pete Jr.	Son	B	M	1898	2		Ga.
		Abe	Father	B	M	1827	75	wd.	Ga.
		McCants, Tildy--G.	Mother*B		F	1820	80	wd.	Ga.
		Johnson, Missouri--M-in-Law**B			F	1847	53	M 30	Ga.

Fig. 7-1. The first listing found of Tildy/Matilda McCants.
* grandmother **mother-in-law

I was led to find the above record during my first family "Roots" trip to Pelham, Ga., the birthplace of my mother, Jewell Moore Jackson. My father, Sylvester Jackson, and I went to the Mitchell County Courthouse for my birth certificate. When my father asked for the death certificate of his father, Horace Jackson (d.1932), I remembered my great grandmother Emma Davis died in 1947, so I requested her death certificate. (See Fig.7-8.) My cousin, Thelma Singleton Hudson, recognized the surname, "Holton" of Emma's father "Abe Holton" on the certificate. Thelma said, "I know a lady named Marcelee Holton. She lives in Macon, Georgia."

My call to Mrs. Marcelee, an old woman over 80 years old and partially blind, revealed that she was the daughter-in-law of +Pete Holton and widow of Pete's son, Edgar Holton. She lived alone. Mrs. Marcelee knew my great grandmother Emma, and her brother +Pete. She spoke to me about their father, Abe Holton (named above) who owned a "shoe factory" in Butler, Georgia.
(See Fig.7-19A.)

I used the Soundex to locate +Pete Holton in 1900. There I found the names of my slave ancestors, Abe Holton, Tildy McCants and Missouri Johnson. Thus my search began. Without the Soundex, an index to the Federal Census Schedules, I would not have known where to begin the search for Pete Holton.

Thelma Singleton Hudson and Mrs. Marcelee Holton passed before the completion of the manuscript. However, I returned to Pelham and thanked Thelma many times. I sat with Mrs. Marcelee at her table twice in her home and listened to her soft voice blending in with the sounds of pecans falling on the tin roof as she spoke of the Holton family. With family oral history, my search gained momentum and never ceased.

Holton, Pete					Vol. 65	E.D. 72	
					Sheet 3	Line 100	
M	Mar	1870	30	Georgia		(Citizenship)	
Taylor		No. 757 Butler					
Butler							

OTHER MEMBERS OF FAMILY

Name	Relationship	Birth Month	Birth Year	Age	Birthplace	Citizenship
Holton, Odd	W	Mar	1874	26	Georgia	
— Annie	D	Aug	1888	11	Georgia	
— Pete Jr.	S	Jan	1898	2	Georgia	
— Ala	F	Feb	1827	75	Georgia	
McCants, Tildy	M mother	Jan	1820	80	Georgia	

1900 Soundex

Holton, Pete

OTHER MEMBERS OF FAMILY — Continued

Name	Relationship	Birth Month	Birth Year	Age	Birthplace	Citizenship
Johnson, Missouri	M L	Feb	1847	53	Georgia	

Fig. 7-1A. 1900 Soundex used to locate the Georgia county, Enumeration District and page for the listing of Pete Holton in the 1900 Georgia Census Schedule.

age two. A 75-year old man lived there too, Peter's father, Abe Holton. There I found the name of my great, great grandfather, Abe Holton. This census find thrust me into my slave ancestral research.

I rushed to view the 1870 Taylor County Census Schedule, the first census to list all inhabitants by complete names. Prior to 1870, only blacks described as "free persons of color," were listed with the general population in the Federal Census Schedules. I found Matilda McCants and wondered who were the others in the household (see Fig. 7-2).

The 1870 Taylor County Census listed first, Matilda age 45, a man Simon age 50, a girl Matilda age 6, Missoury age 17, a man Abraham Johnson age 28, and an old lady, Louisa or Lovinia McCrary age 90. (See Fig. 7-2.) The unclear handwriting made her name uncertain. I wrote both names hoping to later find the correct one. I wondered, who was the 90-year old woman? Relationships were not given in the 1870 Census. Was she the mother or grandmother, aunt or sister of Simon or Matilda?

I saw the family again in the 1880 Taylor County Census, Fig. 7-2B, with relationships given: Matilda's husband, Simon McCants age 65, Matilda age 64, daughters, Isabella age 20, and Matilda age 18 and Simon's sister, Eliza age 20. Since Simon's birthplace was Virginia, and the birthplace of the old woman in the 1870 Taylor County Census, was Georgia, I believed the old woman was the mother of Matilda (Simon's wife). Louisa/Lovinia McCrary was missing in the 1880 Census. Age discrepancies and varied names for former slaves existed throughout the Federal Census Schedules.

I requested the marriage records for Simon and Matilda McCants; and Abel Johnson and Missouri McCants from the Taylor County Probate Court in Butler, Georgia. When I unfolded the copies of their marriage records, what a joy! (See Fig. 7-3.) The marriage of Simon and Matilda was dated 22 December 1866. They had solemnized their marriage soon after it was possible for them to have a legal marriage. (Slaves were legally forbidden to marry.) They received their freedom 1 January 1863 when President Lincoln issued the Emancipation Proclamation. However, history recorded that several months passed before many held in slavery were given their freedom.

The Thirteenth Amendment to the United States Constitution abolished slavery 6 December 1865.

The handwriting on the marriage record of Simon and Matilda was beautiful, with sweeping swirls like a modern-day greeting card, but the words after their names, "Freedman" and "Freedwoman," reflected their past lives, a stark contrast to the beautiful handwriting of James Griffeth, recorder of both marriage documents. The record of Missouri McCants to Abel Johnson was dated 11 March 1870. The notation "col" was written after each name. (See Fig. 7-4.)

I yearned to know Louisa/Lovinia McCrary. What was her kinship to Matilda and Simon McCants? Louisa/Lovinia's age and the notations on the McCant's marriage record assured me--they were not "free persons of color" but former slaves. Eager anxiety drove me down numerous highways to distant libraries and archives searching the past for my slave ancestors. Would I find them?

Mrs. Marcelee Jones Holton
10 Aug. 1899 - 18 May 1986

Mrs. Marcelee, widow of Edgar Holton and the daughter-in-law of Pete Holton, is pictured sharing oral history about the Holton family with the author in her home in Macon, Georgia. She was born in Duval County, Florida and died in a nursing home in Abbeville, Georgia. Her parents were Frank and Mattie Jones.

Chapter Two

SLAVE ANCESTRAL RESEARCH

Slave ancestral research--it's something else! To me, it was an exercise in perseverance on an emotional roller coaster. I began with hope and proceeded with intervening periods of uncertainty. As I searched for *my* kinfolks in the slave records, I sensed the sadness of their hearts and felt their longing for rest at the close of the day. I sensed the suffering of my kinfolks and wondered how they endured.

Matilda, Simon and Louisa or Lovinia, were my slave ancestors, also Abe Holton and his wife, Emily (see Fig. 7-2A). Isabella, Missouri and her husband, Abraham or Abel Johnson were born as slaves. Were they field hands or house slaves? Were they ever sold apart? Was the overseer cruel or kind? Was the overseer, too, a slave "driver" shackled with this scandalous task? Where were they when they received the message of their freedom?

Simon, born in Virginia, a "mulatto," meant his skin color was very light, a product of miscegenation or of mixed races. Who were his parents? He was brought to Georgia from Virginia. When, and by whom? To these questions, I sought answers.

Before I found the 1900 Taylor County Census of Pete Holton and his family with Matilda, etc. (Fig. 7-1), I found Pete and his sister Emma, (listed as Dorcus) in the 1870 Taylor County Census with parents, Abe and Emily Holton (Fig.7-2A). Abe Holton and wife, Emily were both slaves. Emily, I believed, was Matilda and Simon's daughter. She was listed on page 26 before Simon and Matilda on page 27 in the Taylor County 1880 Census. Relatives often lived close to each other as shown in census records.(See Figs. 7-2B and 7-2C.)

8 Slave Ancestral Research

With the following records on hand, I began my search:

1870 Taylor County Georgia Census

Page	Name	Age	Sex	Color	Occupation	Place of Birth
310	McCants, Matilda	45	F	B	Keeps house	Ga.
	McCrary, Lovinia	90	F	B	" "	Ga.
	Matilda	6	F	B	At Home	Ga.
	Johnson, Abraham	28	M	B	Works farm	Ga.
	Missoury	17	F	B	Cooks	Ga.
	McCants, Simon	50	M	B	Works at Mill	Va.

Fig. 7-2. (Typed)

1870 Taylor County Georgia Census

Page	Name	Age	Sex	Color	Occupation	Place of Birth
293	*Holbon, Abe	35	M	B	Farm Labor	Tenn.
	Emily	40	F	B	Keeps house	Ga.
	Baley	8	M	B		Ga.
	**Dorcus	4	F	B		Ga.
	+Peter	3	M	B		Ga.
	Abraham	2	M	B		Ga.
	Riley, Mary	14	F	B	Farm Hand	Ga.

Fig. 7-2A

*Should read Holton.

**My Great Grandmother Dorcus/Emma. Dorcus's name appears as Emma in the 1900 Berrien County Census after the marriage to Charley Ray on 19 May 1888 (see Fig. 7-2D).

+My Great Grand Uncle Pete.

Slave Ancestral Research

1880 Taylor County Georgia Census

Page		Age	Sex	Color	Relationship Occupation	Birth-place
27	McCants, Simon	65	M	Mu^	Farmer	Va.
	Matilda	64	F	B	Wife Keeping house	Ga.
	Isabelly	20	F	B	Daughter	
	Matilda	18	F	B	Daughter	
	Eliza	20	F	B	Sister	

Fig. 7-2B.

1880 Taylor County Georgia Census

Page		Age	Sex	Color	Relationship Occupation	Birth-place
26	Holton, Abram	45	M	B	Boot & Shoemaker	Ky.
	Emily	45	F	B	wife	Ga.
	Bailey	15	M	B	Son	Ga.
	**Dorceus	12	F	B	Daughter	Ga.
	+Peter	13	M	B	Son	Ga.
	Abram	12	M	B	Son	Ga.

Fig. 7-2C.

Census enumerators recorded discrepancies in ages, name spellings, and places of birth. ^M or Mu, mulatto, of mixed white and black parents. Abram Holton born c.1835, worked as a shoemaker in 1880.

1900 Berrien County Georgia Census

Page			Color	Sex	Age birth	Yrs. marr.	No. Child.	Place of birth
303	Ray, Charlton	Head M	M	1874	26	11	4	Ga.
	Emma	wife	B	F	1875 25	11	4	Ga.
	Irene	daughter	B	F	1890 10			Ga.
	Susie	daughter	B	F	1891 8			Ga

Fig. 7-2D.

The birthplace of Charlton Ray's father was given as Kentucky; and his mother's birthplace was Georgia in this census. Charlton's occupation was "preacher." This record stated the birthplace of Emma's mother and father as Tennessee. The birthplace of Emma's mother, Emily in both 1870 and 1880 Taylor County Census Schedules is Georgia. The latter is most likely correct as Emily, her mother, gave the information to the enumerator in the earlier censuses.

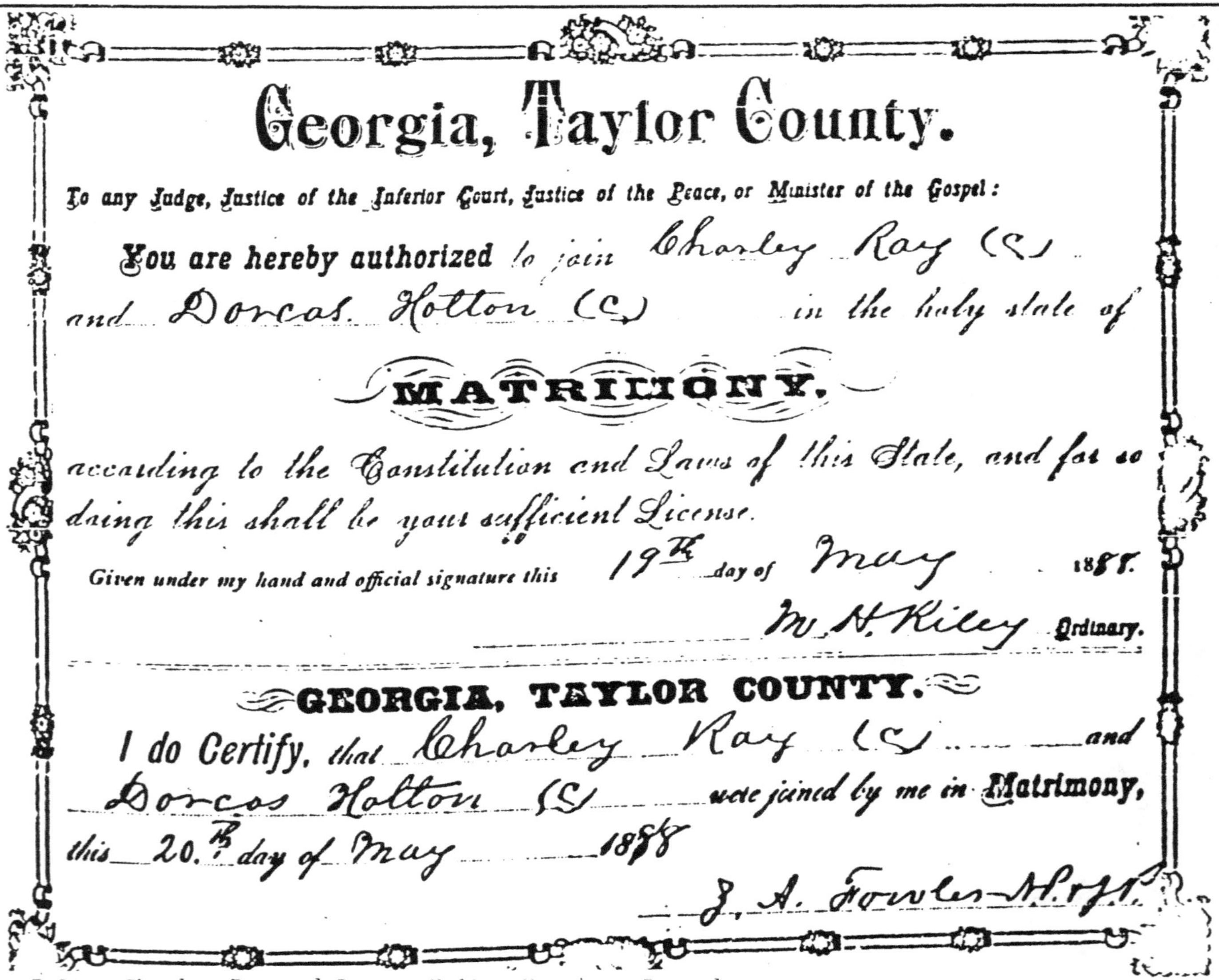

Georgia, Taylor County.

To any Judge, Justice of the Inferior Court, Justice of the Peace, or Minister of the Gospel:

You are hereby authorized to join Charley Ray (S) and Dorcas Holton (C) in the holy state of

MATRIMONY.

according to the Constitution and Laws of this State, and for so doing this shall be your sufficient License.

Given under my hand and official signature this 19th day of May 1888.

M. A. Kiley, Ordinary.

Georgia, Taylor County.

I do Certify, that Charley Ray (S) and Dorcas Holton (C) were joined by me in **Matrimony**, this 20th day of May 1888.

J. A. Fowler, M.P.

Fig. 7-2D. Charley Ray and Dorcas Holton Marriage Record

1900 BERRIEN CO. GA CENSUS

TWELFTH CENSUS OF THE UNITED STATES
SCHEDULE No. 1.—POPULATION

Enumerated by me on the 7th day of June, 1900.

NAME	RELATION	PERSONAL DESCRIPTION						NATIVITY		
		Color	Sex	Month	Year	Age	Marital	Yrs married	Mother of how many children	No. living	Place of birth of this person	Father	Mother
Ray Shelton	Head	B	M	Feb	1845	54	M 18				Kentucky		
Emma	wife	B	F	Oct	1857	42	M 11	4	4	Georgia	Tennessee	Georgia
Lilas	Daughter	B	F	May	1890	10	S			Georgia	Georgia	Georgia
Susannah	Daughter	B	F	Essy	1891	8	S			Georgia	Georgia	Georgia
Anna Spring	Hild	B	F	July	1896	3	M 2 Md			Florida		
	Daughter	B	F									

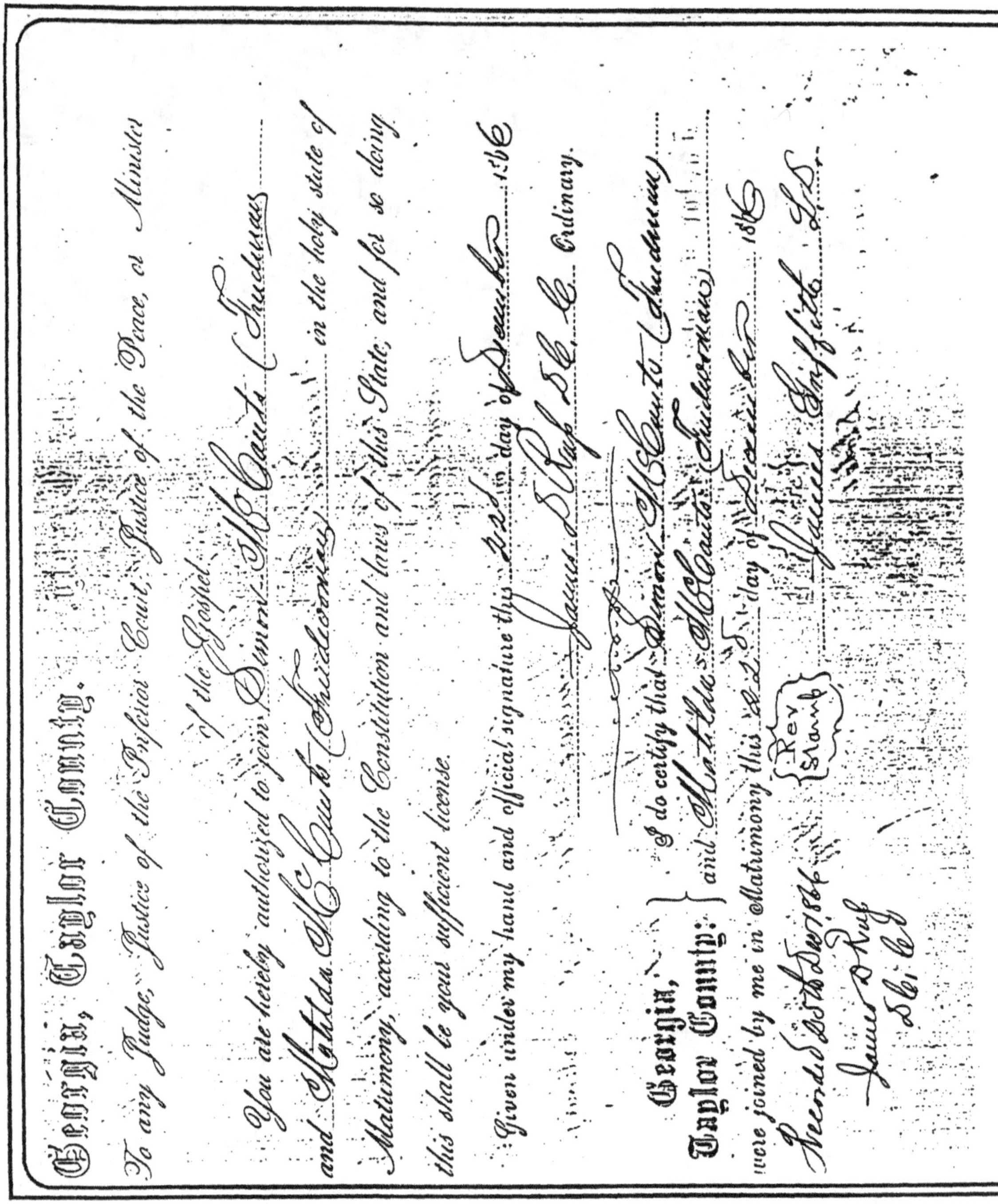

Fig. 7-3. Simon McCants and Matilda McCants Marriage Record.

Marriage record of my Sixth Generation Slave Ancestors, Simon McCants and Matilda McCants. Matilda's maiden name was the same as Simon, implying ownership by the same McCants family.

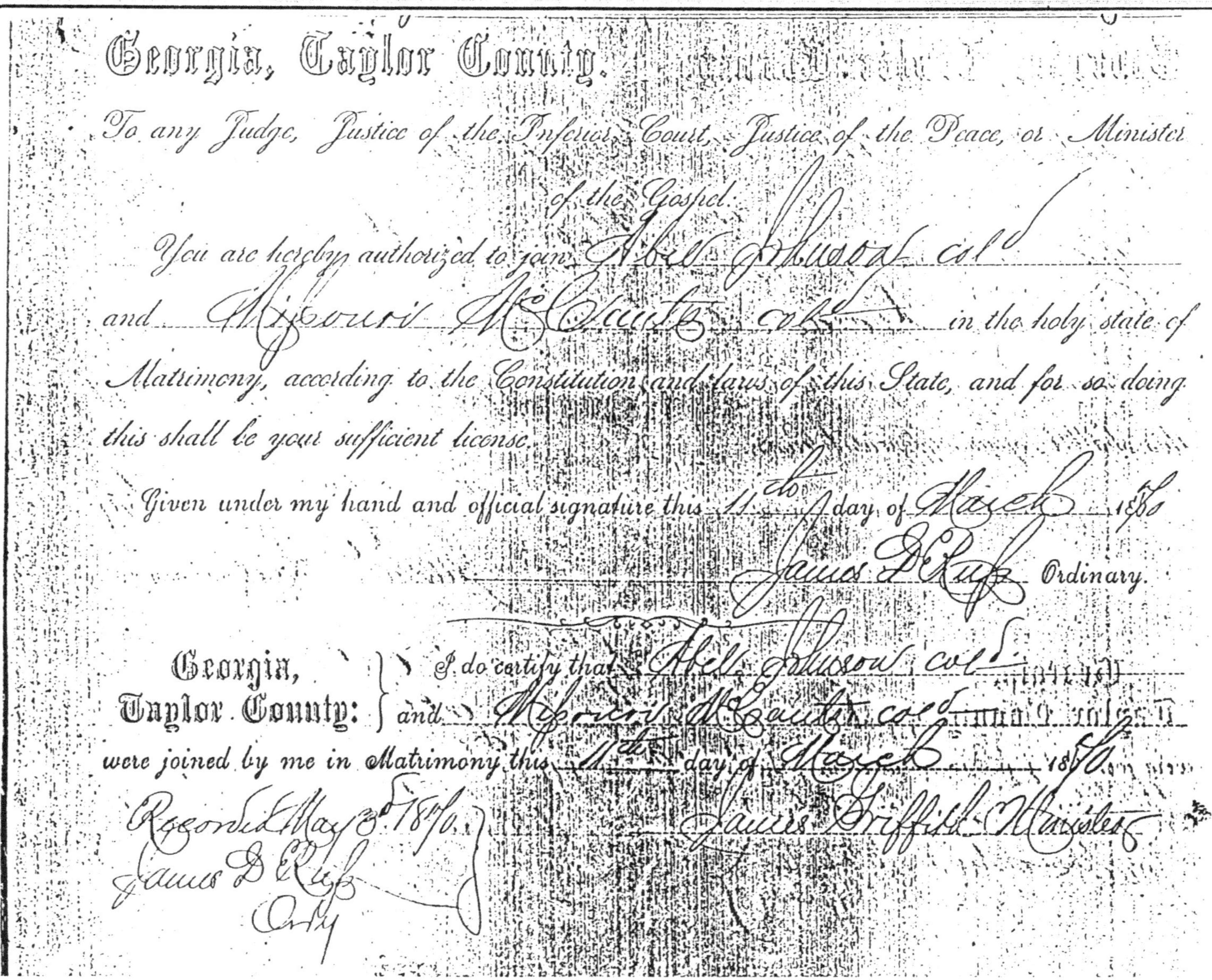

Georgia, Taylor County.

To any Judge, Justice of the Inferior Court, Justice of the Peace, or Minister of the Gospel.

You are hereby authorized to join Abel Johnson col'd and Missouri McCants col'd in the holy state of Matrimony, according to the Constitution and laws of this State, and for so doing this shall be your sufficient license.

Given under my hand and official signature this 11th day of March 1870

James D. Ruff Ordinary.

Georgia, Taylor County: } I do certify that Abel Johnson col'd and Missouri McCants col'd were joined by me in Matrimony this 11th day of March 1870

James Griffith Minister

Recorded May 3rd 1870.
James D. Ruff
Ordy

Fig. 7-4. Abel Johnson and Missouri McCants Marriage Record

14   Slave Ancestral Research

My research objectives were:

1. To find the slave owners of SIMON and MATILDA McCANTS and daughter, MISSOURI McCANTS JOHNSON. (Fig. 7-2).

2. To find the correct name of LOUISA/LOVINIA McCRARY and her relationship to SIMON and MATILDA. (Fig. 7-2).

3. To find EMILY, mother of my Uncle Peter Holton and his sister, (my great grandmother) Dorcus/Emma Holton. The objective was to find Emily listed with her mother, MATILDA McCANTS. (Fig. 7-2A).

To locate my ancestors prior to 1870, I needed to know the *names of the slave owners*. Any written records of slave families would appear in slave owners' records. A leading clue was the marriage record I had of Simon and Matilda McCants. I was unable to find a marriage record of Abram and Emily Holton. This record perhaps, may have verified her maiden name as McCants. Since Matilda had the surname McCants before her marriage, I believed that Simon and Matilda were both owned by a McCants family.

For assistance on how to begin the research, I read *Slave Genealogy: A Research Guide with Case Studies* by David H. Streets, Bowie, MD, Heritage Books, Inc., 1986.
Herbert G. Gutman's research in *The Black Family in Slavery and Freedom*, 1750-1925, N.Y., Vintage Books, 1976, presented a comprehensive study of slave family life and naming practices.[1]
Another very useful reference was *The Source*, Chapter 19, "Black Ancestral Research" by Johni Cerny, Salt Lake City, Utah, Ancestry Publishing Co., 1984. pp.579-594. *Black Genealogy*, a book by Charles L. Blockson with Ron Fry was most helpful to follow as a guide for the research. The book, republished by Black Classic Press, 1991 is essential to the black family researcher.
The authors and historians cited made it clear that information about slaves was available in court records of the slave owners.

Slaves were valued personal property and considered a vital part of the slave owners' estate. State laws gave slaves no legal rights. Their ownership and transference from one owner to another, whether by sale, gift or inheritance through wills, were diligently recorded in court records.

Before plunging into Taylor County Probate Records for wills, deeds, inventories and appraisals of property and other records, as suggested by Cerny and Streets, I searched the 1870 Taylor County Census in pursuit of suspects: white persons with the same surnames as my ancestors and wealth enough to own slaves.

CLUES FROM THE 1870 TAYLOR COUNTY CENSUS

The 1870 Federal Census listed former slaves by complete names. They were listed in family groups in the 1870 census but *not* every one in the household with the same surname was related. Some with a *different* surname were related. I noticed that Mary's surname is Riley. She is living with Abe and Emily Holton in 1870. (See Fig.7-2A.) Louisa/Lovinia's surname is McCrary. She is living with Simon and Matilda McCants in 1870. (Fig. 7-2). But in the 1880 Census, when relationships are stated, neither Mary nor Louisa/Lovinia is in her former household.

I used the surnames Riley, McCrary and McCants as clues to the possible slave owners. I looked closely for those in the 1870 Taylor County Census recorded near my family names.

A clue found! It was the name Henry McCants, age 19, listed near my folks on page 309. Matilda and Simon were on page 310! The 1860 Taylor County Census listed Henry age 10, with his father, Andrew McCants. Andrew McCants was named as a slave owner in the 1860 Taylor Co. Slave Schedule and could have been the slave owner of my family of McCants. Andrew had 13 slaves in 1860. (See Fig. 7-5.) I wondered, what were their names? I needed to see my ancestors' names in a McCants' record. The Slave Schedules did not list slave names, only their gender and ages.

The only clue that I had for locating the slave owners of my ancestors was the surname. The printed 1850 and 1860 Indexes to the

Georgia Population Schedules indicated that the oldest white McCants and McCrary families were in Twiggs, Talbot, Spaulding, and Harrison Counties. They came from South Carolina.

I decided to concentrate on the McCants and McCrary surnames for the slave owners and copy them from the 1850 and 1860 slave schedules. Learning the history of Taylor County became important. There was no 1850 slave schedule for that county. Taylor County was not created until 1852 from the parent counties of Talbot and Marion. There were no McCants or McCrary slave owners in Marion County. From the printed index to the 1850 and 1860 Georgia Slave Schedules, I listed the McCants, McCrary and Riley slave owners in Taylor and Talbot Counties.

1850 Georgia Slave Owners

Name	County	Page	Number of Slaves
McCants, Jeremiah	Talbot	493	12
McCants, Andrew	Talbot	493	3
McCants, Margaret	Talbot	493	4
McCrary, James	Talbot	421	21
McCrary, John	Talbot	367	9
McCrary, John	Talbot	467	33
McCrary, John B	Talbot	401	11
McCrary, William	Talbot	361	16
McCrary, Colon	Talbot	427	2
McCrary, Gilliah	Talbot	503	1
McCrary, William	Talbot	421	4
Riley, Joseph	Talbot	468	29
McCrary, Ruben	Talbot	425	1

1860 Slave Owners

Name	County	Page	Number of Slaves
McCants, John A.	Taylor	26	1
McCants, Andrew J.	Taylor	26	13
McCants, Jeremiah C.	Taylor	26	15
McCrary, John A.	Taylor	26	1
McCrary, Bartley	Taylor	24	44
McCrary, Bartley, Jr.	Taylor	29	18
McCrary, Gillah	Taylor	29	9
McCrary, Henry	Taylor	29	8
Riley, Thomas J.	Taylor	98	24
Riley, Joseph (Jr.)	Taylor	98	9
Riley, William	Taylor	22	2
Riley, Nancy	Taylor	98	7

Fig. 7-5. Slave owners in Talbot and Taylor Co. in 1850 and 1860.

Slave Ancestral Research

My ancestors could have been owned by either of the several slave owners or an owner with a *different* surname who had married into either family. Slaves, after freedom, did not always take the name of the last owner. After making this list, I learned that even after finding a record, unanswered questions glinted. Example: Are there two or three John McCrarys in 1850, or does one John have two lists of slaves? A copy of John B. McCrary's list is shown in Fig. 7-6. I concluded early, even if I found my folks, I might not recognize them. Could a mere age on a list represent my Grandma Matilda?

Mary Riley was 14 years old in the 1870 Taylor Co. Census in Fig. 7-2. Due to her age, she would appear only on an 1860 slave list. Only one Riley slave owner listed a four year old female in Taylor Co., Nancy Riley, page 17. She had 7 slaves listed as follows in the 1860 Taylor Co. Slave Schedule:

NAME	Number	Age	Sex	Color
Riley, Nancy	1	60	F (Female)	B (Black)
	1	34	F	M (Mulatto)
	1	19	F	B
	1	18	M	M
	1	16	M	M
	1	9	M	M
	1	4	F	M

Could the four-year old above be Mary Riley?

My next step was to plunge into the probate records of Taylor County seeking answers.

SCHEDULE 2.—Slave Inhabitants in No. 2 District in the County of Talbot State of Georgia, enumerated by me, on the 25 day of August 1850. John B. McCrary, Ass't Marshal

NAMES OF SLAVE OWNERS.	Number of Slaves	Age	Sex	Colour	Fugitives from the State	Number manumitted	Deaf & dumb, blind, insane, or idiotic		NAMES OF SLAVE OWNERS.	Number of Slaves	Age	Sex	Colour	Fugitives from the State	Number manumitted	Deaf & dumb, blind, insane, or idiotic
1	2	3	4	5	6	7	8		1	2	3	4	5	6	7	8
1. William M Rhodes		14	M	B				1.	John B. McCrary		16	M	M			
2.		11	F	B				2.			13	F	M			
3.		9	M	B				3.			9	F	M			
4.		3	M	B				4.			7	M	M			
5.		1	M	B				5.			4	M	B			
6.		2	M	B				6.			1	F	M			
7.		10	M	B				7.			15	F	B			
8.		6	M	B				8.			1	F	B			
9.		1	M	B				9.	Thomas Hancock		13	F	B			
10.		11	M	B				10.	Mildred Burt		60	M	B			
11.		5	M	B				11.			50	M	M			
12.		2	M	B				12.			44	F	B			
13.		3	M	B				13.			36	F	M			
14.		5	M	B				14.			31	F	B			
15.		11	F	M				15.			20	M	M			
16.		5	F	B				16.			18	M	B			
17.		10	F	B				17.			17	M	B			
18.		3	F	B				18.			14	F	B			
19.		5	F	B				19.			12	F	B			
20.		10	F	B				20.			14	F	B			
21.		5	F	B				21.			12	M	M			
22.		1	F	B				22.			10	M	M			
23.		2	F	B				23.			8	F	M			
24.		5	F	B				24.	Dick		3	F	M			
25.		5	F	B				25.	Richard Pitt		34	M	B			
26.		1	F	B				26.			24	M	B			
27.		5	F	B				27.			16	F	B			
28.		3	F	B				28.			13	F	B			
29.		1	F	B				29.			11	M	B			
30. Alfred Moore		45	M	B				30.			55	F	B			
31.		50	F	B				31.			37	M	B			
32.		35	M	B				32.			35	M	B			
33.		32	M	M				33.			40	F	B			
34.		25	M	M				34.			34	F	B			
35.		15	F	M				35.			30	F	B			
36.		14	M	B				36.			30	F	B			
37.		8	M	B				37.			15	F	B			
38.		7	F	B				38.			24	F	B			
39.		3	M	B				39.			32	M	B			
40. John B McCrary		55	F	M				40.			36	M	B			
41.		20	M	M				41.			28	M	B			
42.		18	M	M				42.			37	M	B			

Fig. 7-6. 1850 Talbot Co. GA. Slave Schedule, John B. McCrary's slave list.

William R. Miller
Name of Estate
Date of Deceased Dec. 1860
 Not Present
Chas./Charley/RAY
or Charlton Ray

Simon McCants

Missouri Johnson

Taylor Co. Ga.   INVENTORIES &
pp. 147   APPRAISEMENTS
                 1852 - 1952
Names being searched:

Abe/Abram/Abraham Holton/Holten

Emily   Matilda/Tildy McCants

Emily with child Mary or Bailey

Dorcus   Peter

==

Man Joe $266.00 Woman Lizza & Child Frank 1000.00
Man Abril 1574.00 "Rhoda & two children Octavia, a girl, Armstead, a boy
" *Carity, a girl and Gabriel, a boy & flip $3,900
" Albert 1500.00 Woman Sheney $400 Woman Harriet $400
Woman Carissa $400.00 Woman Emily $1200 Woman Emeline 1100 Man John
Boy Comas $200.00 $500
Negro woman with children:

Rhoda and 4 children: Octavia, Armstead,
                      Charity, Gabriel

==

boy - b. girl - g. man - m.
==

Man Joe valued at $266.00 was probably old and could not
work very much. * The name in Miller's will was Charity.
1 Boy Mase was valued at $200.00

Fig. 7-7. Inventories and Appraisements of William R. Miller,
deceased. Form used for copying Estate Inventories.

Slave Ancestral Research

Chapter Three

TAYLOR COUNTY COURT RECORDS

I made notes on the McCants, McCrary and Riley families in both 1850-1860 population and slave schedules. While talking to other family researchers about my need for the probate records, a friend, Arlene Echols, suggested using the Lake Mary Library.

I had used the library often for census records. They request records from the Family History Center Library, Church of Jesus Christ of Latter-Day Saints, commonly referred to as the Morman Library or LDS Library of Salt Lake City, Utah. This library has the largest depository of genealogical records in the world preserved on microfilm.

The LDS Library had most Georgia county court records. The Family History Center at Lake Mary, Florida soon became my second home.

I first looked in the "Locality File" for Georgia, Taylor County, Probate Records" and ordered four rolls of film from the LDS Library:

	Order Number
Georgia Taylor Probate Records	
Court of Ordinary	
Inventory and Appraisements 1852-1952	0321098
Estate Sales 1852-1909	0321100
Distribution of Estates 1858-1887	0321099
Wills 1853-1917	0321090

MEANDERING THROUGH THE INVENTORIES

I first threaded the microfilm reader with the film of the "Inventory and Appraisements" with trepidation. It was a film of a journal. At the top of each page in bold, spotty illegible 19th Century handwriting, was the name of a deceased property owner with an inventory of his real and perishable property. A figure at the right side of each item represented its dollar value. I rolled the film from page to page gazing at what seemed absolutely unbelievable. Among the lists of bushels of corn, fodder, horses, cows, household furnishings and kitchen utensils, were people, real human beings listed with their dollar value besides their scribbled names. I had to look hard to distinguish the word "man" from "mare." (Mules and horses had the same names as slaves, Fig. 7-8B.) The dollar value distinguished the difference. A slave carried a higher value.

The experience of looking for my family among lists of farm animals and implements cannot be described in terms of any feelings I had ever had before. I stared at the page images with a mixture of conflicting emotions--hoping to find my family names, yet resentful of the circumstances, while at the same time, bewildered, wondering how they survived the harsh realities of slavery. As I looked at the recording date of the inventory and later found the corresponding record of "Sales" for the same deceased slave owner, I could hear the wailing of families being sold apart. I shuddered, thinking of the life experiences of my own dear kinfolk, Simon, Matilda, Missouri, Louisa/Lovinia, Abram and Emily. Were they somewhere listed among these inventories?

Before I made a thorough search of the inventories for *my* family names, I learned black history as never before from this authentic source. The way the records were written taught much.

Only wealthy people had slaves in large numbers. Slaves with skills in carpentry, iron works, painting, and the like, were valued as high as $1500 to $2000. Negro slaves, the most highly valued property, were often listed first in the inventory.

Rarely was a surname listed with the slaves' given names. Sometimes a relationship was given with a woman's name. Example, "Mary and her child, Susie." A father was seldom given recognition in the records. I saw a few times what appeared to be a family, a listing of a woman's name, then "Buck" and their child, Sarah. Sometimes the woman's name was omitted and the record might read "woman and her child, Rubin." Names were often misspelled or written very poorly and sometimes omitted as one notation read, "53 slaves valued at $350 each." This last notation made it very unlikely that a black researcher could ever be completely sure of identifying his slave ancestors. That is because slaves did not always take the name of their last owner. My McCants ancestors could have been among those 53 slaves, although the inventory was not for a deceased McCants property owner.

An effort was made to avoid having two slaves with the same name. If this happened, a surname might be listed (perhaps the surname of a prior owner) or "big" or "little," or "young" or "old," preceded the name to distinguish the two slaves.

Ages were sometimes given and/or the notation, "a Negro man, a Negro woman, child, boy, girl or infant." Sometimes when no child or adult reference was made, the dollar value could be used as a clue. Fig.7-8A is a partial inventory of Esais Taylor who had 53 slaves. When a woman's age is listed followed by several names and children's ages in descending order about two years apart, one might consider this list a family.

When comparing the "Inventory" listing of the slaves of a property owner with his "Sales," a girl from the inventory may be sold as a woman. I wondered when was a girl, a woman or a boy, a man. A 43 year old man could be listed as a boy. As the man or woman became old and unable to work, his value diminished to $50-100 or was listed as "worthless" or "no value."

THE ADMINISTRATORS AND EXECUTORS OF THE ESTATE

A list of signatures followed at the end of the inventory. These were often names of relatives or trusted friends of the deceased. They hired the slaves out until they were sold or passed to heirs according to the provisions of a will. They sometimes bought some of the property. The Negro property was under the management of the administrator or executor of the estate until the estate was settled.

THE SEARCH BEGINS

The form I devised for copying the Inventories is shown in Figs. 7-7, one with a list of slaves placed at the beginning of this chapter and the unfilled form on page 26. I found the need to devise a form for copying "Returns" as shown in Fig. 7-7. I discovered that the given names of my slave ancestors appeared on many different inventories. I copied each inventory which listed slaves with my ancestors' names. There were dozens of slave owners' inventories to copy.

Slave Ancestral Research/Fears

TALBOT COUNTY RETURNS

Year_____   Film #_____/p._____

_____Estate_____   _____
                                   Guardian ( ) Administrator ( )
Minors:_____

Negro Slaves: Hired to: From
                            _____to_____18_____ $_____
_____
_____
_____
_____
_____
_____
_____
_____

==

                  _____
                      COUNTY RETURNS
Year_____   Film #_____/p._____

Estate_____   _____
                                   Guardian ( ) Administrator ( )

Minors:_____

Negro Slaves: Hired to: $_____
_____
_____
_____

Year_____   p._____
_____
_____
_____
_____

Year_____   p._____
_____
_____
_____
_____

Fig. 7-7.

Slave Ancestral Research/Fears

	Taylor Co. Ga.	INVENTORIES & APPRAISEMENTS
	pp._____	1852 - 1952

Name of Estate
Date of Deceased_____   Names being searched:

Chas./Charley/RAY   Abe/Abram/Abraham Holton/Holten

or Charlton Ray   Emily   Matilda/Tildy McCants

Simon McCants   Emily with child Mary or Bailey

Missouri Johnson   Dorcus   Peter
==

_____   _____   _____   _____

_____   _____   _____   _____

_____   _____   _____   _____

_____   _____   _____   _____

Negro woman with children:_____

_____

_____

boy - b. girl - g. man - m.
==

Fig. 7-7. Inventories and Appraisements Form

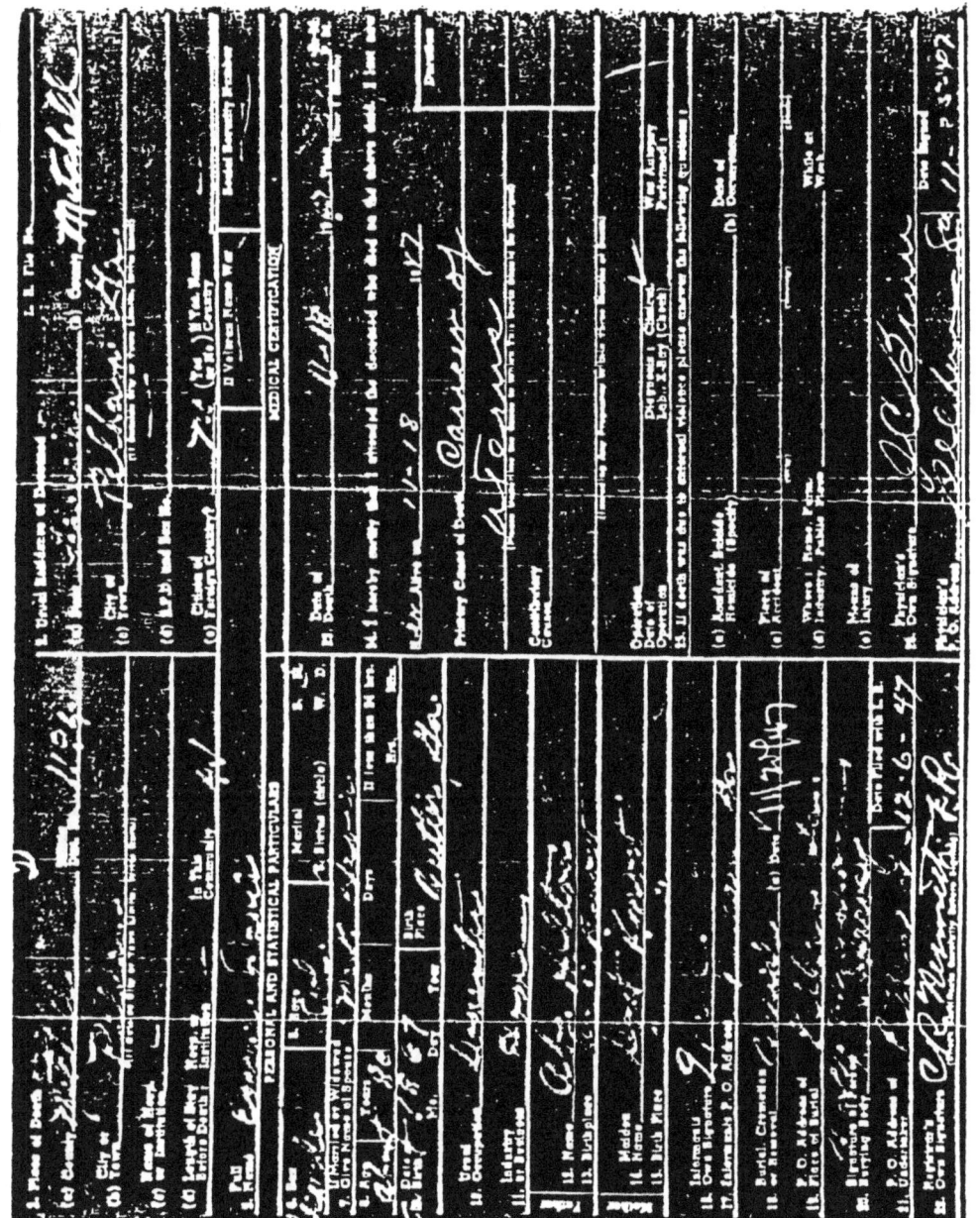

Fig. 7-8. Death Certificate of Emma (Holton) Davis Birthdate, about 1867, Birth place, Butler, GA Her father is Abe Holton. Mother's name, not given. Informant was Irene Durden, her daughter, my grandmother.

This is to certify that this is a true and correct copy of the certificate filed with the Vital Records Service, Georgia Department of Human Resources. This certified copy is issued under the authority of Chapter 89-17, Vital Records, Code of Georgia, annotated, as amended.

Inventory and Appraisement
of the Estate of Esaias Taylor

			Age	Value
1	Negro	Woman Morthia	27	950.00
"	"	girl Linnah	8	625.00
"	"	Boy Washington	5	500.00
"	"	" Charly	3	375.00
"	"	" Anderson	2	175.00
"	"	man Garrow	75	100.00
"	"	" Jack	57	900.00
"	"	" Ben	40	1200.00
"	"	" Sharper	30	1500.00
"	"	" Harries	27	1600.00
"	"	" Rubin	24	1600.00
"	"	" Mingo	20	1600.00
"	"	woman Amy	30	800.00
"	"	child Hannah	5	350.00
"	"	Woman Nelly	38	800.00
"	"	girl Polly	15	1000.00
"	"	" Leah	11	900.00
"	"	" Susanah	9	750.00
"	"	" Lucy	6	350.00
"	"	Woman Harriett	43	800.00
"	"	girl Adaline	7	375.00
"	"	boy Jack	5	300.00
"	"	" Peter	9	600.00
"	"	Woman Charlotte & child	24	1000.00
"	"	child Sallie	3	200.00
"	"	man Robert	62	500.00
"	"	Woman Amy	62	200.00
"	"	girl Margaret	14	750.00
"	"	boy Tom wound	11	600.00
"	"	girl Amy	9	450.00
"	"	boy Robert	7	350.00
"	"	Woman Tilda	90	—

Fig. 7-8 A. Inventory and Appraisements of Esais Taylor, deceased. Slave names are listed apparently in family groups.

No.	61	Gabriel Boy 7 years old		125 00
	62	Martha Woman 28 " "		1200 00
	63	Susanna girl 11 " "		1000 00
	64	Butler Boy 9 " "		750 00
	65	Fanny Girl 5 " "		500 00
	66	Joe boy Boy 12 " "		800 00
	65	Frank old male 5 " " ruptured		150 00
	66	Sullivan " 76 " " ruptured		10 00
"driver" →	67	Randolph man 60 " "		600 00
	68	Lucy " " 60 " "		300 00
	69	Emaline 14 " "		1200 00
	70	Julian Infant 20 " "		1600 00
	71	Mary Hall " " "		600 00
	72	Lucy 24 " "		1800 00
	73	Nancy 45 " "		500 00

Horses

1	Buggy horse Tom		250 00
2	Saddle horse Snow Ball		150 00
→	3 Mare Polly		175 00
mare	" " Lucy		50 00
→	horse colt George		180 00

horse Mules

1	Mule	Fancy	210 00
2	"	Rolah	250 00
3	"	Mariah	275 00
4	"	Nettie	280 00
5	"	Dolly	280 00
6	"	Rachel	210 00
7	"	Brandy	215 00
8	"	Jane Jane	215 00

Distinguishing "man" from "mare" in a part of the Inventory of Sam'l P. Corbin. Slave names numbered 61-73 and names of horses, mules and mares with their appraised value.

Fig. 7-8B. Inventory of Sam'l P. Corbin. Taylor Co. Bk. of Inventories and Appraisements, June 26, 1863, p. 270.

Randolph, the "driver," a slave under the overseer, with duties to enforce slave work in the fields and power to punish with the lash.

I hoped to find my McCants family together as a unit. However, Gutman's work on slave families made me aware of various circumstances of slave family separation. Since former slaves did not always take the name of their last owner, my McCants family could have appeared on any Inventory. It was also possible that their last owner may *not* have died prior to 1870 and my McCants family would *not* appear on any Inventory. The plan I developed was as follows:

1. Copy the McCants, McCrary and Riley slave owners from the Taylor Co. 1850 and 1860 Slave Schedules.

2. Look for McCants, McCrary and Riley deceased property owners on the microfilm, "Inventories and Appraisements." If found, copy their lists of slaves.

   Try to identify the slave names from the Inventories with black families with the same surnames in the 1870 Census Schedules.

3. Copy every "Inventory" which had one or more of my family names.

4. Corroborate each record with data from other records, "Sales" of the property owner, his will, deeds, estate distribution records or other county court records.

5. Locate the property owner in two census years prior to his death to learn the names of his family.

6. Look to see if any member of his family is living close to my family in the 1870 Taylor Co. Census.

7. Use the Index to the 1870 Census of Georgia to locate my names of slaves listed on each Inventory to determine if any of them took the surname of the property owner.

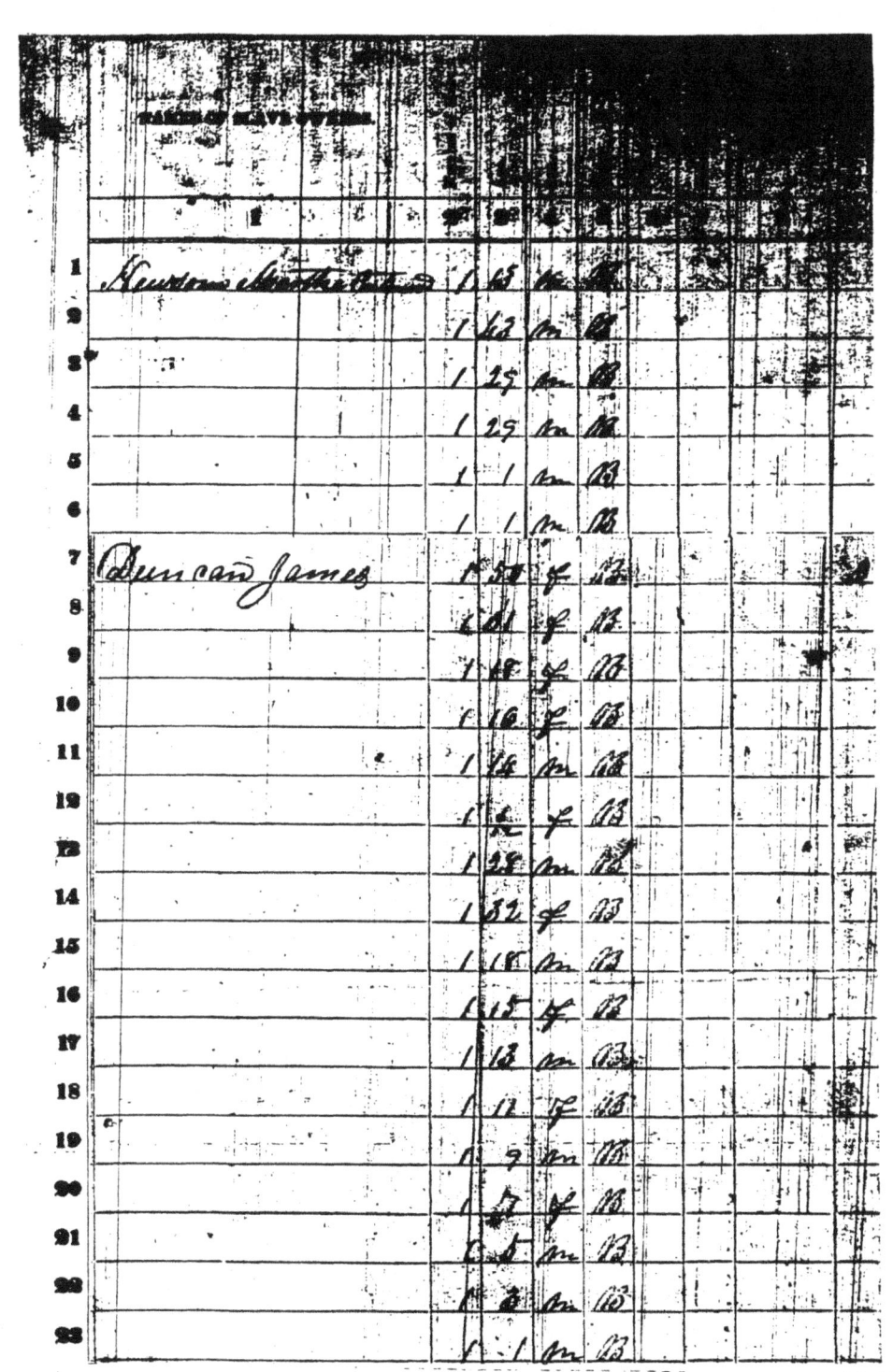

Fig. 7-9A. Slave Schedule of James Duncan

Inventory and Appraisement of [estate]
of James Duncan dec'd.

To	1	Moses about 26 years old		1000	00
"	2	Emily " 34 " "		600	00
"	3	Matilda " 36 " " Child		800	00
"	4	Little Peny " 16 " "		900	00
"	5	Big " " 53 " "		400	00
"	6	Hannah " 7 " "		600	00
"	7	Warren " 19 " "		1200	00
"	8	Green " 13 " "		900	00
"	9	Ben " 9 " "		800	00
	1	Horse Nick		150	00
	1	Do Leo		150	00
	1	Do Do		45	00
	1	Mare Do		100	00
	35	Head Stock Hogs		100	00
	1	Two Horse wagon		60	00
	1	Ox cart		20	00
	1	Buggy & Harness		100	00
	500	acres of Land		3000	00
	1	Patent Ever Watch		18	00
	1	Bedstead, Covering		35	00
	1	Do Do Do		40	00
	1	Bureau		6	00
	1	Bedstead & Mattress		18	00
	1	Lot quilts, counterpanes &			
	1	" Books			
	1	Bedstead & covering			

Fig. 7-9B. Inventory and Appraisements of James Duncan, deceased.

Chapter Four

A DISCOVERY

Is it my family? Yes...Maybe...Perhaps...No...Don't think so.

One of the first Taylor Co. Inventories that grabbed my attention was on page 155, James Duncan, deceased 18 Dec. 1860. He had 12 slaves:

1. Moses	about 26 years old, valued at	$1000	
2. Emily	34	600	
3. Matilda	36 and 3 children	1800	
4. Little Penny	16	900	
5. Big Penny	53	400	
6. Hannah	7	600	
7. Warren	19	1200	
8. Green	13	900	
9. Ben	9	800	
1 Horse Mule...		140	
1 Mare Do ("Do" meant ditto)		100	

Excitement over the find sent me rushing to the *1870 Georgia Census Index* to see if perhaps this was my Matilda and Emily, or if these slaves took the Duncan name. I found the following Index listing:

	Color	Sex	Age	County	page
Hannah Duncan	B	M	16	Houston	145
Green Duncan	B	M	28	Macon	574
Moses Duncan	B	M	37	Macon	536
Ben Duncan	B	M	14	Macon	535
Penny Duncan	B	F	62	Macon	615
Matilda Duncan	B	F	30	Chatham	285
Emoline Duncan	W*	F	48	Lumpkin	419
Emoline Duncan	B	F	12	Taylor	317

*Emoline Duncan, age 48, listed as "white," may or may not be the slave, Emily, age 34, in the Inventory.

34 Slave Ancestral Research

In James Duncan's Inventory, Emily's age 34, was too close to Matilda age 36, to be her daughter. Still I looked in the 1870 Census of each county. I made notes as follows:

Hannah Duncan was listed as a domestic servant with a Charles David White family in Houston County Georgia.

Emeline Duncan, age 12, was a house servant with the James White family in Taylor County. These two "White" families were probably related. My guess is that Emeline was Hannah's daughter. (A researcher would need to locate marriage records which may have shown a relationship between the Duncan and White families.) Since this was not my familly, I did no further research on those families.

Green Duncan was in Macon County with his wife Delcy and five children. Moses Duncan with wife Charlotte were in Macon County with their eight children. (Moses' son Ben age 14, was listed twice. He was among the eight children and also listed as a farm laborer with a white Wyatt Bucks family.)

I found Penny Duncan with her black family, Jane Grizzle and her three children in Macon County.

I was convinced, the slaves took the Duncan name. It was interesting to see. The slaves had left Taylor County and were in other counties after they became free. See Fig. 7-9B, James Duncan's Inventory.

I followed my plan by matching the Duncan names listed in the *1870 Georgia Census Index* with the Duncan slaves of the Inventory. I located James Duncan with his wife Susan and son, James M. and daughter Lucretia in the 1860 Taylor County Census Schedule. Then I located James Duncan as a slave owner in the 1860 Taylor County Slave Schedule (Fig. 7-9A) and noticed that Big Penny was the slave referred to as follows:

Name of Slave Owner	Number	Age	Sex	Color	
Duncan, James	1	50	F	B	(Big Penny)

Slave Ancestral Research

Ages of slaves were not always reported consistently but in this case, "Big Penny" could be identified by her age.

On 18 December 1860, the enumerators listed the number of slaves owned by James Duncan in Taylor County. He had 17 slaves in his 1860 Slave Schedule and 12 in his Inventory at his death. What happened to the other five? A common practice was to hire Negro slaves to help "make a crop" on another plantation while ownership remained with their original owner. Perhaps the five missing were in this category. A search for the will of James Duncan solved the mystery. Below is a typed portion of James Duncan's Will which concerns the distribution of his slaves. James Duncan's Will was dated three months prior to the date his slaves were enumerated in the 1860 Taylor County Slave Schedule.

STATE OF GEORGIA   In the name of God Amen. I, James Duncan of
TAYLOR, CO.   said state and county being of advanced age, but of sound and disposing mind and memory knowing that I must shortly depart this life...make a disposition of the property I make this my last will and testament...

Item 1st...that my body be buried...in a Christian like manner...
Item 2nd...that all my just debts be paid without delay...
Item 3rd...that I give...and devise to my...wife Susan M. Duncan
the plantation...also the following named Negro slaves
to wit-- Moses a man, Warren a man, Green a boy, Ben
a boy, Harrey a boy, William a boy, Harrison a boy,
big Penny a woman, little Penny a woman, Emily a
woman, Matilda a woman and Hannah a girl to have said
property during her natural life or widowhood and at
the death of wife or upon her intermarriage all of
said property to be equally divided amongst my four
children to wit--Thadeus F. Duncan, James M. Duncan,
Martha E. Woods and Lucretia A. Duncan...

Item 4th   I give and bequeath to my son Thadeus F. Duncan a Negro
           girl a slave by the name of Ann and her increase which
           Negro is now loaned to my said son and which Negro
           I value at $1200.

Item 5th   I give...to my daughter Martha E Wooddy a Negro
           woman, a slave named Mary and her child Emily said
           Negroes are now loaned to my said daughter which
           Negroes I value at $1400...

Item 6th   I give...to my son James M. Duncan a Negro boy
           slave named Wiley which Negro is now loaned to my son
           and which Negro I value at $1200...

Item 7th   I give...to my daughter Lucretia A. Duncan Silva
           a Negro girl slave which Negro I value at $800...

Item 8th... Item 9th...Item 10th...

Item 11th I hereby constitute and appoint my wife Susan M. Duncan
           as executrix and James M. Duncan Executor to this my
           last will and Testament this Sept. 4th 1860...

The five slaves not named in James Duncan's Inventory (Ann, Mary and child, Emily, Wiley a boy and Silva, a girl) were already in the possession of his children but ownership did not pass to them until after his death. Even the unborn children of Ann in Item 4th were to become slaves of James' son, Thadeus. Ann, as mother could not claim ownership of her unborn children.

Since this was not my McCants family, I kept the records for the Charley Ray line of research which had a connection to a family of Duncans in Macon County. (Charley, husband of Dorcas/Emma Holton, Fig.7-2D)

Taylor County Inventory & Appraisement of the estate

Catharine Daniel deceased.

	1	Gilbert a Negro boy	$	900.00
Abram	2	Abram " "		900.00
	3	Royal		1050.00
	4	Louisa (Lovyna)		1050.00
	5	Warren		850.00
	6	Emily a Girl		750.00
	7	Lucinda a Child		850.00
	8	Jenny & 2 Children		1500.00
	9	Fanny 1 child is Mary		900.00
				7350.00
	1	Sorrel Horse		100.00
	1	Sorrel Mule		50.00
	8	Hogs		20.00
	1	Buggy & Harness		35.00
	5	head of Cattle		35.00
	2	Beds, Steads and furniture		25.00
	1	Lot of Crockery, Trunks & Chairs		5.00
	1	Grind Stone, large pot		2.00
		Farming Utensils		7.00
				7639.00

Notes & Accounts
4 Notes against John S Jackson 100.00
2 Notes on G B Daniel 32.39
A F Owens acct ....
Mrs E Raglin 15.21
Kilgore 3.51
$8430.20 (approx)

Georgia, We do certify that the foregoing was
Taylor County produced to us by the Adm. the foregoing
is a true appraisement of the estate of Catharine
Daniel dec'd
John Walley J.P.
H Mangham } Appraisers
G B Bulls

I certify that the above appraisement was done
by persons sworn duly to perform same
John Walley J.P.

Fig. 7-10. Inventory and Appraisements, Catharine Daniel

Sale of the Negro property belonging to the Estate of Catherine Daniel Decd of Taylor County the 4th Day of January 1859

Warren	a Boy	Sold	to	Jones Hicks	$1265	
Mary	a girl	"	"	D. W. Morand Agt	666.00	E. Ragland
Abram	a man	"	"	John S. Jackson	1102.00	
Jenny & child		"	"	D. W. Morand Agt	1250.00	E. Ragland
Fanny	a woman	"	"	Will Drane	1255.00	
Lucinda & child		"	"	D. W. Morand Agt	1030.00	E. Ragland
Emily	a woman	Sold	to	S. W. Kilgore	779.00	
Ezekiel	a man	"	"	S. W. Ducham	1450.25	
Royal	a man	"	"	Z. Sterno	1285.00	
Gilbert	a man	"	"	O. E. Daniel	600.00	
					$10682.25	
					404.64	

Fig. 7-11A. Advertising in Georgia Journal and Messenger Leave to Sell Negroes

Chapter Five

ARE THESE MY FOLKS: ABRAM, EMILY, AND MARY ON CATHARINE DANIEL'S INVENTORY AND SALE OF PERISHABLE PROPERTY?

Abram, Emily, and Mary, three of my family names, on a list! My heartbeat quickened when I saw two Taylor County estate records of Catharine Daniel listing their names: her Inventory and Sale of Perishable Property, Figs. 7-10 and 7-11A. Catharine's Inventory, dated 16 Jan. 1857, listed: Abram, valued at $900; Lovynia, $1050; and Emily, a girl, $850. Jenny's two children were listed together in the Inventory and one daughter, Mary listed separately in the Sale. My ancestors Matilda McCants and Simon had a daughter Emily, who married Abram Holton. Could this be my family?

Since Thomas Riley served as Administrator for the sale of Catharine Daniel's property, I used his surname as a clue that 14 year old Mary Riley, Abram and Emily on Catharine's Inventory could be my ancestors. Abram, Emily and Mary Riley were in the same household in 1870, Fig. 7-2A.

T. J. Riley paid $8.50 to advertise the sale of Catharine Daniel's Negro property, 4 Aug. 1858. They were sold five months later. A sad winter day that was, January 4, 1859. Their "missus" had died two years before in 1857, and now they were led away to a new owner. It was a cold day in more ways than one. Each one was sold to a different buyer. (See Fig. 7-11A.)

The names of the new owners should have appeared in the 1860 Slave Schedule with an increase in their number of slaves.

I tried to trail: John S. Jackson, new owner of Abram; S. W. Kilgore, who purchased Emily; and E. Ragland whose agent, D. W. Morand, bought Mary, Jenny and her child along with Lucinda and her child; in the 1860 Census to determine where the slaves were taken. Lovyna was listed in Catharine Daniel's Inventory, but missing from the "Sale." What happened to her? Each record left questions unanswered.

Did Emily, Abram and Mary remain in Taylor County? I checked the 1860 Georgia Census Index for E. Ragland, John S. Jackson and S. W. Kilgore. Neither name appeared in the population or slave schedules of Taylor or Talbot Counties. Since I had not found a marriage record of Emily and Abram Holton in Taylor or Talbot Counties, I reasoned that they were taken away by those who purchased them.

I made an exhaustive search to locate the new owners. I thought that E. Ragland was a male. While searching, I luckily found a marriage record of Eve Steel to Hudson Ragland of Upson County Georgia, dated 12 Dec. 1820. (Married in Wilkinson County Georgia.) The 1850 Upson County Slave Schedule, p. 155, showed Eve Ragland with 14 slaves, John Jackson with 26 and Catharne Daniel with seven, Fig. 7-12A. Is she the same Catharine? Perhaps she moved to Taylor County between 1852, and her death in 1857. Eve Ragland had 27 slaves in 1860, an increase of 13. John Jackson had 26 slaves in 1850 and 24 slaves in 1860. Perhaps Abram was one of them.

In 1860, Eve Ragland was an 87 year old widow in Upson County living with her daughter, Ann Moreman and family. She had sent her grandson D. W. Moreman/Morand, a physician from Upson to Taylor County to purchase Jenny, Lucinda and their children, which totaled five slaves.

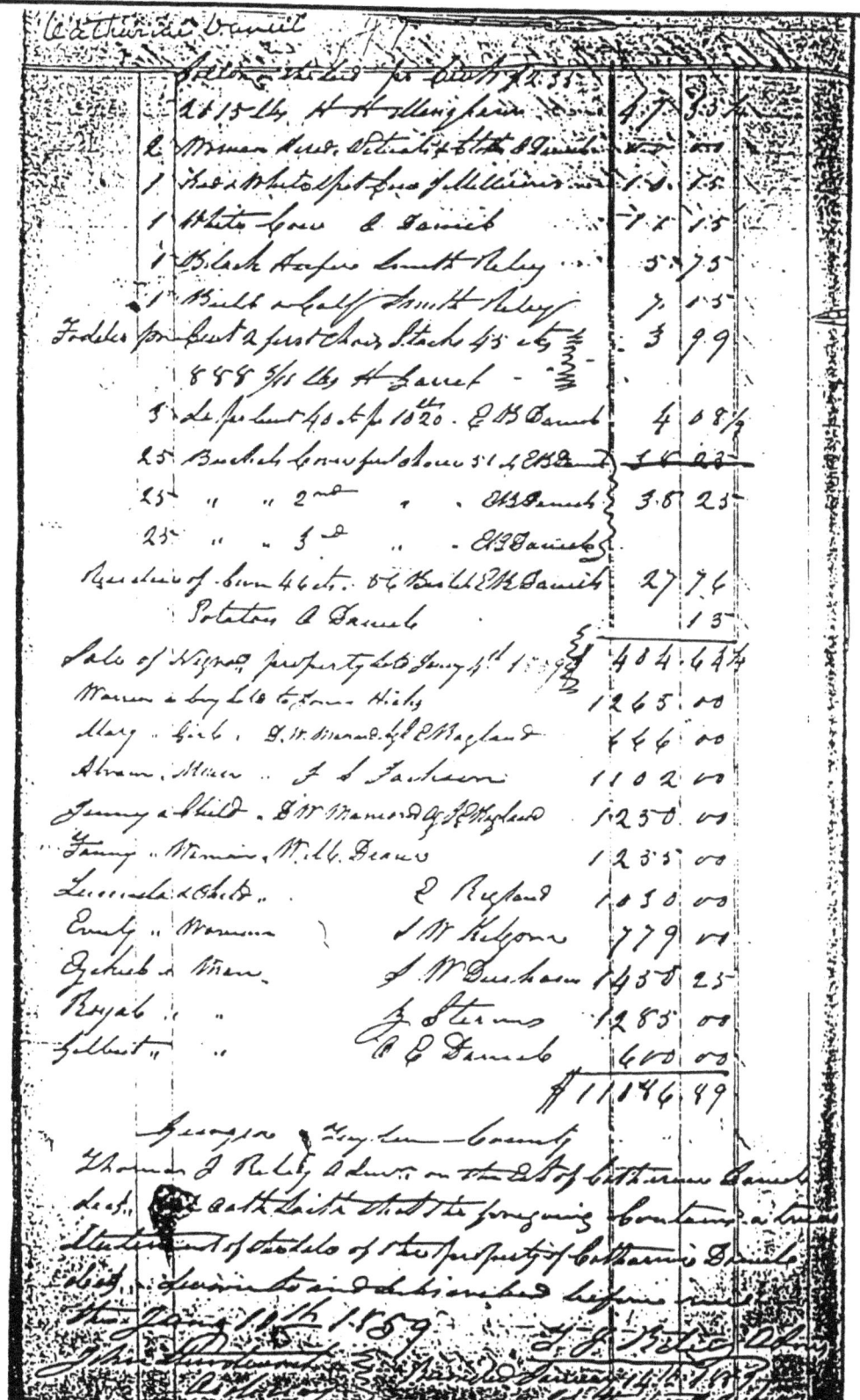

Fig. 7-11A Catharine Daniel's Administrator, Thomas J. Riley, advertises in Georgia Journal and Messenger: Notice to Debtors & Creditors; and "Leave to sell" Negroes. Copy of "Sale of Negroes,...January 4, 1859.

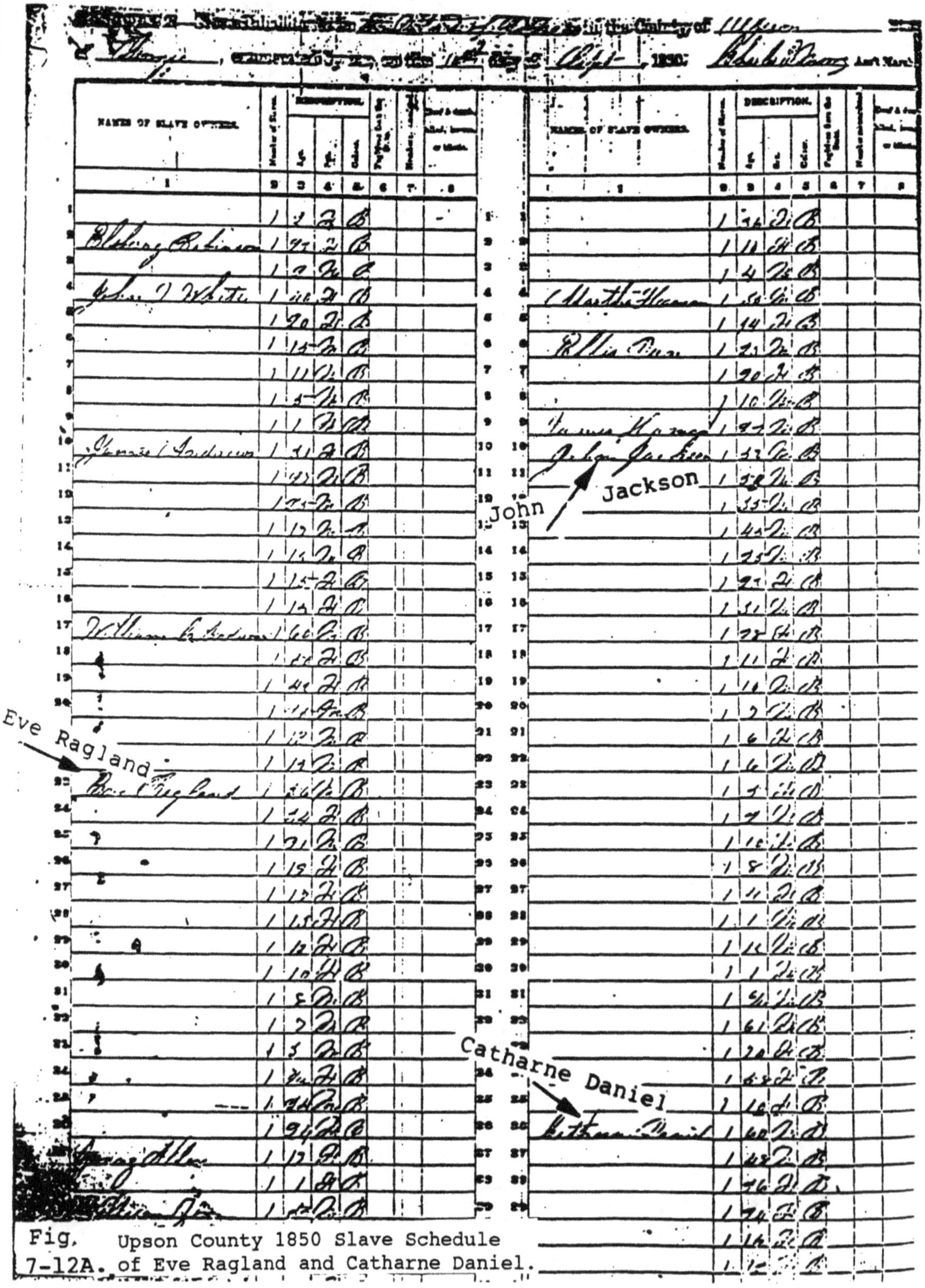

Fig. 7-12A. Upson County 1850 Slave Schedule of Eve Ragland and Catharne Daniel.

Eve Ragland's will dated 8 July 1860, left all property to daughter Ann Moreman and her children. She did not name Negro property in the will. John S. Jackson was a witness to her will. He may be the same person who purchased Abram from Catharine Daniel's estate.

Caroline Daniel age 50, a farmer with two children, lived close to E. Ragland. She had two Negro slaves listed immediately following Eve Ragland's list in the 1860 Upson County Slave Schedule. Perhaps Caroline Daniel was an in-law relative of Catharine Daniel, deceased, in Taylor County. I needed to see a Daniel family history or genealogy, which may have helped.

page 638   1860 UPSON CO. GEORGIA CENSUS

Family Number	Name	Age	Sex	Color	Occupation	Value of Real Estate	Value Personal Estate
709	D. W. Moreman	30	M	W	Physician	$125	$ 1,150
710	James Moreman	20	M	"	Farmer		
	Anna Moreman	58	F	"	Housekeeper	700	1075
	A. W. Moreman	30	M	"	Trader		500
	J. D. Moreman	22	M	"	Overseer	300	
	E. L. Moreman	19	M	"	Farm labor		
	Eve Ragland	87	F	"	Farmer	5400	23,275

Fig.7-12B.   1860 Upson County Georgia Census
              Eve Ragland purchased slaves from Catharine Daniel in Taylor County. She was a very wealthy widow.

I reasoned that the documents on Catharine's Estate might provide clues to trailing my ancestors. A. F. Owens, attorney for Eve Ragland, paid $400 for the purchase of five slaves to Catharine's Estate (see Fig. 7-10). Ann Kilgore paid $8.81. A search for marriage records revealed Ann's marriage to Solomon Kilgore 14 March 1809 in Clark County, GA. However, a *Simon Kilgore* paid $555 to the Estate in Fig. 7-13. *S. W. Kilgore* purchased Emily from Catharine Daniel's Estate in Fig. 7-11A. Solomon and Simon may be the same person. (Name spellings were always inconsistent in the records.) The 1860 Georgia Census Index identified the counties where S. W. Kilgore, Eve Ragland and John S. Jackson lived, but I was unable to find a record listing the names of their slaves.

Georgia } Second Annual Return of [Administrator]
Taylor County } W. S. Riley Administrator of Catharine Daniel dec'd

Amounts Collected Since Last Return

1857 Jan'y 26	Collected	from J. W. Daniel (Per Property)	$19.71
"	"	" " "	7.16
"	"	" O. E. Daniel	301.12
"	"	" E. B. Daniel	512.07
"	"	" John Mathews	12.50
"	"	" Dennis Sheridan	6.45
"	"	" James H. Mills	63.50
"	"	" R. Allen	36.00
"	"	" O. E. Daniel for Negro	602.00
"	"	" Wm. M. Drane	625.12
"	"	" S. W. Dunham	1,450.00
"	"	" C. W. Morrison Ag't for E. Ragland	372.00
"	"	" G. Sternes	1382.00
"	"	" Simon Kilgore	355.00
"	"	" W. S. Riley (per Property)	32.90
June 2	Rec'd of A. F. Owen proceeds of note on E. Ragland		349.42
			5734.07

Amounts Paid out Since Last Return

1857 July 8	Paid	W. P. Mathews as per Voucher	No. 1	4.25
" June 29	"	Edwards & Maines	" 2	3.55
" July 8	"	W. P. Mathews	" 3	3.00
" "	"	"	" 4	64.50
" 6	"	Joseph Brown	" 5	22.15
" "	"	J. L. Brewer Sr.	" 6	10.00
" June 7	"	A. F. Owen Commissions on Notes &c	" 7	27.05
" July 22	"	Margaret A. McLeod	" 8	16.75
Oct 4	"	S. Rose & Co	" 9	2.50
1860 Jan'y 23	"	James E. Ropes	" 10	6.55
1859 June 21	"	O. E. Daniel	" 11	
" Dec 28	"	James W. Daniel	" 12	
" July 31	"	Dennis Sheridan	" 13	
" June 18	"	E. B. Daniel	" 14	
" 12	"	James W. Daniel	" 15	
" 5	"	J. C. McLeod & Co	" 16	
1860 May 14	"	John G. Heath	" 17	2.35
1859 Dec 26	"	O. E. Daniel	" 18	
" "	"	James M. Smith Guardian &c	" 19	
" "	"	Phillip K. Daniel		
" "	"	R. A. Allen		
" "	"	James W. Daniel		
" "	"	J. N. O. Caldwell		
" 24	"	A. Mathews		

Fig. 7-13. Annual Return of Catharine Daniel.

Fig. 7-14A 1910 Taylor Co. Census, p. 33. Missouri Johnson, daughter of Simon and Matilda McCants. Angelina Lockett, mother-in-law, (mother of Abel Johnson), Annie Holton and Edgar Holton are children of Missouri's son-in-law, Pete Holton, my great grand uncle, shown in Fig. 7-1.

Because several of my ancestors' names appeared in the estate records of Catharine Daniel in Taylor County, I believed they were my ancestors and Catharine Daniel was their owner. Since families were often separated during slavery, and I was unable to locate a marriage record of Emily and Abram Holton in Taylor Co., I firmly believed that Abram and Emily were taken to another county.

Matilda and Simon McCants and their daughter, Missouri McCants got legal marriages, I felt that Emily and Abe Holton legally married too. The place was a mystery. I requested their marriage record in Upson County, where I thought they were taken. The response from Upson Co. was "no record."

Year 1920 Soundex No				State Georgia		
Coleman, Janie				Vol. 6	E.D. 43	
Head of Household				Sheet 17	Line 50	
Mu			40	GA		
Color	Month	Year	Age	Birthplace		Citizenship
Bibb						
County						
Macon			Jackson mcd		320	
City			Street		House No.	
Name	Rel.	Birth Mo.	Birth Yr.	Age	Birthplace	Cit.
Johnson, Missouri	Si			70	GA	

Fig. 7-14B. 1920 Soundex, Bibb Co., GA. Federal Census Missouri (McCants) Johnson and sister, Janie Coleman.

Why the name Holton instead of Daniel? Gutman's[2] research on slave naming practices explained that some slaves took the name of a prior owner, the last owner or selected a name of their choice. The Holton descendants that I met during my research did not know the origin of the name. (Holton descendants are discussed in Chapter Four of the companion book to this text, The *Jackson-Moore Family History and Genealogy*, written by this author.)

I learned from the 1920 Census Soundex that Matilda's daughter, Missouri McCants Johnson, was living with her sister Jane Coleman, in the 1920 Bibb County Georgia Census. (Fig. 7-14B) Jane is a nickname for Jenny. If these were my folks on Catharine Daniel's Inventory, then Jane/Jenny and Emily were sisters to Matilda and Simon's daughter, Missouri.

Even though these are assumptions based purely on circumstantial evidence, it was very interesting to find Abram, Emily, Jenny/Jane, and Mary recorded in one record. Future research may prove or disprove my assumption.

My research to find the slave owners of my folks forced me to trace the genealogy of white families. I scanned early Georgia marriage records for names of witnesses and administrators on estate inventories of deceased property owners, the ones I suspected as the possible slave owners of my kin folks. Inevitably, I discovered family marriage connections to the deceased. I looked for their families in the population and slave schedules.

I found the marriage record of Eve Ragland by accident while looking at a list of early Georgia marriages. I learned of her relationship to D. W. Morand by reading her will. I reviewed all court records of Catharine Daniel and saw dates of payments made by Eve Ragland and others for the slaves they purchased. (See Fig. 7-13.) There appeared to be family connections between Eve Ragland, John S. Jackson, S. W. Kilgore, Thomas J. Riley and Catharine Daniel.

The way slaves were pushed and shoved from one owner to another among related families made it very difficult to trace their movements. Only with the intervention of luck and Divine Guidance is a descendant able to find them within a shroud of uncertainty. By scanning indexes in books containing excerpts of Georgia county court proceedings, county histories, Bible records, books of Georgia wills and Georgia genealogical periodicals for the three surnames, I saw family relationships.

Thomas J. Riley, Administrator of Catharine Daniel's Estate, appeared to be a brother-in-law. Catharine's maiden name was Howe. In volume 4, p. 207, of William H. Davis' *Rockaway in Talbot*, I read: "The family Bible of Thomas Jefferson Riley (1815-1878) and wife, Harriet Howe Riley (1819-1850) of the Carsonville community contains a valuable record of births of their slaves." I noticed that Harriet and Catharine had the same "Howe" maiden name. Catharine's name was listed in *Biographical Souvenirs of Georgia and Florida*, p. 213, "M. J. Daniel, MD., one of the oldest... practitioners of Griffin, Ga., was born in Pike County... October 15, 1830, and is a son of E. P. and Catherine (Howe) Daniel..." I found this information by following my plan to browse through any books I saw on early Georgia settlers.

Although names of slaves were not always included in many records, reading records helped identify counties to search for surnames of the slave owners' families. I made a practice to visit city libraries frequently to see books about early Georgia settlers.

Catharine Daniel "seemed" to be the slave owner of my maternal great, great grand parents, Abram and Emily Holton, ID# 30-31 on my Family Lineage Chart. Further research is needed for unquestionable assurance.

I continued my wandering through the Taylor County Inventories for Simon and Matilda McCants and their daughter, Missouri. I found another inventory that seemed promising, John McCrary, dated 25th December 1854.

JOHN McCRARY

Inventory and appraisment of the Estate of John McCrary late of said county dec'd. taken this 25th day of December 1854.

1	Negro	man	Dick	valued	$1600.00
1	"	"	Stephen	"	900.00
1	"	"	Joe	"	1000.00
1	"	"	Hamp	"	1000.00
1	"	"	*(F)lousury	"	1000.00
1	"	"	Ned	"	1000.00
1	"	"	Madison	"	1000.00
1	"	"	Isaac	"	1000.00
1	"	"	Will	"	1000.00
1	"	boy	Peter	"	900.00
1	"	"	Allen	"	900.00
1	"	"	William	"	900.00
1	"	"	Tom	"	900.00
1	"	woman	Cady	"	800.00
1	"	"	Creasy & child		1000.00
1	"	"	Philice & 3 child		1500.00
2	"	boys	Gus and Ruben		1100.00
1	"	"	Horasine		450.00
1	"	woman	Sally & her 2 children		1500.00
1	"	"	*Matilda & Becky & Zussui		1500.00
1	"	"	Litty & Margaret her child		1400.00
1	"	girl	Frances		900.00
1	"	woman	Veny		100.00
1	"	"	Dicey a man Dick		100.00
1	"	"	Casey		100.00
1	"	Negro man	Peter		1500.00

1 Mare Colt valued at		150.00
1 Gray mare & Colt		85.00
1 bay horse named Jane		125.00
1 grey horse mule Allen		75.00
1 " " " Georgie		75.00
1 mare " Gim		75.00

*Writing is not clear.

Fig. 7-15. Partial Inventory of John McCrary, Bartley McCrary, Administrator. Appraisers: Andrew J. Colbert, C. H. Hickler, E. C. Butler and J. C. McCants.

John McCrary
Georgia, Taylor County

Inventory and appraisement of the Estate of John McCrary late of said County dec'd taken this 25th day of December 1854.

				$	
1	Negro man	Drake	valued	1600	00
1	"	"	Stephen	"	900	00
1	"	"	Joe	"	900	00
1	"	"	Harris	"	1000	00
1	"	"	Flournoy	"	1000	00
1	"	"	Nick	"	1000	00
1	"	"	Madison	"	1000	00
1	"	"	Isaac	"	1000	00
1	"	"	Wells	"	1000	00
1	"	boy	Peter	"	900	00
1	"	"	Allen	"	900	00
1	"	"	William	"	900	00
1	"	"	Tom	"	900	00
1	"	Woman	Lucy	"	800	00
1	"	"	Creasy & Child	1000	00
1	"	"	Phebe & 3 children	1500	00
2	"	Boys	Gus & Newton	1100	00
1	"	"	Horace	450	00
1	"	Woman Sally & her children	1500	00
1	"	" Mahulda & 2 children	1300	00
1	"	" Sally & Margaret child	1400	00
1	"	Girl Nancy	900	00
1	"	Woman Rhina	100	00
1	"	" Lucy & Newborn	1000	00
1	"	Woman Crecy	100	00
1	"	Negro man Peter	1100	00
1	Mare Colt & Pined at	150	00
1	Grey mare & Colt	85	00
1	Bay Horse named James	125	00
1	Grey Horse mule Adam	75	00
1	" " Georgi	75	00
1	mare " Jim	75	00

Fig. 7-15. Inventory and Appraisements, John McCrary, deceased c.1854.

Chapter Six

HE'S THE ONE, JOHN McCRARY

"Ah ha, that must be my family on John McCrary's Inventory!" I thought when I first saw my family names. He had a Matilda, Becky and Zussre (Missoury) and an old woman Veny, valued at $100.00. I copied his list, Fig. 7-15. Still, I was not certain and turned my attention to the Talbot County Probate records. (Although John McCrary died in 1854 in Taylor County, he was in the Talbot County 1850 Census.)

Several Returns among the Fanning Estate records in Talbot County named a Matilda with children and a Simon. Three of the Returns with notes are shown in Fig. 7-16. In addition to these, I copied many Talbot County slave lists. It appeared that every slaveholder with a dozen or more slaves always had a "Tildy." That name was very common. The Fanning family, Robert Snellings[3] and Albert Gray had slaves with my family names. See Notes. Other estate records also had one or more of my family names.

Although the Talbot County Returns listed my ancestors' names, I did not find a record transferring them directly to John McCrary. In the absence of that connection, I was uncertain that they were my kinfolks. As I copied the "Returns," I was unaware of the significance of those records in slave ancestral research and did not realize until months later what "Returns" were. See the Chapter, From Pillar to Post.

52 Slave Ancestral Research

With names recorded in various spellings; their owners shifting them from place to place through "hirings" and "sales;" frequent omission of ages; father, mother and child separations, common; and missing surnames, I had nothing to serve as a guide to positively identify the right owner except to seek marriage connections of the slave owners. If there were a marriage to a McCrary, I used that as a clue that the slaves in different households at various times, might be the same ones.

However, a possibility lingered. Perhaps John McCrary inherited my ancestors, had them while in Talbot County, moved to Taylor County, and kept them until his death in 1854. For certain, his Inventory had named my ancestors. He was their owner. However, there was no will which may have included the names of his Negro property prior to his death. A plantation record or Bible record of slave births would have helped. Neither was found.

Although hopeful, my footing was shaky and uncertain. For certain, Veny, Matilda, Becky and Zussre (Missouri) were together on John McCrary's Inventory in Taylor County in 1854. I believed they were my kinfolks. I wondered what happened to them after John McCrary died until they were listed in the 1870 Taylor County Census? Who received John McCrary's Negro property? I aimed to search until I could find the answer.

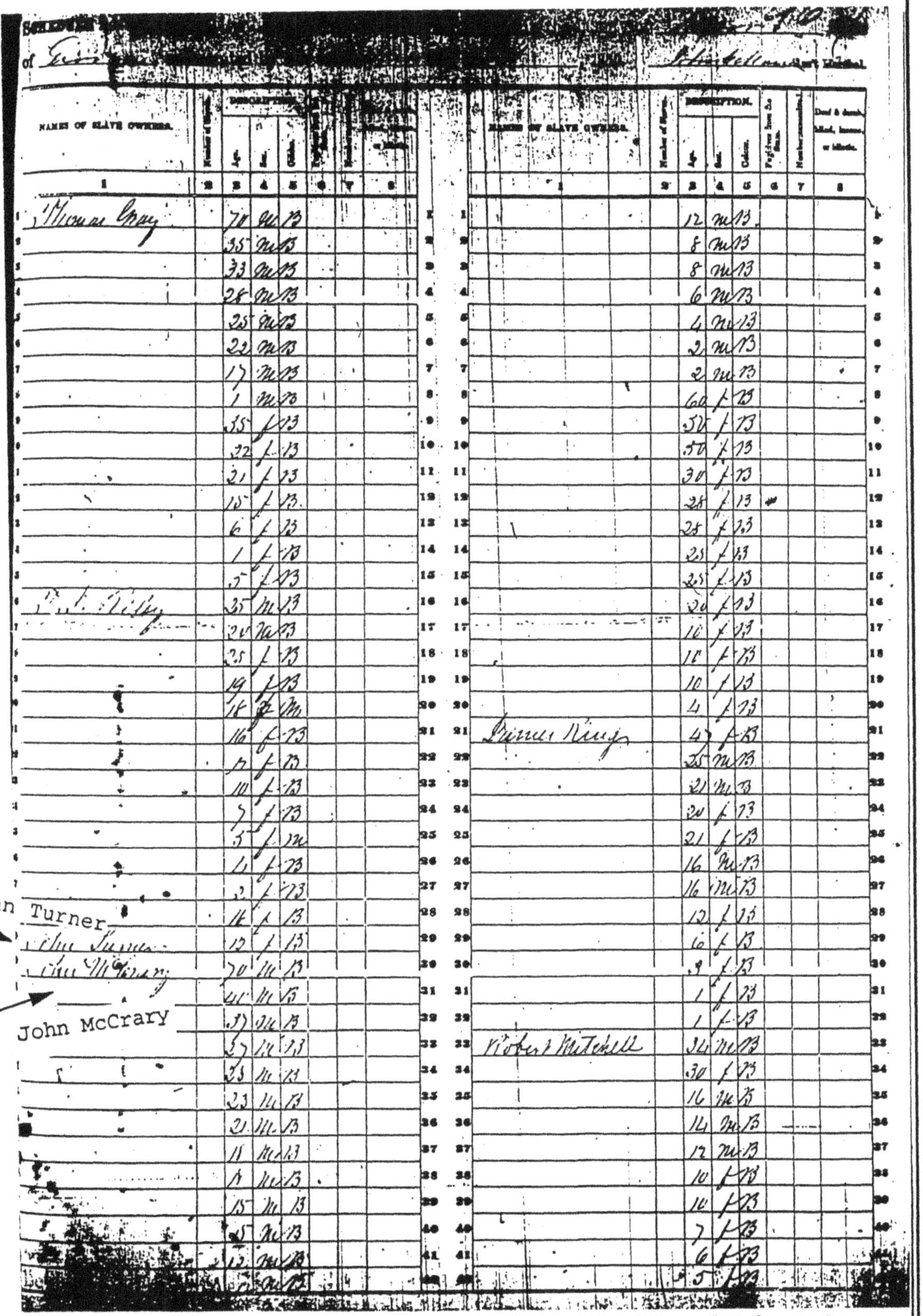

	Names of slave owners	Age	Sex	Colour		Names of slave owners	Age	Sex	Colour
1	Thomas Gray	70	m	B	1		12	m	B
2		35	m	B	2		8	m	B
3		33	m	B	3		8	m	B
4		28	m	B	4		6	m	B
5		25	m	B	5		4	m	B
6		22	m	B	6		2	m	B
7		17	m	B	7		2	m	B
8		1	m	B	8		60	f	B
9		35	f	B	9		50	f	B
10		32	f	B	10		50	f	B
11		21	f	B	11		30	f	B
12		15	f	B	12		28	f	B
13		6	f	B	13		25	f	B
14		1	f	B	14		25	f	B
15		5	f	B	15		25	f	B
16	[illegible] Riley	35	m	B	16		20	f	B
17		20	m	B	17		10	f	B
18		25	f	B	18		10	f	B
19		19	f	B	19		10	f	B
20		18	f	M	20		4	f	B
21		16	f	B	21	James King	45	f	B
22		12	f	B	22		25	m	B
23		10	f	B	23		21	m	B
24		7	f	B	24		30	f	B
25		5	f	M	25		21	f	B
26		4	f	B	26		16	m	B
27		2	f	B	27		16	m	B
28		14	f	B	28		12	f	B
29	John Turner	12	f	B	29		10	f	B
30	John McCrary	70	m	B	30		9	f	B
31		41	m	B	31		1	f	B
32		37	m	B	32		1	f	B
33		27	m	B	33	Robert Mitchell	34	m	B
34		25	m	B	34		30	f	B
35		23	m	B	35		16	m	B
36		21	m	B	36		14	m	B
37		18	m	B	37		12	m	B
38		18	m	B	38		10	f	B
39		15	m	B	39		10	f	B
40		5	m	B	40		7	f	B
41		13	m	B	41		6	f	B
42		[illegible]	m	B	42		5	f	B

Fig. 7-15A. ***1850 Talbot County Slave Schedule of John McCrary, d.1854. Above McCrary, John Turner has one female slave, age 12.

54 Slave Ancestral Research

COULD THIS BE THE SLAVEHOLDING FAMILY OF MY KINFOLKS?

1850 Talbot Co. Census Schedule of John McCrary, dec'd. 1854.

1850 TALBOT COUNTY, GA CENSUS SCHEDULE

Dwelling house numbered in order of visitation	Family number		Age	Sex	Occupation	Place of Birth
1000	1000	John McCrary	60	M	Farmer	Sc
		Balty	23	M		Ga
		Jane	21	F		Ga
		Jonathan	17	M		Ga
		John	17	M		Ga
		Henry	16	M		Ga

Fig.7-15B. Talbot County, GA Census Schedule of the John McCrary family.

I read the history of both Talbot and Taylor Counties and learned that Taylor County was created in 1852 from Talbot County. The Carsonville District of Talbot County became Taylor County. Robert H. Jordan reported in his book, *There was a Land, a Story of Talbot County, Georgia and Its People*, that the 1850 Census of Talbot County showed 8,723 slaves. If John McCrary were the slave owner of my kinfolks, then they were among the 8,723 slaves. John McCrary was among the first settlers in Taylor County, GA. He died in 1854, two years after the creation of the county.

Slave Ancestral Research 55

Chapter Seven

TALBOT COUNTY RETURNS

Although I felt fairly certain that my ancestors were listed on John McCrary's Inventory in 1854, I wanted to know where they were *before* that year. Perhaps they would be in Talbot County Inferior Court records, I reasoned. I searched there because Taylor County was created from Talbot in 1852 and John McCrary and his family were in the 1850 Talbot County Census Schedule. (See Fig. 7-15B)

At the Family History Center (see page 13), I looked at their "Locality File" on microfische which listed all films available from the LDS Library under the topic, "Georgia, Talbot County, Probate Records, Court of Ordinary." Under this topic were many kinds of probate records including Books of: Wills, Inventories and Appraisements, Sales, Vouchers, Marriages and Annual Returns.

From time to time I ordered over two dozen rolls of microfilm, while having no idea what I would find. I ordered the film covering the years from 1827 through 1854 and searched each one for my family names. Talbot County was created in 1827. I soon learned to look for the index at both the beginning and end of each roll. I spent long hours sitting with weary eyes copying every estate record with one or more of my family names.

From those records I learned what happened to the slaves when their owners died. The executors of wills or, if the owner died intestate (without a will), court-appointed administrators were required by law to have the county clerk record all matters concerning the estate of the deceased. The clerks listed the slaves

56 Slave Ancestral Research

in Estate Inventories and recorded what happened to them, whether they were sold, their value, names of the buyers or if they were hired out, to whom and for how much, also if they were transferred to heirs.

If I felt that any of my folks were named in a record, I would follow those estate records closely, then check early Georgia marriage lists to see if there were a marriage to a McCrary, McCants or Riley. The names of the slaves from an estate were repeated in several different records. In one of the records, a mother-child relationship might be given. This enabled me to dismiss some names as no kin.

With each visit to the Family History Center to view the microfilm, the list of slave owners who had slaves with my family names grew longer and longer, while my files bulged higher and higher. However, I was drawn to consider the Fanning Estate records.

The Returns in the Fanning Estate Records listed my names in their "hiring" records. I thought perhaps the Fanning family once owned Matilda and Simon as shown in Fig.7-16. As the notes explain, even after seeing the names Simon and Matilda together in the same record I could not be sure. Slave ancestral research is by no means an exact science. Three Fanning Returns are in Fig. 7-16. The 1850 Talbot County Slave Schedule of John McCrary, d.1854 is Fig. 7-15A.

Slave Ancestral Research

TALBOT COUNTY RETURNS

SEPARATE RETURN FOR THE HIRE OF THE NEGROES IN THE ESTATE OF JAMES G. FANNING FOR MINORS, MARY, JOHN AND ELIZABETH FANNING. THOMAS GREEN, GUARDIAN

1840				
	Randal a Negro man hired to		James E. Smith	267.50
	Basen	" "	Archibald Norrid	150.00
	Matilda & child**	"	John Turner***	80.00
	Lucy, a girl	"	William Barnett	87.00
	Nancy, girl	"	J. B. Bateman	27.00
	Martha, old woman	"	Rob Wynn	41.00
	Charlotte, woman	"	Jas Carter	80.00
	Ciller & 2 children	"	B. Bethune	71.00
	Dinah & child	"	Thomas Green	76.00

1840   RETURN FOR MARTHA B. FANNING   FELIX GREEN, *GUARDIAN

	Dennis	$ 147.00
	Peter	140.00
	Simon	55.00
	Patience & 2 children	45.00
	Annis	35.00

SEPARATE RETURN FOR THE HIRE OF NEGROES FOR MARTHA B. FANNING IN ACCT. WITH FELIX GREEN, *GUARDIAN

1842	Dennis	$ 56.00
	Simon Peter	63.00
	*Patience and Children	.00
	**Matilda and children	15.00

Fig. 7-16. Talbot County Returns

Notes on Fig. 7-16

*When names of other persons who hired the Negroes were not listed in the Return, the guardian hired them or the clerk omitted the names from the records and recorded only the amounts received from the hire. Many of the Talbot Returns only printed the amount received from the "hire."

**After 1842, Matilda no longer appeared in the yearly Fanning Returns. At this point she and her children may have been sent to live on John McCrary's plantation where she is listed in his estate records of 1854. My ancestor Simon McCants became the spouse of Matilda McCants legally 22 December 1866 (Fig.7-3) in Taylor County. Since the record above lists no surnames and I did not find a record transferring them to John McCrary, there is only the *possibility* that they were my ancestors.

***In the 1850 Talbot County Slave Schedule, Fig. 7-15A, John Turner is a slaveholder listed immediately above John McCrary with his 33 slaves. *Matilda above, was hired out to work on the adjoining plantation to John McCrary.

Chapter Eight

A LIGHT AT THE END OF THE TUNNEL

The mountain of copied records ceased to grow when my frequent trips to view Taylor and Talbot County records at the Lake Mary Family History Center came to a halt. I took a two-week pause to plan a celebration for my 25th Wedding Anniversary.

On Sunday morning, July 19, 1992, my husband Joel and I left our home in Daytona Beach for Georgia in our motor home. It was the morning after our Silver Wedding Anniversary. I wanted no part of a cruise as a gift, but a trip to Butler, Georgia in Taylor County, where my roots began. My hope swelled with sustained anticipation--the hope of locating where my folks, Louisa/Lovenia McCrary, Simon and Matilda McCants, Emily and Abe Holton and Mary Riley had lived and worked as slaves.

As we rode along the highway entering Taylor County, I thought, "My folks worked somewhere around here. Louisa/Lovenia McCrary, 90 years old in the 1870 Census is buried somewhere under this Georgia soil. They're all here somewhere." A trip to the oldest cemetery where Blacks were buried revealed old broken stones bearing surnames of the slave owners that I had seen in both Taylor and Talbot County Records. We found the oldest Negro cemetery in Butler, Georgia. My ancestors were now sealed beneath the soil they had worked so hard to till.

BENEATH TAYLOR COUNTY SOD

I stepped around scattered ant hills in wild grass dodging crawling insects to brush rain-washed sand from crumbling stones in the old black cemetery. I saw surnames of slave owners staring at me just as they had from estate inventories and sales listing their slaves. Only a few stones bore scribbled names lying between sunken graves, a stark contrast from the smooth stones of their slave masters in other cemeteries. We left the Butler "Colored" cemetery having found no trace of Matilda, Simon or any of my ancestral kin.

After lunch, as I entered the Taylor County Courthouse in Butler to search through the Deed Books for some record of John McCrary, the possible slave owner; and some information about my great, great grandfather, Abram Holton; friendly faces spoke and offered help.

"My ancestor was reported to have had a "shoe factory here and owned property" I told the clerk. "An old lady, Marcelee Holton, told me that. It was her father-in-law Abe Holton. Do you think I can find anything about that in your court records?" I asked.

The man smiled and shook his head, saying, "Perhaps it might show in the tax records."

I looked through the huge heavy volume of early tax records for Taylor County but found no record on that day. (See Fig. 7-19A for a record found a year later.)

Before leaving Butler, we visited the public library to see if there were a published family history of the McCants or McCrary families. We did not find one. The library had a special edition of a newspaper with the story of the creation of Taylor County in 1852 with detailed biographical sketches of its early citizens.

The special edition of the *Taylor County News* reported that the people with the surnames (McCants, McCrary and Riley) I was searching were prominent citizens in the early years. They were wealthy farmers, some had large slave holdings. T. J. Riley was a judge of the Inferior Court; J. M. McCants, Clerk of the Superior Court 1852-1856; L.Q.C. McCrary was Sheriff, 1858-1860; Peter E. Riley, Surveyor 1854-1856; M. L. Riley, Sheriff, 1895-1906; J. P. McCrary, Clerk of the Superior Court, 1866; J. M. McCants, Clerk of the Superior Court, 1852-1856. Even the land for building the first courthouse was purchased from Andrew McCants and others. Were any of the unpaid skilled slave artisans a part of the work force that helped to build the early town buildings and churches? I wondered.

As these prominent citizens were busy organizing a town, building a courthouse, erecting places of worship, and their first family dwellings, hundreds of slaves, including my folks were laboring, unnoticed, without prominence in the hot sun tilling the soil, gathering the crops, taking care of the housework and minding their children. At the same time trying to keep soul and body together in spite of their living condition. In the 1850's, 1860's, 1870's and on through to 1900, had they walked where I was now standing? Probably so. In their later years, perhaps there was a reason to visit the courthouse. A feeling of having found a long lost relative came over me and I felt closely tied to my people of years past. I learned later that slave "sales" were made in front of the county courthouse in many Georgia counties.

ON TO TALBOT COUNTY

Since Taylor County was created from Talbot, we traveled to Talbotton, the county seat of Talbot County. We spent the afternoon looking through the deed books. Since John McCrary died two years after Taylor County was created, I belived the record of where he got his slaves was in Talbot County.

There were many references in the Index for John McCrary and other McCrary names but each entry was for land sales. "They sure did purchase a lot of land not only in Talbot but also in surrounding counties," I thought as I scanned the records. I concluded that the McCrary and McCants' families acquired large land holdings for planting and selling.

The clerk remained a few minutes past the closing hour, but we were unable to locate any references to slaves on the long handwritten pages of land transactions. She said that she was unaware of any records pertaining to slaves in any of the deed books. The second day of our trip was spent in Columbus, Georgia. At the library, I was still unable to locate a McCants or McCrary family history. Our third day visit in Georgia found us at the LaGrange Archives in LaGrange. My husband Joel's slave ancestors had come from Troup County, Georgia and were taken to East Texas in 1859. The original deed books of Troup County were at the LaGrange Archives. Joel used the index to locate the slave owner named Henry Long. Joel experienced moments of elation when he discovered the original document showing the date of purchase and actual transfer of his ancestors, his great grandmother, Bedie Fears, his grandfather, Gus Fears and sister, Caroline to Henry Long's daughter, Sarah Battle Long Fears, "for $5.00 love and affection." (See Fig.7-17) Our spirits soared like a kite in Spring when we read this original document. Now we knew that the records sought were in the deed books.

Our next two days would be spent in Atlanta at the Georgia Archives. I vowed to spend the time there searching Talbot County Deed Books reproduced on microfilm. I still had hope that I would find them during this trip. All hope was not lost.

As I sat in the LaGrange Archives reading through Talbot County history books, cemetery records and early marriage records trying to piece the slave owners' families together, a young archivist came to my table to offer assistance.

I explained, "I'm trying to locate the family of John McCrary. My ancestors, Matilda and Missouri are listed in his Inventory in Taylor County in 1854, recorded after his death. There are several McCrary slave owners in the 1860 Taylor County Slave Schedules but the same names appear in Talbot County 1850 Federal Census Schedules and the 1850 Talbot County Slave Schedules. I was in hopes of finding a family history published but I haven't found one. My ancestors' surnames were McCants and McCrary. My folks could have been owned by either of them."

The young man left the table saying, "Let me see if I can help." He returned with a book showing that Bartley McCrary and a John McCrary were in the 1810 Baldwin County Tax Digest and John McCrary had seven slaves. "This John may be a relative of the John McCrary I had who died in 1854 in Taylor County," I thought.

BOOK M

State of Georgia } Know all men by these presents that I Henry Long of
County of Troup } the State and County aforesaid, for and in consideration of the sum
of Three Dollars cash in hand to me paid, as well as in consideration
of the natural love, regard and affection I have and bear towards
my daughter Sarah Ann Battle Hearn, and her children now living and
which may hereafter be born hereafter, hath given, granted, aliened & conveyed
and doth, by these presents, give, grant, alien, and convey unto my said
daughter Sarah A.B. Hearn and her children now living and which may
hereafter be born, the following property, to wit: Lewis a man aged about (62)
sixty-seven years of dark complexion; Pat a man aged about (30) thirty years
of dark complexion; Archer one a boy aged about (6) sixteen years of copper
complexion; Winny a woman aged about (30) thirty years of dark complexion;
Betsy a woman aged about (22) twenty-two years of dark complexion; Betty
a girl aged about (11) eleven years of copper complexion; Ellen a girl aged
about (5) five years mulatto; Lue a boy aged about (3) three years a mulatto;
Caroline a girl about (1½) one, and one half years old to and to her and
their only use separate and exclusive of any future husband her interest therein to
consist of her present or any future husband. I, to be forever absolve & bound to have
and to hold the said property to her & their proper use & to their use
as above set forth. In testimony whereof I have hereunto set my hand and
affixed my seal this the fifth day of November A.D. 1859—
Signed sealed & delivered in presence of

R.A.T. Kidd   Henry Long (Seal)
Benj. N. Bigham
    Notary Public

Fig. 7-17. Troup Co., GA Deed recorded Nov 5th 1859

@C COL. LONG TO SARAH A.B. FEARS, DEED OF GIFT

State of Georgia }
County of Troup }   Known all men by these present that I
Henry Long of the State and County aforesaid, for and
in consideration of the sum of Five Dollars Cash in hand
to me paid as well as in consideration of the natural
love, regard and affection I have and bear towards
my daughter Sarah Ann Battle Fears and her children
now living and which may hereafter be born, hath given
granted alliened & conveyed, and doth by these presents -
give, grant allen and convey unto my said Daughter
Sarah A B Fears, and her children now living and
which may hereafter be born, the following property towit
Lewis a man aged about (67) sixty seven years of dark-
complexion, Job a man aged about (30) thirty years
of dark complexion, Anderson a boy aged about (16)
sixteen years of copper complexion, Winney a woman
aged about (30) thirty years of dark complexion, Bedy
a woman aged about (22) twenty two years of dark complexion, Betsey a girl aged about (11) Eleven years of
copper complexion, Ellen a girl aged about (5) five years
a mulatto, Gus a Boy aged about (3) three years a mullato,
Caroline a girl aged about (1 1/2) one and one half years

@C COL. LONG TO SARAH A.B. FEARS, DEED OF GIFT

old. To and for her and their only sole and seperate use
forever free from the debts liabilities and control of her present or of any future husbands her interest therein to
constitute her seperate estate & to be for her exclusive use
benefit, to have and to hold the said property to her and them
forever limited to their use as above set forth. In testimony where of I have here unto set my hand and affixed
my Seal this the fifth day of November AD 1859
Signed Sealed & delivered in presence of }   Henry Long {Seal}
R A G Ridley
Bing H Bingham Notary Public
Georgia
Troup County   Personally appeared before one Henry Long
whose signature is affixed to the foregoing deed of Gift -
being personally known to me, and after being duly sworn
deposith and saith that he signed, sealed and delivered
the same for the purposes therein contained and that he
acknowledeged the sam(sic) to be his own set and deed.
Sworn to (described) before me and acknowledged in
my presence this the 28th day of February 1860. }   Henry Long
Orville A Bull Judge Supr Court

Fig. 7-17. Troup Co., GA Deed

Georgia | I Know all men by these presents that for and in consideration
Troup County | of five Dollars cash in hand to me paid & for divers other
goods & valuable considerations me hereunto knowing, I William P. Beasley
of said State and County have transferred sold & delivered & relinquish
and doth by these present transfer sell deliver and relinquish to Henry
Long of said County his being administrator Executor and asigns
all of my right-title and interest in and to the following property towit
Lewis a man aged about (67) sixty seven years of dark complexion,
Job a man aged about (30) thirty years of dark complexion Anderson
a boy aged about (16) sixteen years of copper complexion, Winny a
woman aged about (30) thirty years of dark complexion Bidy a woman
aged about (22) twenty two years of dark complexion, Betsey a girl aged
about (11) Eleven years of copper complexion, Ellen a girl aged about
(5) years mulatto Gus a boy aged about (3) three years a mulatto
Caroline a girl about (1 1/2) one and one half years old. So that from this
time henceforth all of my interest in this property doth cease determine
& vest as above. Witness my hand and seal- this 5th day of November
A.D. 1859. Signed sealed and delivered in presence of
R A. T. Ridley
Benj. H. Bigham Not. Pub.   Wm P. Beasley (seal)
                              Recorded Dec 20 1859
                                   WmM Latimer clk

Fig. 7-17.   Troup C. GA Slave Sale
              William Beasley to Henry Long

Georgia   } Know all men by these presents that for and in consideration
Troup County } of Five Dollars cash in hand to me paid & for various other
good & valuable considerations me hereunto moving, I William P. Beasley
of said State and County have bargained sold delivered & relinquish
and do by these presents bargain sell deliver & relinquish to Henry
Long of said County his heirs administrators Executors and assigns
all of my right title and interest in and to the following property to wit:
Lewis a man aged about (6y) sixty seven years of dark complexion,
Jacob a man aged about (30) thirty years of dark complexion, Wesley a
boy aged about (16) sixty two years of copper complexion, Betty a woman
aged about (30) thirty years of dark complexion, Betsy a girl aged
about (22) twenty two years of dark complexion, Eliza a girl aged about
(11) Eleven years of copper complexion, Ellen a girl aged about
(6) five years twelfth Lee a boy aged about Three years a mullatto
Caroline a girl about (1½) one & one half years old, I do that from this
time hence forth all of my interest in the property does cease & determin
& vest as above. Witness my hand and seal this 8th day of December
A.D. 1857 Signed sealed & delivered in presence of_

R. R. Ridley   Wm. P. Beasley (seal)
Benj. H. Bigham Not. Pub. 3

                                    Recorded Dec 20th 1857
                                    Wm H Latimer? Clk?

I said, "Perhaps I could find where John got those slaves." He did not think so as he thought that the early Baldwin County Courthouse had burned. He also found that Bartley McCrary received land in the 1805 Georgia Land Lottery. Now I had another county to search, Baldwin County. When he went to the shelves, I was looking through four volumes of *Rock Away in Talbot*, by William H. Davidson, Hester Printing Co., 1983. These volumes had several pages written about the McCrary family. They had come from Laurens County, South Carolina and Baldwin County. They went from the latter county to Talbot County in the early 1830's. I needed next to search Baldwin County and trace records into Talbot County. I would begin that search at our next stop, the Georgia Archives.

ON TO ATLANTA AND THE GEORGIA ARCHIVES

At the Georgia Archives I rushed to locate the drawer and box number for the General Index to the Deeds of Talbot County. I hastily recorded the index pages for all McCrary entries, rewound the index microfilm and threaded the machine containing the Deed Books. "If John McCrary's slaves are recorded in these deeds, I am going to find them today!" I said with determination.

I turned the crank to roll the microfilm forward. My heart sank. The top part of each printed page was completely black and not a page number could be read! With page numbers in the hundreds, it was clear, it was an impossible task to locate pages with invisible numbers. Within tightly spaced lines of handwriting I could read: "parcels of land" and see a few references to "Negro slaves" but I could not read the page numbers. I sat in agony grumbling, refusing to roll the film and count page by page up into the hundreds in order to find the pages noted from the index. I soon turned my attention to the Baldwin County records.

I copied eight pages of the General Index to the Baldwin County Inferior Court. The index referred to pages in the court minutes, inventory and sale records, returns, appointment of administrators and guardians of minor children for deceased members of the McCrary

68 Slave Ancestral Research

Baldwin County, Georgia Tax Digest

Year		Number of Slaves	
1809	*John McCrary Sr.	*7	
	Bartley McCrary (Sr.)	15	
	Isaac McCrary	5	Wilkinson County
	Ann McCrary	4	Jones County
1810	Bartley McCrary (Sr.)	14	... This name was given to me at the LaGrange Archives.
	Administrator of Jonathan McCrary, Deceased		
	*John McCrary (Sr.)	7	...*This record was brought to my attention by the librarian at the LaGrange Archives.
	**John McCrary, Jr.	0	
1811			
	*John McCrary (Sr.)	7	
	Wm. McCrary	2	
	Isaac McCrary	4	
	**John McCrary, Jr.	0	
1818			
	Barlett McCrary	17	Notes added after further research:
	**John McCrary (Jr.)	2	... John McCrary, Jr. acquired his first slave CLARY from
	Isaac McCrary Deceased	9	the Estate Division of Jonathan McCrary in 1815.
1822	Bartley McCrary, Sr.	28	... Had acquired 32 by the date of his death, 1826.
	Bartley McCrary, Jr.	1	
			Added after further research:
1822	+James McCrary	1	...+James McCrary acquired his first slave LUVESER, my slave ancestor in 1822 when he married his cousin, Jane McCrary, daughter of Jonathan McCrary, d.1808.
1823	Bartley McCrary, Sr	28	
	Bartley McCrary, Jr.	2	
	Admr. William McCrary	10	
1825	+James McCrary	1	
	**John McCrary, (Jr.) Guardian, Isaac McCrary's Orphans	10	
1828	...+James McCrary	10	
1831	+James McCrary	15	... Number of Slaves increased.

Fig. 7-18. Excerpted from Baldwin County, Georgia Tax Digest.

and McCants families who died in Baldwin County. I planned to order the rolls of microfilm from the Lake Mary Family History Center when I returned to Florida. I did not have enough time to look at all of the pages referred to in the index during our two-day visit to the Georgia Archives.

I decided to look at the Baldwin County Inventories and Sales records. First, I copied the Inventory Slave lists of Bartley McCrary, and John McCrary. They were the two McCrarys listed in the 1810 Baldwin County Tax Digest. Fig. 7-18. I also copied several other records of McCrary family members who had purchased slaves, transferring ownership of the same slaves within the McCrary family. See Record Groups 1-7.

I left the Georgia Archives on the last day of our trip to Georgia without knowing where John McCrary had gotten Matilda, Becky and Zussre (Missouri). I did not know the relationship of Bartley McCrary and John McCrary of Baldwin County, nor their kin to the John McCrary, who died in 1854, whose record I had and was researching. Yet, I did not feel that my Georgia trip was unsuccessful. At least I learned that the McCrary family had come from South Carolina to Baldwin County, Georgia and I had visited the places where my slave ancestors lived. It was amazing to learn that in only a few hours drive from my Daytona Beach, Florida home, I could travel to where my slave ancestors worked and died in Taylor County, Georgia.

A RUDE AWAKENING

One morning early, a few days following our return home, I awoke early and the thought came to me, "Get up and look at Bartley McCrary's list of slaves, see if there is a name similiar to any of my family names." I got up and went to my genealogy room where I did my studying and writing and saw the name "Lovenia and 4 children" hired out to A. G. Beckham for $1.00." I thought, "Four children and their mother for only one dollar. Beckham must be a relative." (See Fig.7-20 in RECORD GROUP 1.) I searched through my files for a copy of the 1870 Taylor County Census.

I remembered having seen the name of an old woman living with Matilda McCants and Simon who was 90 years old. I did some quick figuring. She could have been living in 1826 when Bartley McCrary died. Few slaves knew their exact ages or birthdays. I stared at the handwriting on the 1870 Taylor County Census, and asked myself, "Could this 90-year old woman possibly be Lovenia? I always recorded the name as Louisa/Lovenia because the census enumerator's handwriting was not clear. (See Fig. 7-19.)

Without pausing for breakfast after taking my son to school, I flung my notebooks in my car and headed for the one hour drive to the Orlando Public Library. I stopped by the desk and shared my find with the librarians saying,"I think I've found my oldest slave ancestor. I'm not real sure, I've got to check the spelling of the name in the 1870 Taylor County Census." I showed them Bartley's Inventory and the copy of the "Hiring" of his slaves, pointing to Lovenia and A. G. Beckham. I left the desk saying, "I'm willing to bet that Beckham's wife is a McCrary."

It did not take long to locate Matilda and Simon and the 90-year old woman on the 1870 Taylor County Census as I had found it ten years before in 1983 when I met Mrs. Marcelee Holton. (See Chapter One.) I made several copies of the names and looked closely with a magnifying glass. For ten years, all through my written records, I had recorded the name as Louisa/Lovenia. The 1870 Georgia Census Index recorded the name as Louisa. It seemed that the 90-year old woman's name was not Louisa, it was written "L o v i n i a." That sounded the same as "Lovenia" on Bartley McCrary's hiring list!. The first "i" was faint but there definitely was no "s" before the "a." I sat back in my chair, clasped my hands in my lap, my eyes glued to the writing and said with certainty, "I've found my slave ancestor! She's my great, great, great, great grandmother! Her name is Lovinia! Then it suddenly dawned on me. That's *my* middle name, Louvenia. My *maiden name* is Mary Louvenia Jackson! My thoughts were uttered aloud and by this time, fellow researchers sitting at machines nearby were each staring at me. (See Fig. 7-18.)

EXTRACT FROM 1870 CENSUS

State: Georgia   County or Parish: Taylor   Township, Ward or Beat: _____   Post Office: Butler

Index compiled by: _____   Extract by: _____   Date of Enumeration: _____   Publication No.: _____   Reel No.: _____

Page	Dwelling No.	Family No.	Names	Age	Sex	Color	Occupation, etc.	Value of real estate	Value of personal property	Birthplace	Father foreign born	Mother foreign born	Month born in year	Month married in year	School in year	Cannot read	Cannot write	Impairment	Male eligible to vote	Male ineligible to vote
310	116	116	McCants Matilda	45	F	B	Keeps house			Ga										
311			Mc Cants Lovinia	90	F	B	Keeps house		40	Ga						1	1			
			" Matilda	6	F	B	at home			Ga										
			Johnson Abraham	28	M	B	Works farm			Ga						1	1		1	
			" Margaret	17	F	B	at home			Ga						1	1			
			McCants Lionel	50	M	B	Works at trade			Ga						1	1		1	

Fig. 7-19. What's the name? Is it Louisa or Lovinia or Lovenia? 1870 Taylor Co., GA. Census, p. 311. Fig. 7-2 is the same census record.

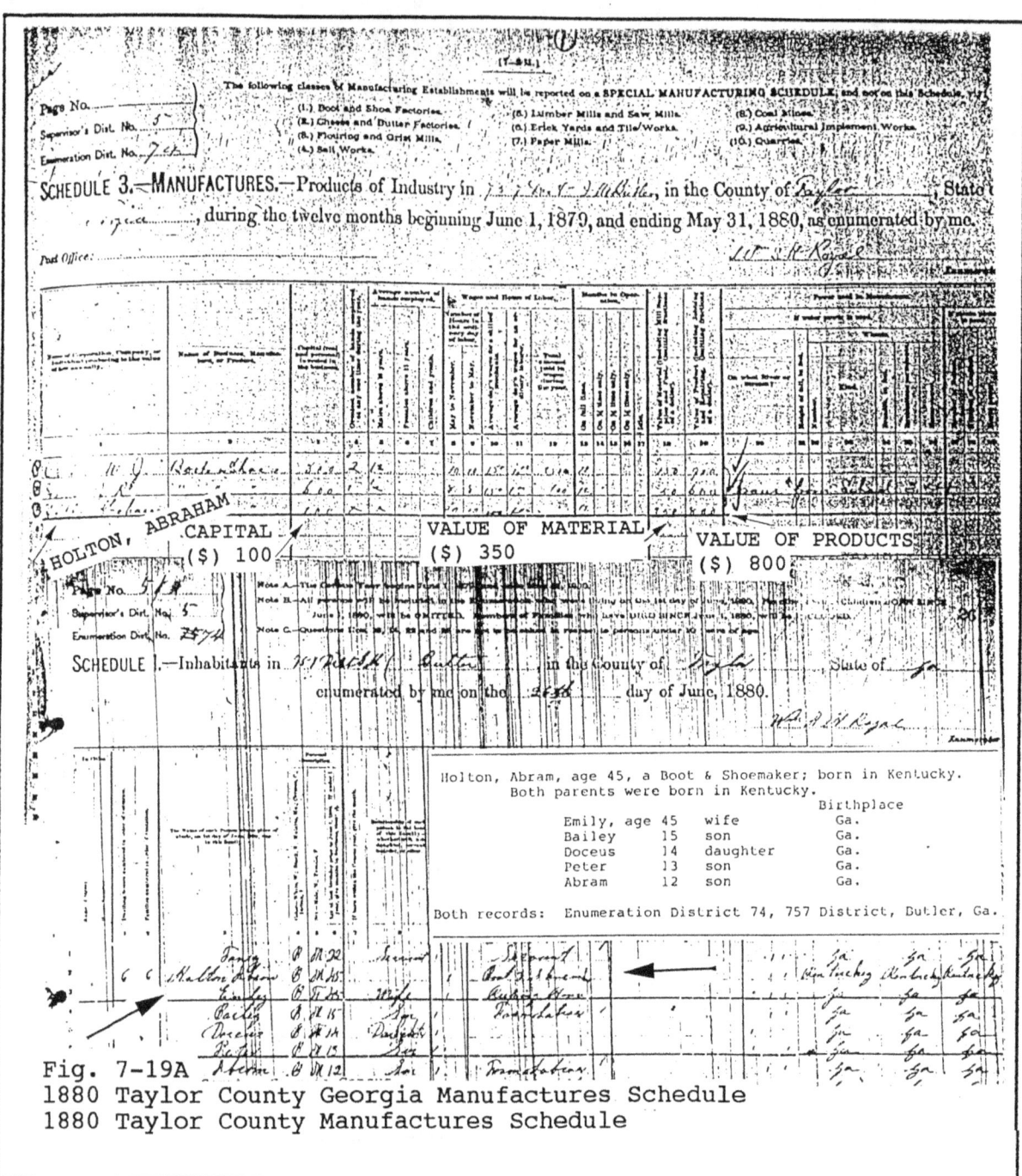

Fig. 7-19A
1880 Taylor County Georgia Manufactures Schedule
1880 Taylor County Manufactures Schedule

Note: I found the Manufactures Schedule in April, 1993 during a trip to the National Archives. The 1880 Taylor County Census Schedule listed the occupation of Abraham Holton, my great great grandfather as a "boot and shoemaker." Mrs. Marcelee Holton told me during the early years of this research that "Abe Holton owned a shoe factory."

Oh, if I could just find Lovenia with the names of her four children. Would one of them be Matilda? Matilda's age was given as 45 in 1870. In 1826, the year of Bartley McCrary's death, Matilda would have been one year old and possibly one of Lovenia's four children. Although the 90-year old woman was listed in the census with Matilda and her husband, Simon, I felt that Lovinia was not the mother of Simon, because he was born in Virginia and both Lovinia and Matilda were born in Georgia. See Fig. 7-2. and Fig. 7-19. After this discovery, I *thought* that I had discovered the correct name of the 90-year old woman.

QUESTIONS. QUESTIONS. QUESTIONS.

I had many questions after I discovered the name Lovenia. Who was the father of Lovenia's four children? Was he one of the slave men on Bartley McCrary's Inventory? I thought perhaps he was Peter, since Matilda's daughter Emily Holton and Abram Holton had a son Peter. It was Peter in the 1900 Census of Taylor County (Fig.7-1) whose grandmother, Matilda McCants lived with him that led me to find Matilda, Simon and Lovenia in the 1870 Taylor County Census. How did Matilda get the surname McCants before her marriage to Simon McCants? If she were a daughter of Lovenia, was she sold away to a McCants? Did Lovenia have other children? If so, what were their names?

On John McCrary's Inventory of 1854, Fig. 7-15, there is a slave woman, "Veny, valued at $100." Her dollar value implied that she was very old. "Veny" is a nickname for Lovenia or Lovinia. Could this Veny be the same Lovinia in the 1870 Taylor County Census living with Matilda and Simon and the same "Lovenia with four children" on Bartley McCrary's "Hiring" list of Slaves in Baldwin County in 1828? I HAD FOUND THE LIGHT AT THE END OF THE TUNNEL! (See RECORD GROUP I)

However, one question burned to be answered, did A. G. Beckham, eventually purchase "Lovenia and her four children" after hiring them for $1.00? I exhausted many hours trying to find that answer. I learned from a list of early Baldwin County marriages that Albert G. Beckham married Mary McCrary April 7, 1825 in Baldwin County, one year before the death of her father, Bartley McCrary.

74 Slave Ancestral Research

In 1840, Albert was listed in the Muscogee County, Georgia Census. I could not locate him in a census after 1840. In later research within Revolutionary War records, I learned that Albert died in Elmore County, Alabama, c.1869. (See Chapter 15, "Revelations from Revolutionary War Records.")

A few weeks after my return home, without realizing it, I entered the last phases of my slave ancestral research when I received microfilm rolls of the Baldwin County Probate records from the LDS Library through the Lake Mary Family History Center. The credit goes to a librarian at the Georgia Archives. While in Atlanta, I discovered that asking just the right question sent my research in the most revelant direction, as explained in Chapter Nine.

Chapter Nine

FROM PILLAR TO POST

After I found the Inventory and "Hiring" record of Bartley McCrary at the Georgia Archives, I asked Ms. Jan McLendon, a librarian," What's a "Return?" I had just finished reading the General Index to Proceedings of Estates--Court of Ordinary, Baldwin County, Georgia, listing pages about Bartley McCrary in the Minute Books, Book of Sales, Inventory and Appraisements, Guardian Bonds and *Returns*. Back home, my vast accumulation of copied records from Talbot County included many Returns, but in the excitement of doing research at the Georgia Archives, I was not thinking about those records. I had not fully realized the significance of those Returns.

Ms. McLendon explained, "Minor children of a deceased property owner had a court-appointed guardian. The guardian was required to record annually a financial account of the income and expenditures for the minor children, called orphans of the deceased, to the court. This accounting was called a "Return." Income from the hiring of slaves was often used for the support of the minor children." The librarian added, "I helped a black researcher follow her slave ancestors through several generations by using the Returns."

After my return home, I ordered Baldwin County Returns for the years 1813-1831 on microfilm #41517 at the Lake Mary Family History Center. Records of hirings, sales of slaves and the final distribution of shares in the McCrary estates were included on the microfilm. With these records I viewed lists of their Negro property and saw how they were consistently shifted between McCrary households. I divided the records into seven groups on the pages that follow. The records revealed how the Negro slaves went from "pillar to post," with my kinfolks among them.

Springfield & Strickl...	M. D. Huson	9.50
Barley patch	Co Co	3.25
Woodfolk field	Bartley McCrary	18.00
Matthews plantation	Co Co	15.00
Dwelling & Springfield	A. G. Beckham	26.00
Small field neat creek	Co Co	2.00
Negro field	Co Co	12½

Negroes Hired

Peter	John McCrary	80.00
Arch	A. G. Beckham	60.00
Sam	Co Co	80.00
Joe	Bartley McCrary	63.00
Lou	Co Co	87.00
George	A. G. Beckham	72.00
Old Jano	Wiley McCrary	61.00
Cesar	A. G. Beckham	71.25
Ben	Co Co	80.00
Dick	Iaw Pendaiter	40.00
Hardy	Ia. McCrary	17.00
Clark	M. D. Huson	42.00
Patience & children	A. G. Beckham	11.00
Lovenia & 4 children	Co Co	1.00
Betsey	W. McCrary	10.00
Lacey & children	A. G. Beckham	11.00
Mary	Inw Pendaiter	6.00
Balens	Co Co	31.50
Patrick	Co Co	8.50
John	N. Digby	2064

Fig. 7-20 Hiring record of Bartley McCrary, dece'd 1826. Baldwin Co., GA.

Chapter Ten

BALDWIN COUNTY PROBATE RECORDS

I observed that the Negro property in the McCrary estate records was listed in their Inventories and Appraisement records, Sales, Division of Estate and Returns records. I listed them all not knowing family or marital relationships. After a trip to the DAR Library in Washington, DC, I returned home and *added* in a different type script, notes that explained family relations. The notes are based upon my interpretation of the information submitted by persons who filed applications for DAR membership as descendants of four McCrary Revolutionary War soldiers.[4]

I have written notes about the transferrence of the slaves among the McCrary family and others as follows: I placed together related groups of records of each slave owner's estate, with the year of his or her decease, and used the page number of the various court records to help identify each record as it is explained in the text.

I began with Bartley McCrary in Baldwin County because his was the first records that I found. Notes of explanation follow each group of records.

Inventory and Appraisement of the Estate of Bartley McCrary deceased

No.		
1	London a negro man	250.00
2	Cesar a man	400.00
3	Young Sam a man	500.00
4	Old Sam	200.00
5	Pater a man	500.00
6	Jo a man	500.00
7	Arch a man	400.00
8	Ben a man	500.00
9	Hardy a Boy	300.00
10	George a Boy	500.00
11	Patience, Alfred, Bird & Peter	900.00
12	Josey, Hampton, Ben & Jim	700.00
13	Mary a Girl	200.00
14	Patrick a Boy	200.00
15	John a Boy	200.00
16	Orange a Boy	400.00
17	Vicey, Josh, Ned & Lindy	700.00
18	Dick a Boy	300.00
19	Clark a Boy	400.00
20	Barka a Girl	350.00
21	Betsey a Girl	250.00
22	Elick a Boy	150.00
23	Winney a Old woman	10.00
	fourteen Senters	10.50
	One lot of Old Shovel plows	
	Four Jugs	
	One lot of Wool	
		8918.25
No. 1	One Bay Horse	
2	One Sorrel Horse	
3	One Dark Bay Horse	
4	One Yellow Bay Horse	

Fig. 7-21. Inventory and Appraisements, Bartley McCrary.

Slave Ancestral Research

RECORD GROUP No. 1, page 309 — BARTLEY McCRARY, Estate Records. Deceased in 1826. Baldwin Co. <u>Inventories & Appraisements</u>

Bartley's Inventory had: 9 male adult slaves, 4 adult women, and 19 children. Patience had 3 children: Alfred, Bird and Peter

Joicy had 3 children: Hampton, Ben and Jim

Vicy had 3 children: Josh, Ned and Sindy

page 202 — BARTLEY MCCRARY "NEGROES HIRED"

A. G. Beckham hired slaves from Bartley's list including my slave ancestors, "Lovenia & 4 children" for $1.00. (Vicy/Lovenia, believed to be the same person; a child is added by the date of the "hiring.") This unnamed child is believed to be "Matilda," who married Simon Mccants.

Fig. 7-21. Other McCrary family members hire the slaves: John, Bartley (Jr.), Wiley, James, and W. M. McCrary. A.G. Beckham is the spouse of Mary McCrary. Jane was the daughter of Bartley McCrary.

RECORD GROUP No. 1 page 154 — BARTLEY McCRARY <u>Distribution of Estate</u>, 1827, Jan. 5
The slaves are divided among relatives.

Robert McCrary gets London, Hardy, Alfred and Bird.

William McCrary gets Peter, Old Sam, and John.

Bryant Bateman, spouse of Charity McCrary, gets George, Patsey, and Ellick.

Albert G. Beckham, spouse of Mary McCrary, gets Patience, Clark, and Peter.

James McCrary gets Young Dick, Sam and Hampton.

Bartley McCrary (Jr.) gets Cesar, Balkus and Ned.

Jenny Poindexter gets Orrange, Mary, Patrick, and Joshua.

William Colbert gets Ben, Joicey, Jim, and Little Ben.

Fig. 7-22. David Moses gets Vicey and child and Sindy.

page 155 ... Cash found with the deceased $87.00

The Estate of Bartley McCrary Senr. decd.

Georgia } Pursuant to an order of the Honorable the
Baldwin County } Inferior Court of the county aforesaid when
sitting for ordinary purposes, requiring us to allot and
distribute such part of the Estate of Bartley McCrary Senr.
decd. as should be produced to us by the administrators on said
estate, after first being duly sworn. We have appraised and
allotted the same as follows:—

Lot No. 1. To Robert McCrary containing London, Hardy,
    Alfred and Bird, valued at — $875.—

Lot No. 2. To William McCrary's Orphans; containing Peter,
    old Sam and John valued at — $850.

Lot No. 3. To Bryant Bateman containing —
    George, Patsey and Ellick valued at — $800

Lot No. 4. To Albert G. Beckham containing Patience,
    Clark and Peter valued at — $800

Lot No. 5. To James McCrary containing Young, Dick,
    Sam, and Hampton valued at — $850.

Lot No. 6. To Bartley McCrary containing —
    Ceasar, Balkus and Ned, valued at — $865.

Lot No. 7. Jenny Poindexter, containing — Orrange,
    Mary, Patrick and Joshua valued at — $875

Lot No. 8. Wm. Colbert containing Ben, Joicey, Jim
    and Little Ben valued at — $980

Lot No. 9. David Moses, containing Vigey & child
    and Sindy valued at — $885

Amounting in all to the sum of — $7780

Given under our hands and seals this 5th day of January
1827.—
    Jno. Rutherford (Seal)
    Joshua A. Bigham (Seal)
    Barney Ivey (Seal)
    James Bivins (Seal)

Georgia }
Baldwin County }
    I certify that the above petitioners were duly
sworn before me on the fifth of January 1827 before
making partition of the before described property.
    Shadrack Burns J.P.

Fig. 7-22. Estate Division, Bartley McCrary

I observed that Patience was allowed to keep her son, Peter with her when she went to Albert G. Beckham, but her sons Alfred and Bird were taken away to go with Bartley's son, Robert McCrary.

Joicey was also unfortunate. Joicey, a woman and Ben, a man on Bartley's inventory, went with Little Ben and Jim to William Colbert. This seemed to have been a family. But Joicey's son Hampton was transferred to James McCrary, Bartley's son.

Added: *Bartley McCrary, (c.1767-1826) died in Baldwin County, Georgia, a Revolutionary War soldier from Laurens, South Carolina. His father, John McCrary, born, c.1735, died 1814, Baldwin County, Georgia, (Both were Revolutionary War soldiers) Bartley McCrary and his father, John McCrary were listed in the 1810 Baldwin County Tax Digest. Fig. 7-18.*

Albert G. Beckham left Baldwin County. He was listed in the 1840 Muscogee County, Georgia Census. He died in 1869 at Elmore County, Alabama. His wife, Mary, died in Smith County, Texas, c. 1870. I wonder did Patience and son, Peter, ever see her sons, Alfred and Bird again after they left Baldwin County.[5]

RECORD GROUP
No. 1   page 320   JENNY POINDEXTER, deceased. ESTATE SALE in 1847, Feb. 2nd.   BALDWIN COUNTY SALES BOOK

The Negro slave girl "Mary" from Bartley's Inventory was observed again in the Sales records of Baldwin County. Jenny Poindexter received her from her father, Bartley McCrary, after his death. I looked at the document of Jenny Poindexter's "Sales of Negroes...," remembering the words of the old Negro spiritual, "Lord, How Come We Here?" The beautiful handwriting recorded in harsh reality, the plight of the slave girl, Mary, 21 years after she left the plantation of Bartley McCrary.

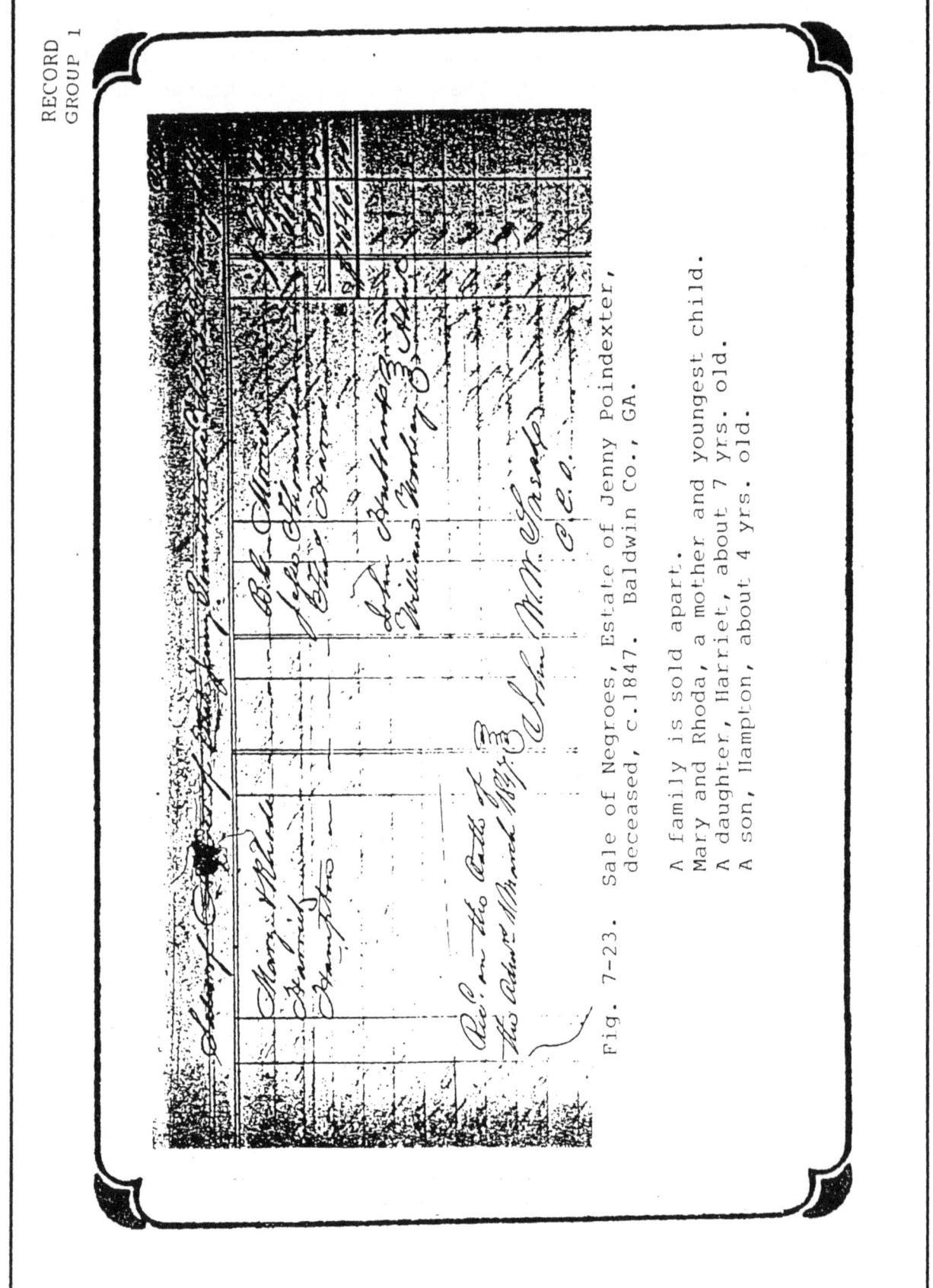

Fig. 7-23. Sale of Negroes, Estate of Jenny Poindexter, deceased, c.1847. Baldwin Co., GA.

A family is sold apart.
Mary and Rhoda, a mother and youngest child.
A daughter, Harriet, about 7 yrs. old.
A son, Hampton, about 4 yrs. old.

"OH LORD, HOW COME WE HERE?"

I breathed the words of the old Negro spiritual, "Lord, How Come We Here?" when I stared at the writing. It recorded the cruel fate of the slave girl, Mary, from Bartley McCrary's Inventory and "Hiring" list. On 5 Jan. 1827, Mary belonged to the estate of the deceased Bartley McCrary. As children, Mary, Patrick and Joshua were contained in "Lot No. 7" with a total value of $875. Joshua was Vicey's child. They were given to Jenny Poindexter. Mary was hired out to Jenny for $6.00 in 1828. (See RECORD GROUP 1).

By 24 July 1846, Mary had become the mother of three children. They were listed in the inventory of deceased Jenny Poindexter:

Negro woman Mary about 26 valued at		$500
Harriet, a girl, 6 yrs.	"	300
Hampton, a boy, 3 yrs.	"	300
Roady 2 yrs.	"	150

A mere six months later, 2 February 1847, Mary and three year old Rhoda (Roady) are sold to B. G. Morris for $675; (Fig. 7-23). Harriet, about seven, sold to Jessie Thomas for $368 and 4 year old Hampton is sold to Thomas Harris for $300. Mary's two small children are sold away. Oh Mary, I say to her, how much did you weep? For how long, for days and nights? Could you ever forget that February day in 1847? Was there any way to find a place in your heart to forgive John Hubbard and William Woolsey, the men who sold your children away? Were you standing with your two small children clinging to your skirt, and holding little Rhoda, while they pulled them away, crying and reaching for the hand of their mother to hold them back, or were you in your cabin and they just came and took you and your children away? The records don't tell how it happened.

Was it for you, Mary, and thousands of other slave mothers, that this Negro spiritual came to be? Did you fold your hands around little Rhoda, with tears streaming down your face, asking, Oh, Lord, what's going to happen to my children, will I ever see them again? Did you hum the words as little Rhoda tried to wipe the tears away? "Oh Lord, they took my children away, I wish I never was born."

Where was the father of Mary's three small children? He had to be close by. He had no say in what was happening to his family.

My name is "Mary" too and I can't determine if you were related to "Lovenia and her 4 children." All of you were listed together in Bartley McCrary's Inventory in Baldwin County in 1826. But I have written your story just as if you were related. The evils of the system deny the possibility of uncovering the complete story of our slave inheritance.

Mary was listed as a girl on Bartley McCrary's Inventory directly beneath the names: Joicy, Hampton, Ben and Jim. Since Mary named a child Hampton, he may have been her brother, or perhaps, a man Hampton may have been the father of Mary's children. The records made no reference to fathers.

What name shall I take? If Mary lived until freedom, she was priviledged to say that she had a surname. Did she choose McCrary, Poindexter or Morris or, was she sold again?

Slave ancestral research--*it's something else.*

Frederick Bancroft in *Slave-Trading In The Old South* explained the Georgia Code, 1861 Section 2523, p.483:[6]

> "In Georgia, administrators, executors, guardians and other trustees for the purpose of sale or distributions were forbidden to separate children not above eight years from their mothers, or to sell separately husband and wife, recognized as such by the deceased master when both belonged to his estate. These provisions were advantageous to the slaves concerned but did not affect a living master's property rights. It remained entirely legal for him to sell separately any slave of any age whatsoever." pp. 198-199.

Inventory and Appraisement Est. Jenny Poindexter

A List of the Property of Jenny Poindexter, Dec'd. Appraised by R. F. Ivey, Charles Ivey & Furney Ivey the 24th July, 1846.

Negros

Woman Mary about twenty six years old — Appraised to	$500.00
Harriet a Girl Six years old	310.00
Hampton a Boy 3 years old	300.00
Rondy two years old	150.00
One Horse and Wagon	7.50
One Red Cow and Calf	10.00
One Brin Cow and Calf	8.00
Sideboards	3.00
One Spinning Wheel	1.00
Two Beds and furniture	20.00
Two Chests $1.00 — One Lot Pot ware $2.00	3.00
One Table and Chairs	1.50
	$1304.00

Certificate

We do certify that as far as produced to us by the Administrator the foregoing contains a just and true Appraisement of the goods and Chattels of Jenny Poindexter deceased. to the best of our judgement and understanding.

  Furnia Ivey
  R. D. Ivey
  Chas. Ivey

I do certify that the above Appraisers were duly sworn to perform their duties as such before me this 24th day of July 1846.

  Samuel Hall J.P.

Fig. 7-24. Inventory & Appraisements, Jenny Poindexter, 1846 Baldwin Co., GA.

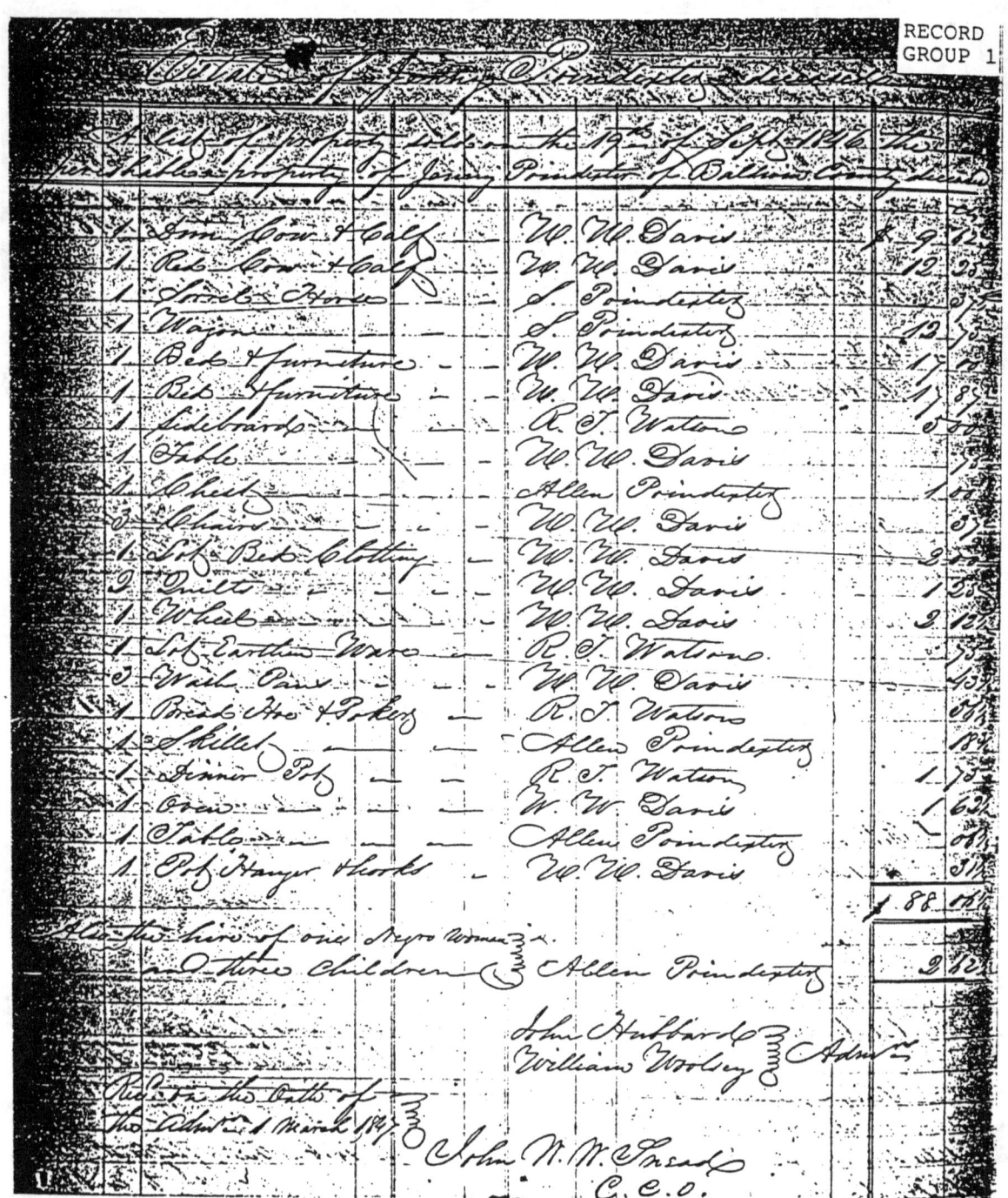

Fig. 7-25. Estate Sale of Jenny Poindexter, 1847 and "The hire of Negro woman and three children to Allen Poindexter." $2.62 1/2.

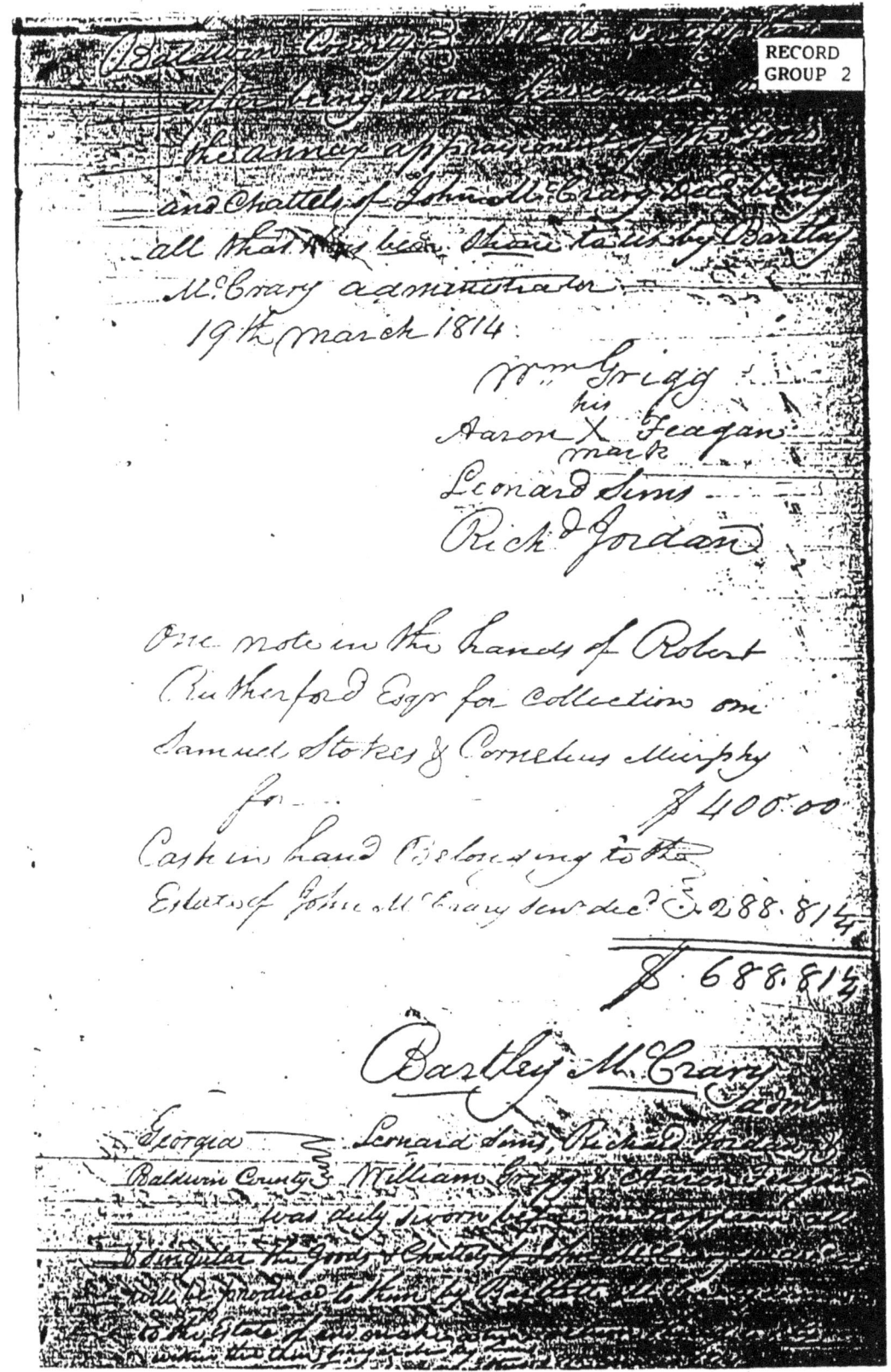

the sum of appraisment of the goods and Chattels of John McCrary deceased all that has been shewn to us by Bartley McCrary administrator

19th March 1814

Wm Grigg
Aaron X (his mark) Feagan
Leonard Sims
Rich'd Jordan

One note in the hands of Robert Rutherford Esqr for collection on Samuel Stokes & Cornelius Murphy for — $400.00

Cash in hand belonging to the Estate of John McCrary senr decd — $288.81¼

$688.81¼

Bartley McCrary admr

Georgia } Leonard Sims, Rich'd Jordan
Baldwin County } William Grigg ...
...was duly sworn...

Fig. 7-26. Names of property appraisers and Bartley McCrary, Administrator, of John McCrary's (d.1814) Estate.

Property of John McCrary Sen'r (Dec'd)

London a fellow	450
Dick " "	500
Ceasar " "	450
Eaden " "	470
Cassey " Woman	350
Pyesu & two Children Bill & Stephen	575
Rachel a Woman	360
Wynney & Child John	500
Dick a Boy	160
Betty a Woman	5
26 Head Hogs	37 50
26 Head Stock Cattle	180 —
1 Grind Stone	1 —
1 Set Blacksmith Tools	55 —
1 Small Parcel of Flax	75
4 Raw Cow Hides	3 —
Supposed 650 Bushels of Corn	325 —
" 1600 lb Fodder	7 50
1 Waggon and Gear & Saddle	40 —
1 Spinning Wheel	50
1 Large Sorrel Mare	80
1 " " "	
1 Dark Bay Horse	125
1 Sorrel Colt	35
1 Large	

Fig. 7-26. Property of John McCrary, deceased, 1814. Baldwin Co., GA.

Slave Ancestral Research

```
RECORD GROUP              JOHN McCRARY, Senr. Estate Records.  Deceased in
No. 2    1814             Baldwin County Inventory and Appraisements
     page 128             Negro slaves:                      x on Bartley's
                                                                Inventory
                          London, a fellow   valued at $ 450 --x
                          *Dick, a fellow        "        500
                           Ceaser     "           "       450 --x
                          *Eaden      "           "       470
Casey..+............Cassey, a woman               "       350
Dicey..+............Dycea & 2 children
Will...+............ Bill and +Stephen            "       575
                          *Rachel, a woman        "       350
                           Wynney & child, John   "       500 --x
        +............ Dick, a boy                 "       160 --x
                           Betty, a woman         "         5 ?--x
```

Fig. 7-26.

* On Bartley McCrary's "Hiring" list in 1826.

+ On John McCrary's "Inventory" in 1854

This "Inventory" of John McCrary shows the transfer of McCrary slaves within the family.

The 1810 Tax Digest of Baldwin County showed a John McCrary with 7 slaves (unnamed). Another "John McCrary" is deceased in 1854 in Taylor County, the same one who had my folks, Matildy, Becky and Missouri. Some of the same named slaves above appeared on his Inventory. (+This latter John McCrary family moved from Baldwin County and is listed in the 1830-1850 Census schedules of Talbot County, Georgia and lived in Taylor County after the latter county is created in 1852 until his death in 1854.)

x See also RECORD GROUP 1 Bartley McCrary, deceased 1826

+ See also RECORD GROUP 7 John McCrary, deceased 1854

Division of the Estate of John McCrary

Pursuant to an Order of this Court of ordinary of Baldwin County, We the undersigned having divided the Estate of John McCrary dec'd as late of Baldwin Co have find each Legatees part as followeth (vizt)

Mildred McCrary — 1 Negro man Cosom $450
1 Do Cesar 450
Notes 175
Cash 113.25
$1188.25

Legy McCrary — 1 Negro woman Cyb 350.00
1 Negro boy Dick 160.00
Notes 565.00
Cash 113.25
$1188.25

Isaac McCrary — 1 Negro man Beck 500.00
1 Negro woman Sylvi & 2
Children Billy & Stephney 575.00
Cash 113.25
$1188.25

The Orphans of Jonathan McCrary — 1 Negro Girl Hanner 3500.
Notes 575.00
Cash 113.25
$1188.25

Bentley McCrary — 1 Negro boy Edwd 475.00
1 Negro girl Rachel 360.00
Notes 240.00
Cash 113.25
$1188.25

Given under our hand the 26th day of Sept 1814.
Henry Jones
James Stripling

Georgia
Baldwin County — Personally appeared before me this within written Jas Stripling & Henry Jones & being duly sworn deposeth & saith the within division of the Estate of John McCrary dec'd agreeable to equity as within stated
sworn to before me
the 29th of September 1814
William Johnston JP

John Stripling
Jas Stripling
Henry Jones

I delivered the cash in this part to Bentley McCrary as Admr of this Estate of John McCrary dec'd

Abner S. Reid

Slave Ancestral Research

RECORD GROUP JOHN McCRARY, (c.1735-1814) Estate Division
No. 2   Baldwin County, Book of Returns 26 Sept.
   page 41   1814

Matthew McCrary receives Negro	man,	London x
" " " "	man,	Cesar x
Letty McCrary receives "	woman	Cass
" " " "	boy	Dick
Isaac McCrary receives "	man	Dick x
" " "	woman	Dicey
Orphans of Jonathan "	girl	Winny x
McCrary receive "		John x
Bartley McCrary receives "	Boy	Eden
" " "	girl	Rachel

Fig. 7-27

The Negro slaves identified with an "x" were listed on Bartley McCrary's Inventory after his decease in 1826. It is reasonable to assume that even though the ownership of Negro slaves is passed to minor children, the slaves would be given work to do by a family plantation owner and listed later by that owner as shown by Bartley's Inventory. (See RECORD GROUP No. 1)

When is a girl a woman and a boy a man? The date of the above record is 1814. In the "Inventory" of this estate, dated 1808, "Wynney and child, John" are listed; "Eaden, a fellow;" Rachel is listed as a woman; and Dicey is recorded as "Dycea and two children, Bill and Stephen." In the "Division" record above:

        Winney becomes a "girl"
        Eaden, a fellow, becomes Eden, a "boy"
        Rachel, a woman, becomes a "girl"

ADDED from DAR Record National Number 656131. This John McCrary, a Revolutionary War soldier, came from South Carolina. His wife was Jane, who predeceased him. John moved to Georgia after the war around 1789 or 1790. His children are named in the above record. The key to my understanding McCrary family relationships was the Data File on this John McCrary.

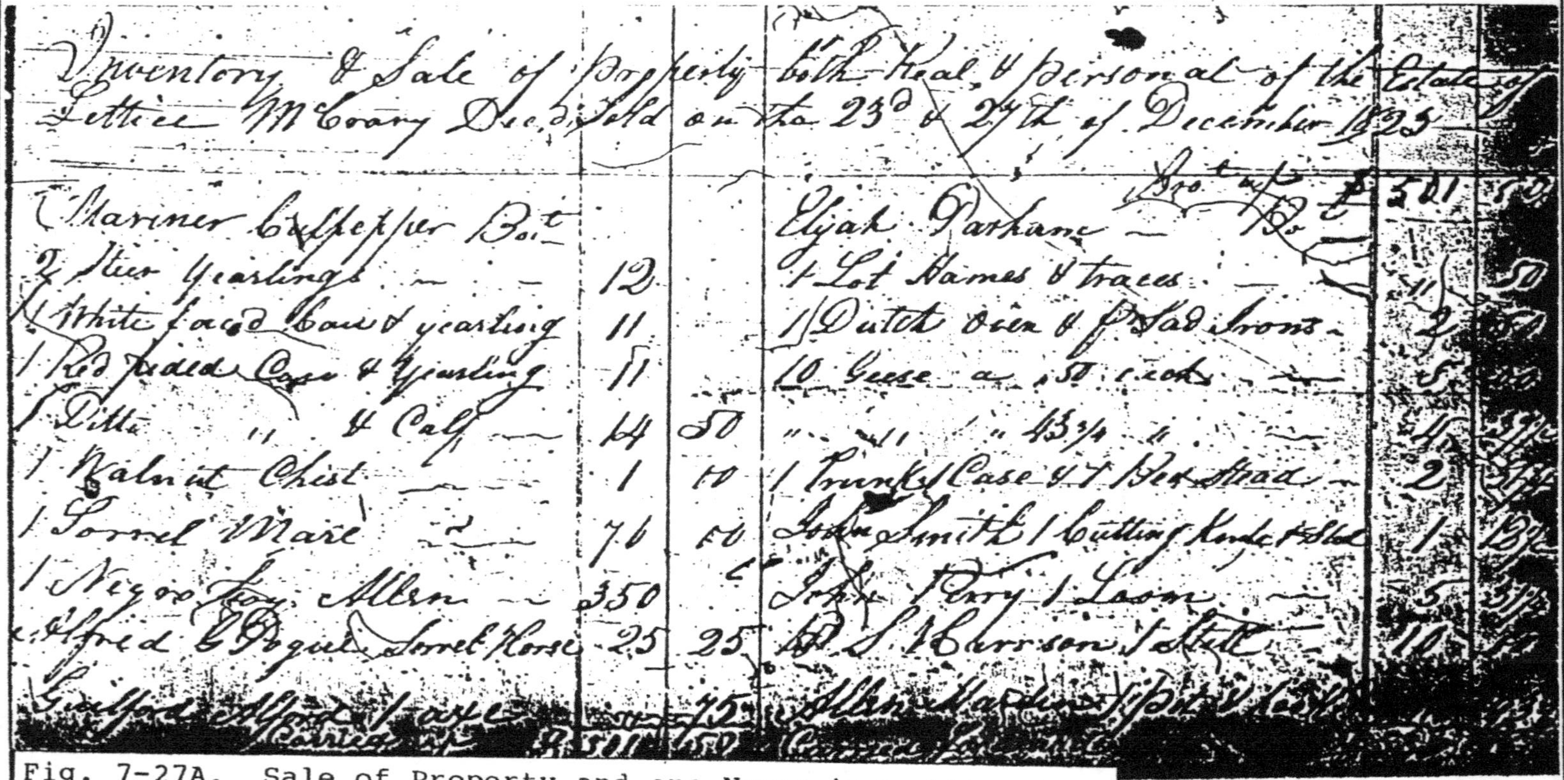

Fig. 7-27A. Sale of Property and one Negro boy, Allen to Mariner Culpepper. Estate of Lettice McCrary.

Slave Ancestral Research

WARREN COUNTY RECORDS

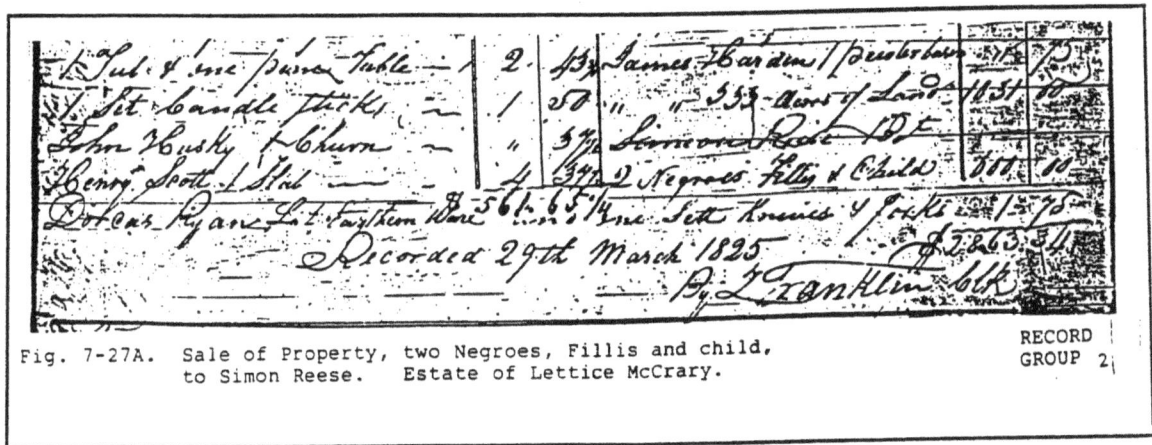

Fig. 7-27A. Sale of Property, two Negroes, Fillis and child, to Simon Reese. Estate of Lettice McCrary.

RECORD GROUP 2

Matthew McCrary and Letty McCrary were heirs of their father's estate. (John McCrary, Sr., RECORD GROUP 2) Matthew lived in Warren County, Georgia and was very wealthy. His sister, Letty, also lived in Warren County and was a widow of a Matthew McCrary who died in 1809 in Warren County. Her husband, Matthew was the son of Robert McCrary. In the Inventories of the brother and sister, Matthew and Letty, at the time of their decease, neither listed the slaves received from their father's estate. Matthew's Inventory did not have the Negro slaves *London* and *Cesar* and Letty did not have *Cass* and *Dick*. The four slaves remained in Baldwin County. London and Cesar went to Bartley McCrary. Although Eden was allotted to Bartley, his name is in Matthew's Inventory in Warren County. (Fig. 7-27B).

Since this was the case, I believe that some slave transfers within the McCrary family were not always recorded in court records. The TRANSFER CHART in Chapter Sixteen illustrates the recorded transfers within the McCrary family.

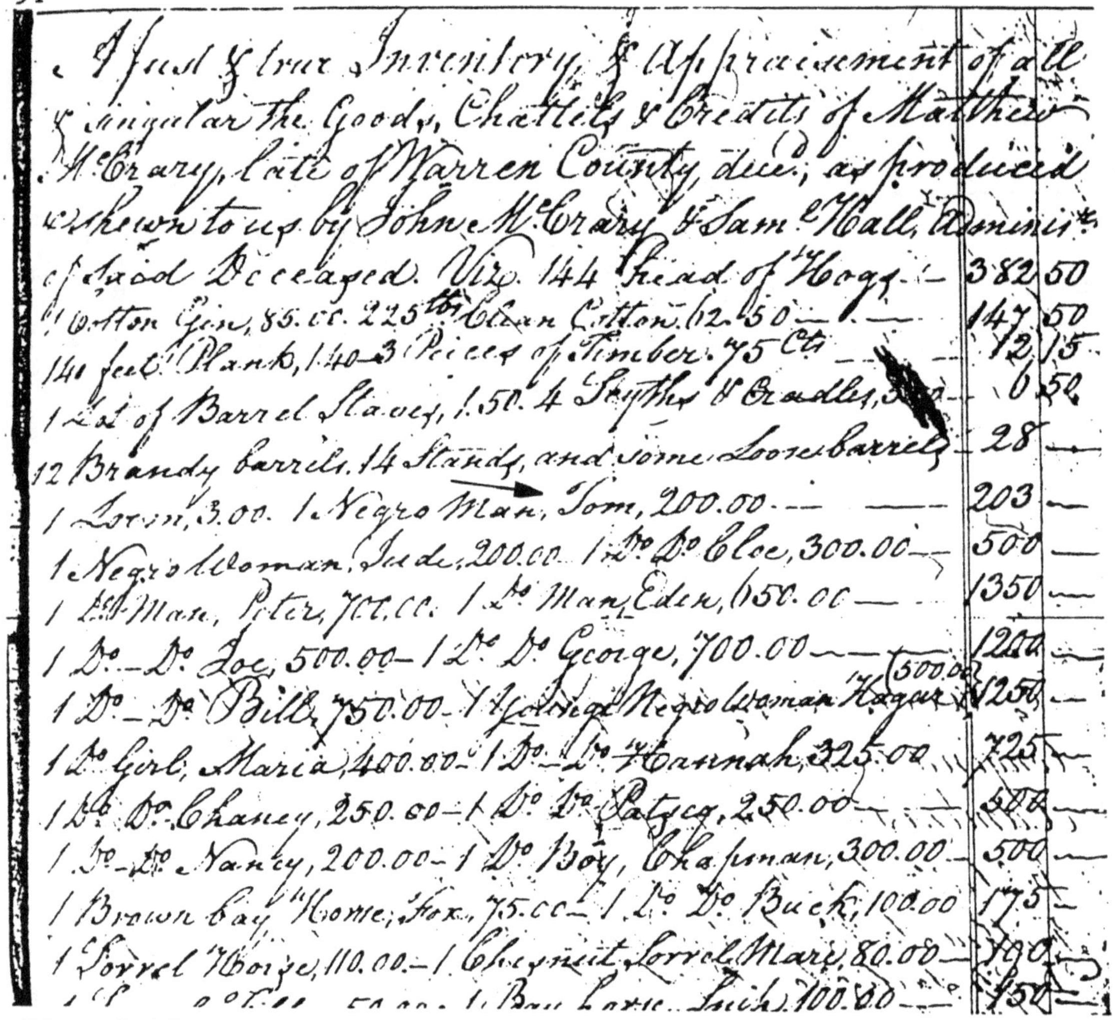

A Just & true Inventory & Appraisement of all
& singular the Goods, Chattels & Credits of Matthew
McCrary, late of Warren County, dec'd; as produced
& shewn to us by John McCrary & Saml. Hall, Adminis.
of said Deceased. Viz. 144 head of Hogs — 382 50
1 Cotton Gin, 85.00 225 lbs Clean Cotton 62.50 — 147 50
140 feet Plank, 1.40 3 Pieces of Timber 75 Cts — 2 15
1 Lot of Barrel Staves, 1.50 4 Scythes & Cradles, [illegible] — 6 50
12 Brandy barrels, 14 Stands, and some Loose barrels — 28 —
1 Loom, 3.00 1 Negro Man, Tom, 200.00 — 203 —
1 Negro Woman, Jude, 200.00 1 Do Do Cloe, 300.00 — 500 —
1 Do Man, Peter, 700.00 1 Do Man, Eden, 650.00 — 1350 —
1 Do Do Joe, 500.00 1 Do Do George, 700.00 — 1200 —
1 Do Do Bill, 750.00 1 young Negro Woman Hagar (500.00) 1250 —
1 Do Girl, Maria, 400.00 1 Do Do Hannah, 325.00 — 725 —
1 Do Do Chaney, 250.00 1 Do Do Patsey, 250.00 — 500 —
1 Do Do Nancy, 200.00 1 Do Boy, Chapman, 300.00 — 500 —
1 Brown bay Horse, Fox, 75.00 1 Do Do Buck, 100.00 — 175 —
1 Sorrel Horse, 110.00 1 Chesnut Sorrel Mare, 80.00 — 190 —
1 [illegible] 50.00 1 Bay [illegible] 100.00 — 150 —

Fig. 7-27B. Inventory and Appraisements. Partial Inventory of Matthew McCrary, dec'd. 1816. Warren Co., Ga.

Negro slaves:

man, Tom	$200	woman, Jude	$200
woman, Cloe	300	man, Peter	700
man, Eden	650	man, Joe	500
man, George	700	man, Bill	750
young Negro woman, Hagar	500		
girl, Maria	400	girl, Hannah	325
girl, Chaney	250	girl, Patsey	250
girl, Nancy	200	boy, Chapman	300

Brown Bay Home Fox 75.00
Do Do Buck 100.00 (Do means ditto)
Sorrel Horse 110.00
Chestnut Sorrel mare 80.00 ...

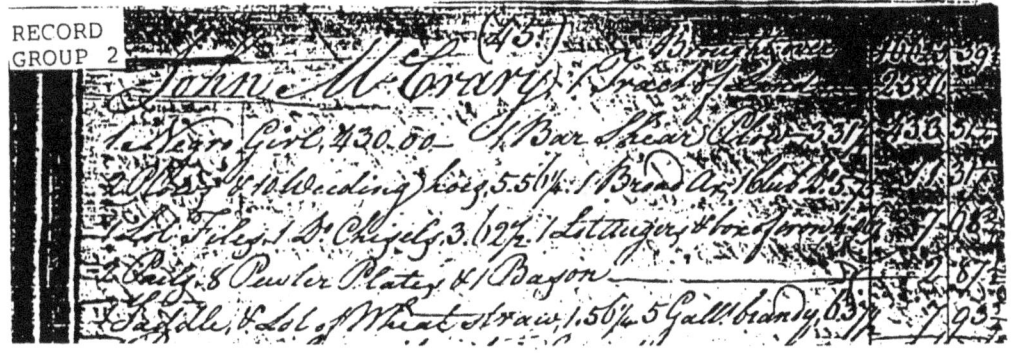

```
                    (45)           Brought Over
                                   $ 16,625.39

John McCrary        Track of Land                 2,516
1 Negro girl   430.00    1 Bar Shear Plow   331 1/4
2 Plows & 10 weeding hoes   5501 1/4  Broad ax club Do 5.75
1 Lot Files Do Chisels 362 1/2   1 Lot Auger & Box of Iron
2 pails   8 Pewter Plates & Bason   287 1/2
1 saddle & Lot of wheat straw 1.50 1/2  5 gall brandy 6.37 1/2
```

John McCrary is perhaps a son of Matthew McCrary, d. 1816. The above shows his share in the Estate Division. The Negro slaves were not named in the record. The names of the new owners who received the 15 slaves (See Matthew McCrary's Inventory & Appraisement) are named in the TRANSFER CHART in this chapter.

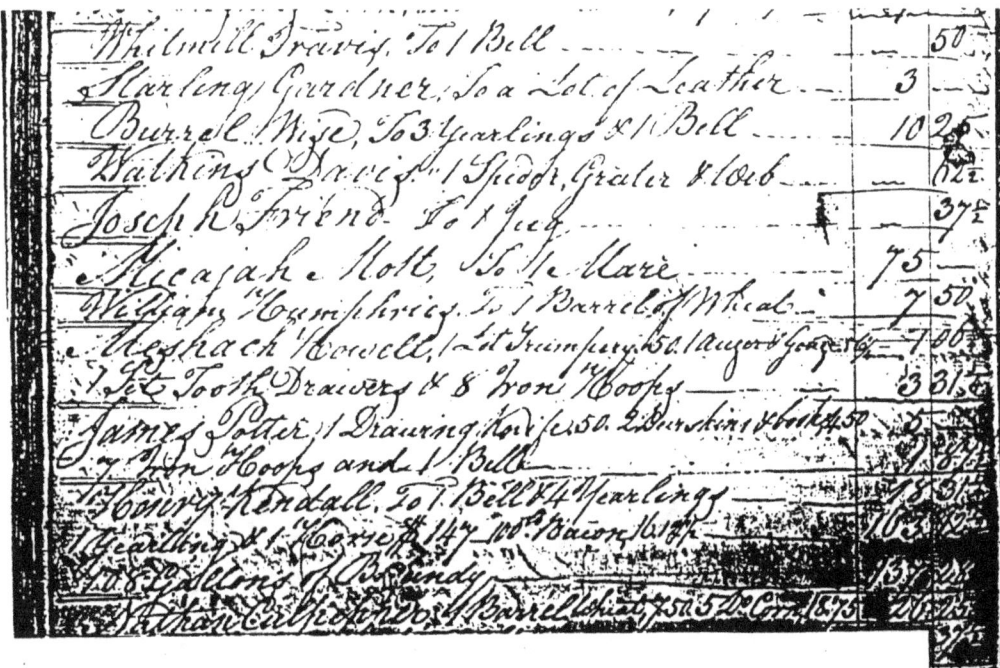

Fig. 7-27C. Estate Division. Partial division of Matthew McCrary, dec'd 1816, Warren Co., GA. to John McCrary.

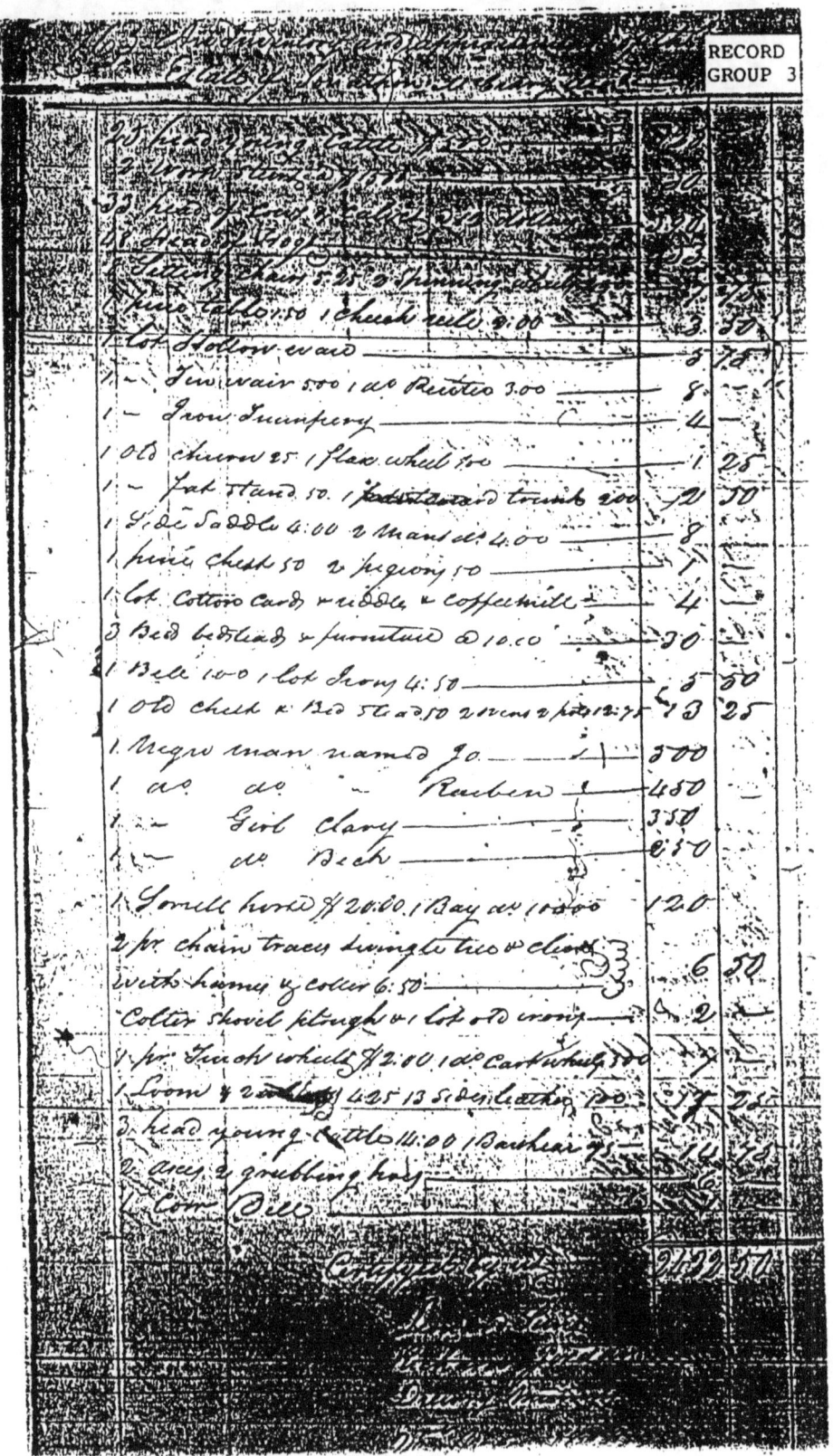

Fig. 7-28. Inventory and Appraisements. Jonathan McCrary, dec'd. 1808 Baldwin Co., GA.

Slave Ancestral Research

RECORD GROUP　　　　　JONATHAN McCRARY, Estate Record.
NO. 3　　　　　　　　　　ca. 1808 Baldwin Co., GA. <u>Inventory and
　　　　　　　　　　　　　　Appraisement</u> 25 January 1809

    page 163

          ...

          1 Negro man Jo $500
          1　　do　　do Reuben 450
          1　　--　　girl Clary 350
          1　　--　　do　 Beck.................. 250
          1 sorrel horse....................... 20
          1 Bay　　　Do.......................$100

          ... "do" used for ditto.

Fig. 7-28.

    This Inventory of Jonathan McCrary named four slaves. Jonathan McCrary's Estate was not settled until 1815. By this date, a Negro woman Winny and two Negro children, Luveser and Jack are a part of the Estate. See Fig.7-29. Although Winny is allotted to Sary Calton, Winny's name appeared as "an old woman" in Bartley McCrary's Inventory in 1826. See RECORD GROUP 1.

ADDED: *If I could determine which of the three Negro women was the mother of Luveser, I would know the name of my Eighth Generation ancestor. By conjecture, I believed that Clary or Beck was Luveser's mother. Reuben might have been the father because the name "Reuben" was given in two generations of Luveser's descendants. After my visit to the DAR Library, which enabled me to make connections in the slaveholding family, I began the search to determine Luveser's mother.*

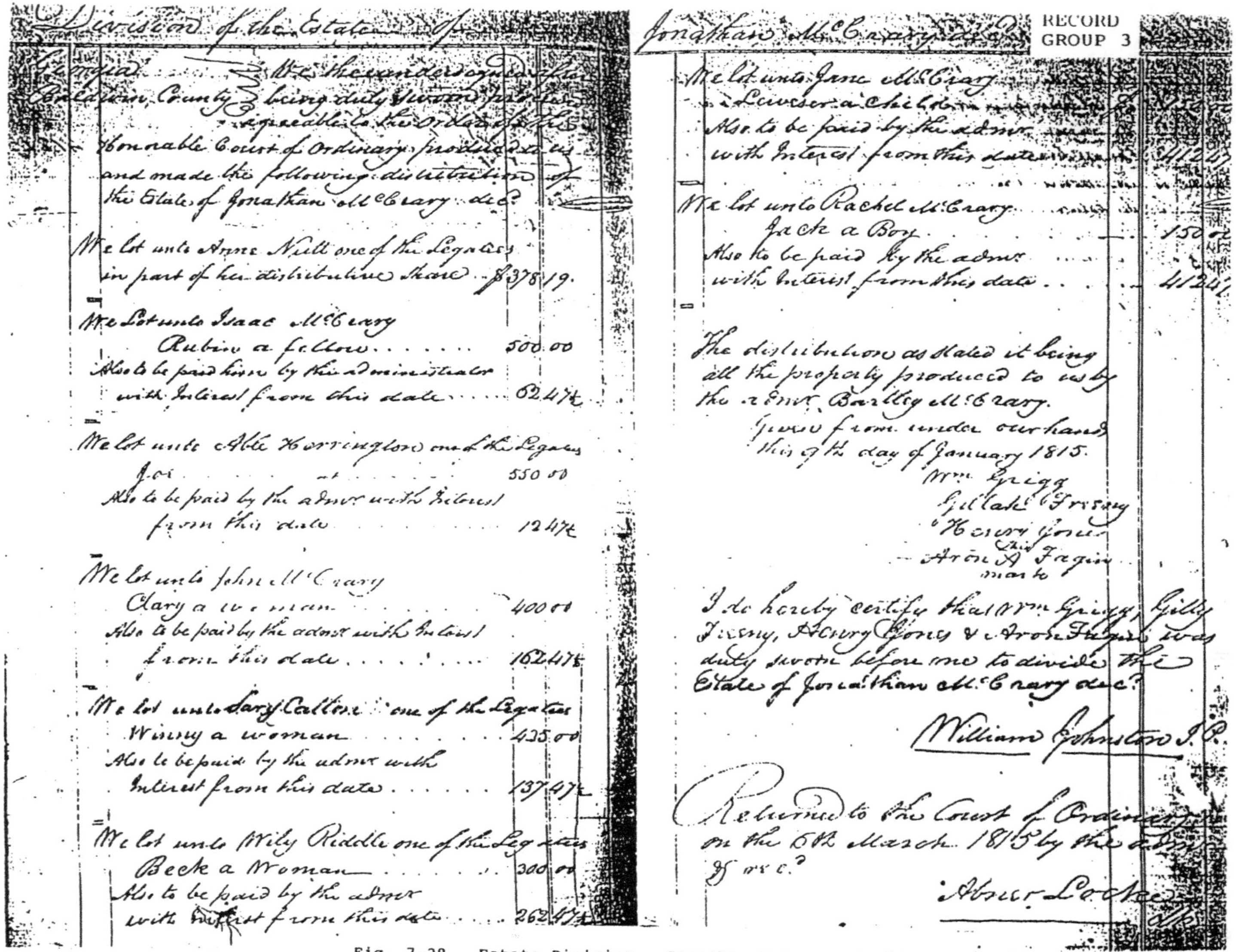

Fig. 7-29. Estate Division. Jonathan McCrary, dec'd. 1808 Distribution to heirs, 1816.

Slave Ancestral Research

RECORD GROUP No. 3, pages 46-47

JONATHAN McCRARY, Estate Records. Deceased ca. 1808 Baldwin Co. Returns. <u>Distribution of Estate</u> in 1815.

Ann Nutt, a Legatee, receives	$378.19
(m) Isaac McCrary receives	Rubin
Able Herrington receives	Joe
^John McCrary receives	Clary
Sary Calton receives	Winny,*a woman
Wiley Riddle receives	Beck, a woman
(m) ** Jane McCrary receives	Luveser, a child
(m) Rachel McCrary receives	Jack, a boy
Bartley McCrary, Administrator	

Fig. 7-29.

Bartley (d.1826) was the administrator of the estate. (m) Minor children of Jonathan McCrary were Isaac, Jane and Rachel. Each received one Negro slave. *Winney is the "old woman" listed on Bartley McCrary's Inventory. From this Jonathan McCrary, deceased in 1808, **Luveser may be the Negro girl who becomes "Lovenia" on Bartley McCrary's Hiring list and the old woman "Viny" valued as $100 on John McCrary's Inventory in 1854 in Taylor Co. (See RECORD GROUPS 1 & 7)

ADDED: *This Jonathan McCrary (1735-1814), is the son of John McCrary, Revolutionary War soldier whose records are in RECORD GROUP 2. My grouping of all McCrary records, and writing of the above paragraph were done prior to my visit to the DAR Library. After I read the Data File there on Jonathan's father, John McCrary, I learned that my thinking was right about the slave child "Luveser." ^John McCrary, who has "Veny" in his 1854 Inventory, was John McCrary's son.*

This is the record that shows my ancestor Luveser McCrary, the 90-year old woman in the 1870 Taylor County Census when she was a small child. AT LAST, I FOUND HER! SHE WAS IN MY RECORDS A LONG TIME, BUT I DID NOT MAKE THE CONNECTION UNTIL MY VISIT TO THE DAR LIBRARY 13 YEARS AFTER I BEGAN MY SEARCH!

RECORD GROUP 3

In act with Wm Grigg guardian

		By Interest one year on $553.18¾ is	[illegible]	[illegible]
		Ballance due the Minor is	[illegible]	[illegible]
		Act. with Wm Grigg gardian		
		By Int. one year on $522.46¼ is	41	77
		Ballance due from the Minor is	17	83
		Act. with Wm Grigg guardian		
		By Int. one year on $561.81¾ is	44	94
		Ballance due the Minor is	"	91¼
		Jane McCrary		
1819		By one Bonnet & Band box	6	17
		Trimmings for the same	2	51
		Cash hand her to pay for shoes & other articles	5	10
		1 Dress bt. George Reeves	6	75
		Cash pd. Thos. H Keenan Clk	"	25
		Boarding for this year	47	62½
			68	12½
1819		Isaac McCrary		
		By 2 School Books	1	37½
		" 1 quire of Paper	"	25
		" mending pr. shoes	"	37
		" George Reeves pr. shoes	2	12
		Cash pd. Thos. H Keenan Clk	"	25
		Boarding this year	[illegible]	[illegible]
			[illegible]	[illegible]
1819		Rachel McCrary		
		By 1 school Book	[illegible]	62½
		" 1 pr. shoes & mending pr.	2	12
		Cash pd. Thos. H Keenan Clk	[illegible]	25
		Boarding this year	[illegible]	[illegible]
			[illegible]	[illegible]

Fig. 7-30. Returns of Wm. Grigg, Guardian of minor children of Jonathan McCrary, dec'd. 1808.

Slave Ancestral Research

RECORD GROUP	JOHNATHAN McCRARY Returns Baldwin Co.
No. 3 pages 53-54	1818-1819

Wm. Grigg is the court-appointed guardian of the minor children of Johnathan McCrary. Each year, the guardian is required to file a "Return" in the court records showing how much money was spent on the minor children, called, "orphans" or "minors" and the income for their care. I observed that income from "hiring out" the slaves; tax on the slaves; clothing, boarding of the minors, school supplies and income from interest on their distributive share of the estate are included in the "Returns." In one Return for Johnathan McCrary, dated July 17, 1812, the notation reads: "To hire of Negroes for 1811 to Ann Nutt $357.25." The "Returns" were filed annually for the minor children.

RECORD GROUP 3

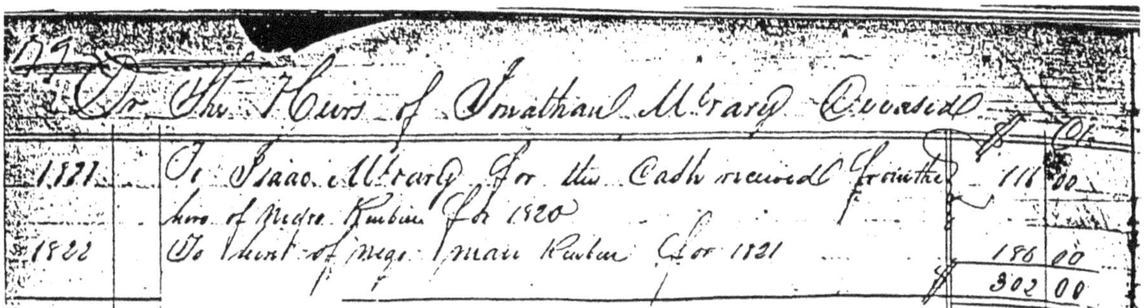

Fig. 7-30.

Dr. In account with William Grigg Guardian 18[illegible] Cr

Date		Item	$	c
1808 Jany 21st.		By Cash paid James McCrary the Guardian & a negro girl by the name of Louesa it being in full for all the property in my hands as guardian of Jane McCrary as per his Receipt		
	1	By Cash pd Daniel McCord for Books & tuition	29	50
1820	1	By Ciphering Book 50 & quire of paper 37½		87½
	2	Cash pd Robert Fletcher for 3 months tuition	4	10
	3	" " H. L. Jones tax for 1819		47½
		" Boarding for the year 1820	31	00
		$	65	85
1821	4	By Cash paid Henry L. Jones tax for 1820		47½
	5	By Cash paid A. Greene [illegible]	1	00
	6	" Cash paid A. W. Chamberlain for Schooling	4	00
	7	" " George Lewis a/c	12	12½
		2 pr Shoes	4	25
		Boarding & washing for 1821	80	00
		Making One suit of Clothes	3	00
	8	Mark M. Brown a/c	104	85
		Dr. By money paid away $	13	90½
		Cr. By money paid away for Rachel McCrary 1820	178	75½
1820	1	By Cash paid Daniel McCord for tuition & Schooling		
		1 quire of paper		37½
	2	" " Robert Fletcher for Schooling	4	10
		1 quire of paper		37½
	3	" H. L. Jones tax for 1819		47½
		" For Boarding 1820	31	00
		For 1821 turned over $	5[illegible]	47½
		By tax to H. L. Jones for 1820		47½
		" George Lewis a/c	9	12½
		1 pr Shoes	1	12½
		½ quire paper & pr Shoes	1	23
		" Boarding for 1821	31	00
		" Mar M. Brown a/c	5	87
		$	47	93½

Fig. 7-31. William Grigg, Guardian of Jane McCrary, transfers "Negro girl by the name of Louesa..." S518

Slave Ancestral Research

RECORD GROUP   JONATHAN McCRARY. Estate Records. Baldwin
NO. 3   County, Ga. RETURNS Book B.

page 180   In account with William Grigg Guardian $518.64
                   By Cash paid James McCrary the Heir-at-Law
1822   Viz an Negro girl by the name of Louesa at
Jany 26th   hand in full for all the property in my hands
                   as guardian of Jane McCrary as per his recept
                   ...
                   This Return shows that Jane McCrary, minor
                   of Jonathan McCrary, married James McCrary and
                   her husband paid William Grigg $518.64 for the
                   slave girl Louesa, my slave ancestor. The
                   Return shows payments for books, paper,
                   schooling, clothing, boarding and taxes paid
                   for the years 1819-1822. Item 5 in 1821 reads:
                   "By cash paid A. Crane of crying negro man
                   $1.00." "Crying" meant verbally advertising the
                   sale or hiring of a Negro slave.

Fig. 7-31.

Georgia ~~~~~ Jonathan Colbert
~~~~ County ~ Aaron Teagan, Henry
Jones and John Parker, being duly sworn
sayeth that the following is a just and true
appraisment of all the goods and chattles
of Isaac McCrary decd produced to them
by John McCrary and William McCrary
or come within their sight or knowledge
to the best of judgement Sworn to and
Subscribed before me this 13th day of March
1817

Wm. Gridge, J.P.

     Johnathan Colbert
     Aaron Teagan
     Henry Jones
     John Parker

Appraisment of the goods & Chattles of Isaac McCrary decd in Dollars and Cents

Item	Value
One Negro man Peter apprd to	600.00
One Negro do Dick	700.00
One Negro woman Jude	600.00
One Negro man Sam	550.00
One Negro girl Lucy	350.00
1 Negro woman Frey	500.00
1 Negro girl Betsy	250.00
1 Negro Boy Stephen	250.00
1 Negro boy Lewis	150.00
1 Oven $2.00 1 Large Pot $3.00	5.00
1 Small oven $2.00 1 Pot Hooks $2.00, 1 Spider $1	5.00
2 Pot racks 1 Skillet & 1 Griddle	2.50

Fig. 7-32. Appraisement of the goods and Chattles of Isaac McCrary in Dollars and Cents. 1817 Baldwin Co., GA.

Slave Ancestral Research

      Georia   Jonathan Colbert
   Baldwin County   Aaron Fegan, Henry
Jones and John Parker, being duly sworn
sayeth that the following is a just and
true appraisement of all the goods and chattles
of Issac M'Crary decd produced to them
by John McCrary and William M'Crary
or comes within their sight or knowledge
to the best of judgement Sworn to and
subscribed before me this 15th day of March
1817

Wm. Grigg J P

                 Johnathan Colbert
                 Aaron Feagan
                 Henry Jones
                 John Parker

Appraisement of the goods & Chattles of Isaac
McCrary decd in Dollars and Cents--

RECORD GROUP   ISAAC McCRARY, Estate Records. Deceased in ca.
No. 4   1817 Baldwin Co. <u>Inventory and Appraisements</u>
page 13

one Negro man	Peter	appr. to	$	600
one Negro "	Dick	"		700
one Negro woman	Jude	"		600
one Negro man	Saml	"		550
one Negro girl	Lucy	"		350
1 Negro woman	Dicy	"		500
1 Negro girl	Betsy	"		250
1 Negro boy	Stephen	"		250
1 Negro boy	Luvis	"		150

Fig. 7-32.

Relatives John McCrary and William McCrary presented the appraisement of the goods and chattles.

Account of rent of the land & hire of the Negroes belonging to the
Estate of Isaac McCrary Dec'd for the year 1817

John McCrary to the old house field	26 00
" " the stubble do	10 00
" " J McCrary do	20 00
Parthy Shuffield Six acres	15 00
John Northington to old Bottom do	30 00
" " Stoney field	31 00
Parthy McCrary to New ground field	16 00
Hanah McCrary to House & orchard	30 00
William Dunn to hire of negro man Peter	147 00
John McCrary to Do Do Sam	113 00
William McCrary to Do Do woman Jude	87 00
" Do Do Girl Lucy	22 00

From the first of January 1818 to the third of March 1818
Parthy McCrary to Dido and his family for their support
William McCrary to the hire of Sam	20 00
" to " Jude	12 00
" to Lucy	4 00
John McCrary to Peter a man	24 00

Isaac McCrary Dec'd on account of property sold the 11 day of March 1817

Parthy McCrary Jr to a Square of Land N° 196	905 00
Mathew McCrary to 1 Square of land N° 190	1800 00
Wiley McCrary to 1 Square of Land N° 198	550 00
John Clark to 50 acres of land N° 199	200 00
" to 144 acres of land N° 119	1000 00
Parthy McCrary to 26½ acres part lot N° 196	150 00
John McCrary to one negro man Dick	1015 00
" to woman Grey	701 00
" to Boy Stephen	333 00
" to Girl Petsey	350 00
" Boy Lewis	200 00
William McCrary to one negro woman Jude	670 00
" Girl Lucy	600 00
" man Peter	1113 00
Parthy McCrary to one negro man Sam	755 00
William Grigg to two Cows and one yearling	37 00

Fig. 7-33. Returns, Negro Hirings and Sale of Property.
Isaac McCrary, Baldwin Co. Ga., 1817.

Slave Ancestral Research

RECORD GROUP   ISAAC McCRARY, BALDWIN COUNTY RETURNS, BK. B
No. 4   1817   Account of the rent of land and hiring of the
     page 11   Negroes for the year 1817.

```
          William Dean  hire of Negro man Peter    147.00
          John McCrary    "     "    "   man Sam   103.00
          William McCrary "     "    "  woman Jude  87.00
                          "     "    "   girl Lucy  22.00
```
From the first of January 1815 to the third of March of the same date.
Bartley McCrary to Dick and his family for their support.

```
          William McCrary  to the hire of Sam    20.00
          _____  to _____ Jude    12.00
          _____  to          Lucy       4.00
          John McCrary     to   Peter a man      24.00
```

Fig. 7-33.

Isaac McCrary's Negro slaves were hired out for the year 1817 before being sold in 1818.

RECORD GROUP   ISAAC McCRARY. BALDWIN COUNTY RETURNS BK. B
No. 4   2 March 1818 Account of Property Sold.
     page 12

```
       * John McCrary    to one Negro man  Dick    $1015.00
       * _____   to  _____ woman   Dicey     706.00
       * _____   to  _____ boy     Stephen   333.00
       * _____   to  _____ girl    Betsey    350.00
       * _____   to  _____ boy     Lewis     200.00
         William McCrary to one   woman    Jude      670.00
         _____   to  _____ girl    Lucy      600.00
         _____   to  _____ man     Peter    1003.00
         Bartley McCrary to one Negro man  Sam       755.00
```

Fig. 7-33.

* This JOHN McCRARY is the important one to my search for the slave owners of my ancestor, "Lovenia," See Record Group No. 7.

Georgia Baldwin County

We the undersigned commissioners agreeable to an order to us directed from the Honorable the Court of Ordinary for the County aforesaid meet agreeable to request and made the following distribution of the Estate of Isaac McCrary Dec'd after being duly sworn Viz

that the Several Legatees whos names are hereunto Enexed be paid by the Adr of said Dec'd the Several Sums that is opposit there names with Intrest from the Eight day of May 1820

	$	cts
To John McCrary, sr.	1060	02¾
The Heirs of William McCrary, Dec'd	1060	02¾
Bartley McCrary, jr	1060	02¾
Mathew McCrary	1060	02¾
Jonathan McCrary	1060	02¾
Hanah McCrary	1060	02¾
Benjamin Culpepper	1060	02¾
Elizabeth McCrary	1060	02¾
John McCrary jr	1060	02¾
Isaac McCrary	1060	02¾
Lettice McCrary	1060	02¾
Sarah An. McCrary	1060	02¾
	12720	33

Given under our hands & Seals the 8 day of May 1820

    Wm Grigg (Seal)
    Simon Brooks (Seal)
    Rich'd Jordan (Seal)
    Mark M. Brown (Seal)
    A Young (Seal)

Georgia Baldwin County } I do Certify that Wm Grigg Simon Brooks Rich'd Jordan

Fig. 7-34. Estate Division. Isaac McCrary. Baldwin Co., GA., 1820.

Slave Ancestral Research

RECORD GROUP   ISAAC McCRARY.   Baldwin Co. <u>Distribution of</u>
No. 4   1820 May 8   <u>of Estate</u>.   Bk. of Returns
    page 167

Fig. 7-34.

       This record shows the final distribution of the estate of Isaac McCrary. I observed that each Legatee (heir) is a member of the McCrary family and receives an equal share. No relationships are given and several have the same name. Benjamin Culpepper married into the family which makes it necessary to search marriage records and other probate records to trail the McCrary slaves.

       By 2 Feb. 1837, Benjamin Culpepper was deceased in Talbot County. His property was purchased by Isaac McCrary, Jr., Mathew McCrary, William Durden, Geo. Jameson and James Culpepper. Isaac McCrary, Jr. was the administrator of the estate. Benjamin's Inventory listed two slaves, a woman Edy and a boy, Austin. This information came from Talbot County Sales Book, pp.293-294, and p. 264 of Talbot County Inventories and Appraisement Book.

ADDED: *Isaac McCrary was the son of John McCrary, the Revolutionary War soldier (1735-1814). John McCrary who died in 1854, bought the slave family: Dick, Dicey, Stephen, Betsey and Lewis. This family appeared on John McCrary's Inventory in 1854, as shown in RECORD GROUP 7. Isaac McCrary received the Dick and Dicey family from his father, John McCrary as shown in RECORD GROUP 2. (To distinguish between the McCrary names, individual death dates are used.)*

The Sale of those Negroes belonging to the Estate of Robert McCrary deceased, Sold on this 6th day of March 1827.

One Negro boy Hardy purchased by Willie McCrary at $360.00

One negro man London purchased by Bartley McCrary at 311.00

Two negro boys Alfred & Bird purchased by James McCrary at 350.00

                                                                          $1021.00

May 9th 1827.
                                                James McCr[ary]

1827 Money paid to different persons on the Estate of Robert McCrary Dec'd

No. 1 Paid William S. Davis for letters of dismission
   2 Paid William S. Davis for recording appraisement
   3 Paid R. A. Greene for a copy order to sell negroes
   4 Paid M. W. Perry Robert McCrary Tax for 1827
   5 Paid John McCrary on note principal and interest
   6 Paid to M. W. Perry on note principal and interest
   7 Paid to Thomas B. Stubbs on note principal and interest

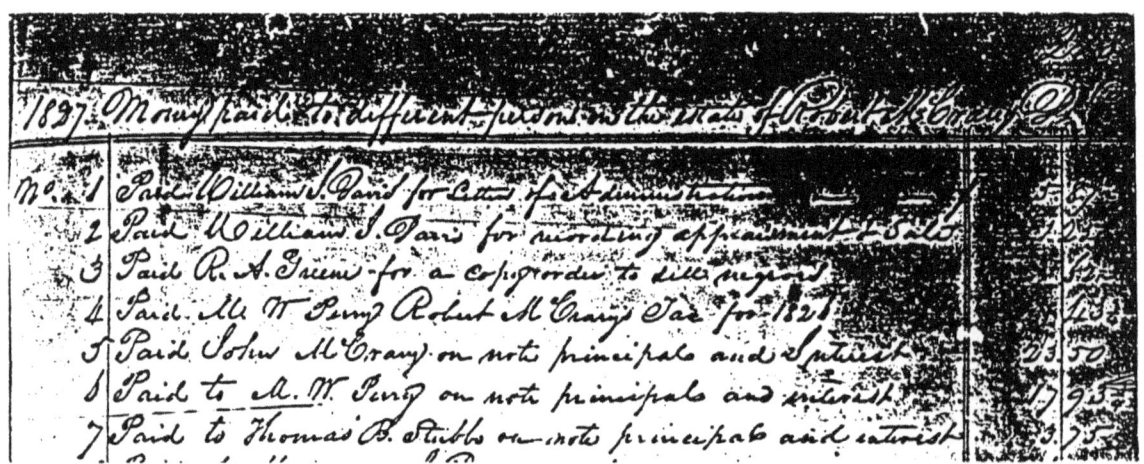

Fig. 7-35. Sale of Negroes. Robert McCrary, dec'd. 1817, Baldwin Co., GA. 1827.

Item 3. Payment made for a copy order to sell Negroes.

Slave Ancestral Research

RECORD GROUP   ROBERT McCRARY. Estate Records. Deceased c.
No. 5   1827   Baldwin County Book of Sales
        page
        187   Sale of the Negroes belonging to the Estate of Robert
                 McCrary...6th day of March 1827

                 Negro boy Hardy purchased by Willie McCrary

                 "   man London   "   " Bartley McCrary (Jr.)

                 Two Negro boys, Alfred & Bird purchased by James
                 McCrary

Fig. 7-35.

The three boys and man, London, were on Bartley McCrary's Inventory of slaves and Hiring list in 1826. (RECORD GROUP 1) In 1814, London was in John McCrary's estate and when divided, London went to Matthew McCrary. (RECORD GROUP 2)

In 1827, London and Hardy went from Bartley McCrary's Estate to Robert McCrary. Also Alfred and Bird went to Robert McCrary. After the decease of Robert McCrary, the two boys are purchased by James McCrary, as indicated above. Alfred and Bird were sold away from their mother Patience, a woman belonging to Bartley McCrary.

RECORD GROUP   ROBERT McCRARY. Baldwin County Returns.
No. 5   1828 Money paid to different persons in the
        page   estate of Robert McCrary, deceased.
        222

Fig. 7-36.

The next record shows five of the Legatees of Robert McCrary: William Colbert "in right of my dec'd wife, Lettice Colbert;" Albert G. Beckham (spouse of Mary McCrary); Jane Poindexter; Bryan Bateman, "in right of my wife;" and David Moses. This type of record increases the demand for more research. Each new surname has to be explored for probate records in search of the McCrary slaves.

ADDED: *Robert is a son of Bartley McCrary, Sr. (d. 1826), also James and Bartley McCrary, Jr., Administrators of his Estate.*

Estate of Robert McCrary &c continued

Burke County (No 55.)
Rec'd 5th May 1828 of James & Bartley McCrary adm'rs of Robert McCrary dec'd one hundred and eighty five dollars in full for my distributive share of the estate of said dec'd in right of my dec'd wife Littice Colbert

Wm Colbert

Test
Wm Grigg
S. Bivins

(No 56.)
Rec'd of James & Bartley McCrary adm'rs of Robert McCrary dec'd in full of my distributive share of said estate being the one eighth part of said estate say one hundred and eighty five 3/100 dollars.

Albert G. Beckham

Test John Williams

(No 57)
Rec'd of James and Bartley McCrary Adm'rs on the estate of Robert McCrary dec'd in full of my Legacy on said estate
Feb'y 20th 1828.

her
Jane X Poindexter
Mark

Test John Wilson
John Hubbard

(No 58.)
Rec'd of James & Bartley McCrary administrators of the estate of Robert McCrary deceased one hundred and seventy two dollars and ninetien cents in full of my Legacy of said estate in right of my wife

Bryan Bateman

January 30th 1828.

Archer D. Steele.

Note. The foregoing five receipts Numbered 54-55-56-57 and 58 are endorsed as Recorded and are returned to the Admin'rs by order of this Court (see minutes July Term 1828) for the settlement with heirs & legatees on page 217 of this book —

Fig. 7-36. Estate Division. Robert McCrary, dec'd. 1817. Heirs are the same as for his father, Bartley McCrary, deceased 1826, See RECORD GROUP 1, Fig. 7-22.

Slave Ancestral Research

By trailing the ownership of the McCrary slaves, a researcher could trace the McCrary family. For example: the Negro slave London was transferred from John McCrary, (deceased c.1814) to his son Bartley McCrary, Sr. (deceased c.1826) to his son, Robert McCrary (deceased 1826) to Robert's brother, Bartley McCrary, Jr. in 1827. Since the record does not read "Jr." the Bartley McCrary named in the above record could possibly be a son of Robert McCrary. The repetition of names in the McCrary family appeared to be patterned after a common naming practice.

During the years, 1700-1800, in many families among the free population, first sons were often named after the father's father; the second son after the mother's father and the third son, after the father. The first daughter was named after the mother's mother; the second daughter was named after the father's mother and the third daughter was named after the mother. The fourth son was named after the father's eldest brother and the fourth daughter was named after the mother's eldest sister. In the McCrary family, there seemed to be a daughter Jane or Jenny (nickname for Jane) for each of John McCrary's (d. 1814) sons. A "Jane" was named as the wife of John McCrary, Sr., the Revolutionary War soldier from South Carolina in his DAR Data File.

Within the slave population, this strict naming pattern was impossible to maintain as the slave families were often split apart. Even small children were sold apart from their mothers.

Georgia
Wilkinson County

We the undersigned appraisers being duly sworn do certify that the annexed appraisement, are inventory of is a true list of the property shown to us by the widow of Wm McCrary and taken under our hands this 9th of March 1819.

Daniel Clark
Alexander McCook
Daniel McCook

State of Georgia
Wilkinson County

Appeared George ..., Daniel Clark, Alexander McCook and Daniel McCook who being duly sworn to appraise the property of Wm McCrary, decd, late of the County of said deceased this 9th of March 1819.

Philip Pittman J.P.

An Inventory or register of the property of William McCrary decd. appraised by Daniel Clark, Alexander McCook and Daniel McCook, this 9th of March 1819.

Negroes	Valuation
John	950.00
Jude	500.00
Tom & her child	700.00
Lucy	400.00
Ned	450.00
Bazzel	500.00
Benjamin	300.00
Peter	200.00
Samuel	500.00
	450.00
Household and kitchen furniture	120.00
Three feather beds & furniture	
1 Bureau	10.15
Lot of ware, pewter, glass & earthenware	10.00
1 Smoothing augur & saw, candle...	

---

1 Pitcher & plates	2	4
1 Looking glass	1	17
1 Lot of Wm McCrary's clothes	20.10	25
2 Coats cut down		10
2 Smoothing irons & yard	1	50
24 Head of hogs & ...	24.10	

$757.05 ¾

Fig. 7-37. Inventory, William McCrary, dec'd. 1819
Wilkinson Co., GA.

Slave Ancestral Research

RECORD GROUP No. 6

Fig. 7-37

WILLIAM McCRARY. Estate Records. Recorded in 1819 on 9 March in Baldwin County. Inventories and Appraisements. (Residence was in Wilkinson County, Georgia)

The Inventory of William McCrary listed nine slaves. Below are two hiring records of William McCrary in Record Group No. 6. Baldwin County Returns Bk. B pp. 231, 243

Name of Negroes		Hired by	For the Year of	of
Peter	man	John McCrary	1823	1827 to John McCrary
Ned	boy	James McCrary	1823	1827 to D. M. Hall
Lucy	girl	Ezekiel Miller	1823	1827 to Mathew McCrary
Sam	boy	Willie McCrary	1823	1827 to William John
Bazel	boy	Britton Willis	1823	1827 to Samuel Montgomery
Jude*	woman	Bartley McCrary Jr.	1823	1827 to Wm. Durding
John	man	William Hansel	1823	1827 to S. Bivins
Jude and 3 children			Bartley McCrary Senr. 1823	
Patience			1827	to William Colbert
Ben			1827	to William Durding
Sam			1827	to A. Black
Peter			1827	to A. G. Beckham

*Jude is named with a child, Henry, in the 1827 record when she is hired by Durding.

Since the McCrary slaves were hired out yearly, apparently after each McCrary slave owner was deceased, slaves were almost constantly "on the move" working under various taskmasters and overseers. What a life that must have been, never knowing to whom they would be hired or sold, nor when. And in addition to that, their children were scattered in different directions to work under the same cruel system.

Rec'd 11th December 1826 from Bartley McCrary Adm'r of William McCrary dec'd as Guardian of the Orphans of said dec'd nine negroes to wit Peter, Ned, John, Bazil, Ben, Henry, Jude, Lucy, Patience. One tract of Land in the dis't Wilkinson, notes to the amount of one hundred and thirty eight dollars and five cts — from the Estate of Shelly McCrary dec'd three negroes to wit Peter, Told Sam & John

Mathew McCrary
Guardian
5th March 1827

243	Matth. McCrary Guardian of the Orphans of William McCrary deceased	Dr
1827	To cash rec'd from the Administrator of Bartley McCrary dec'd	930.50
	To the hire of the negroes for 1827.	
	Patience to William Colbert	11.25
	Ben to William Purding	6.00
	Bazil to Samuel Montgomery	37.00
	Sam to Wm John	46.00
	Ned to D. M. Hall	70.00
	Lucy to Self	40.00
	Jude & Henry a child to Wm Purding	13.25
	Peter to John McCrary	55.50
	Sam to A Black	41.00
	Peter to A. G. Beckham	70.14
	John to S. Bivins	4.12
		$1324.71

Fig. 7-38. Transfer of Guardianship of William McCrary's minor children from Bartley McCrary, Jr. to Matthew McCrary and Hiring Records of the nine Negro slaves.

Slave Ancestral Research

Baldwin County Returns Bk. C, page 148 showed the following record which included children.

The hiring of the Negroes belonging to the Estate of William McCrary dec'd for the year 1826.

Nathaniel Nicholson	boy Ned	$73.25
William John	boy Sam	47.25
William Durden	boy Bazel	22.87
James C. Hay	boy Ben	11.00
John McCrary	Man Peter	61.00
William Colbert	Girl Lucy	50.25
Thos. Lee	Jude & Child	33.12
William Colbert	Girl Patience	6.12

RECORD GROUP No. 6   WILLIAM McCRARY. Estate Record. Deceased c. 1819. Baldwin County Returns Bk. C

page 191   Rec'd. in December 1826 from Bartley McCrary, Administrator of William McCrary dec'd's guardian of the orphans of said dec'd, nine Negroes to wit: Peter, Ned, John, Bazel, Ben, Henry, Jude, Lucy, Patience, one tract of land in the dist. Wilkerson, (County) notes to the amount of one hundred and thirty eight dollars and five cents-from the Estate of Bartley McCrary dec'd, three Negroes to wit: Peter, Old Sam and John.

                                       Mathew McCrary,
                                             Guardian
                                       5th March 1827

Fig. 7-38

ADDED: *William was a son of Bartley McCrary, Sr. (died 1826). William's slaves were brought to Baldwin County from Wilkinson County, Georgia. Bartley McCrary, Jr. became administrator of William's Estate after Bartley Sr. died, then his brother, Matthew McCrary became the guardian.*

118 Slave Ancestral Research

   This record (numbered "191") shows that Bartley McCrary, Jr. is the Administrator of William McCrary's Estate. William's nine slaves passed to his minor children after William is deceased. Peter, Old Sam and John, are taken from the estate of Bartley McCrary (Sr.) deceased in 1826 in Baldwin County and added for the support of William's minor children. Bartley McCrary, presenter of this information to the court is a Junior, son of Bartley who died in 1826. Matthew McCrary is serving as the guardian of the minor children of William McCrary. So Mathew would decide what to do with the Negro slaves. Matthew McCrary transferred all court records on his brother William's Estate from Wilkinson and Baldwin Counties to Talbot County, (court records) where he lived and served as guardian of William's minor children. The nine slaves were hired out annually for many years to support the minor children.

   The record numbered 243, dated 1827 is one of many hiring records on William's nine slaves (Fig. 7-38).

ADDED: *Matthew McCrary was the son of John McCrary, Sr., d.1814, the Revolutionary War soldier.*

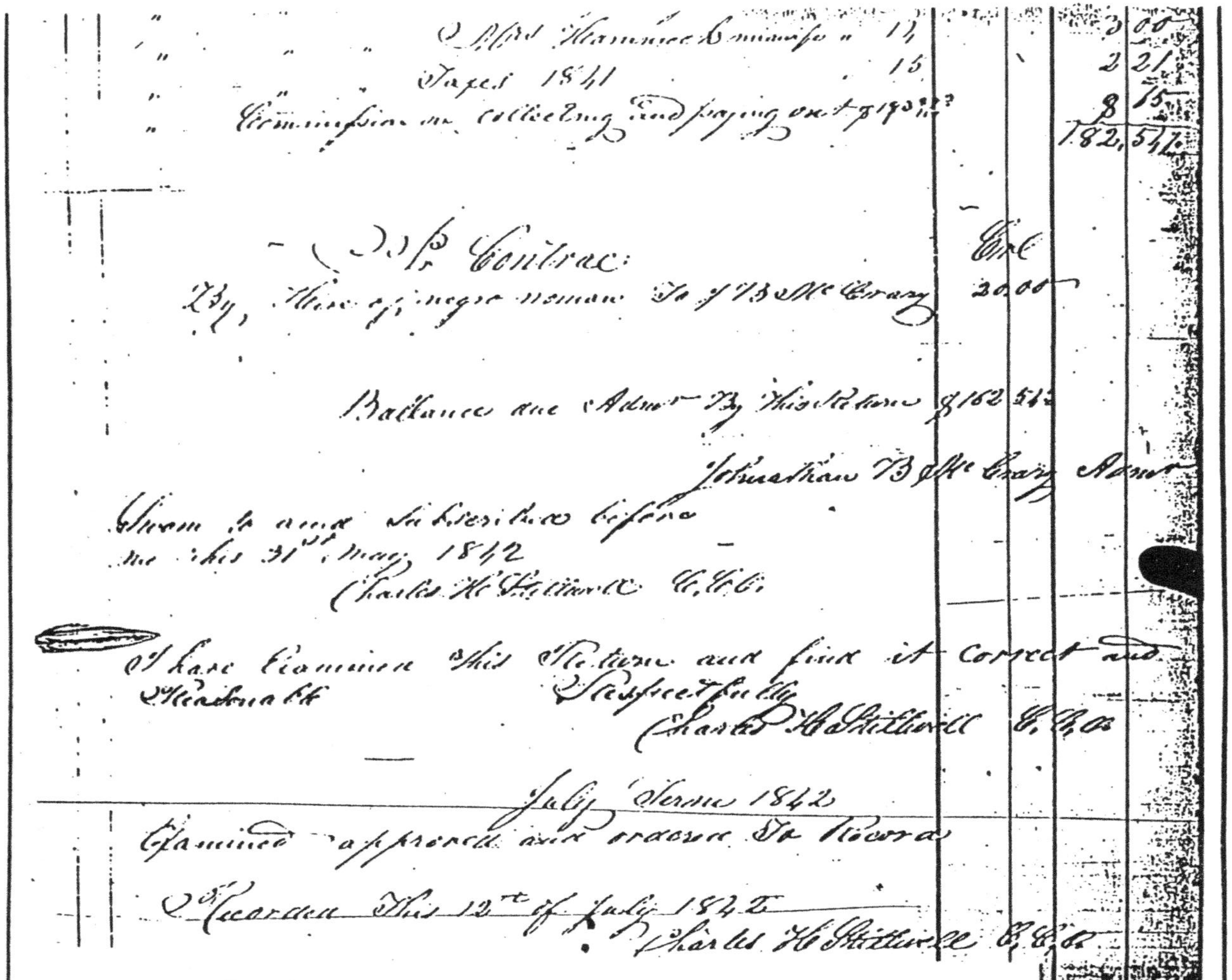

" Mrs Hammock Commission " 17 — 3 00
" Taxes 1841 " 15 — 2 21
" Commission on collecting and paying out $190.33 — 8 75
182 54½

Contra Cr
By Hire of negro woman To J B McCrary 20 00

Ballance due Admr By this Return $162 54½

Jonathan B McCrary Admr

Sworn to and subscribed before
me this 31st May 1842
Charles H Stillwell C.C.O.

I have examined this Return and find it correct and
reasonable
Respectfully
Charles H Stillwell C.C.O.

July Term 1842
Examined approved and ordered to Record
Recorded this 12th of July 1842
Charles H Stillwell C.C.O.

Fig. 7-38. Sample Talbot Co, Ga. Hiring record of a Negro woman to J. B. McCrary. Her name is omitted.

Sally McCrary Minor Dr. Hannah H. McCrary Guardian

1822 No 1 To Thomas H. Kenan Clk		
2. George Lewis ap		
Boarding & Clothing for 1822	40	25
	$ 42	37½

Hannah McCrary Guardian

3d Jany 1823

The admr of William McCrary Dec'd to Mary McCrary Dr. to Boarding & Clothing of five orphans for the year 1822 at 50$ each — 250.00
Mary McCrary

Rec'd of Bartley McCrary admr of W. McCrary Dec'd two hundred & fifty Dollars in full of the above February 12th 1823 / Mary McCrary

---

231

The Hiring of the Negroes belonging to the Estate of William Mc.

John McCrary a man Peter	70	00
James McCrary a boy Ned	125	10
Ezekiel Miller a girl Lucy	30	25
Willie McCrary a boy Sam	12	10
Brittin Willis a boy Bazel	3	00
Bartley McCrary Jr. a woman Jude	36	10
William H. Housel John man	53	10
Bartley H. McCrary Senr. Jude & 3 children	1	00
	232	25

Credit on the Estate of Wm McCrary dec'd for the year 1823

1823	Paid Willie McCrary for board No 1	$ 18	00
	John McCrary for Tuition 2	11	10
"	Samuel Hitt Do 3	4	66
"	William Durden for working on a horse 4	2	11
"	A Duburg for one pair shoes 5	1	25
"	Wiley and Baxter " " 6	1	25
"	A Finley for one " " 7		57
"	John Morton Taxes for 1822 8		62½
"	Thos P Kenan 9		6½
"	one arithmetic for Johnathan		57½
"	one pocket Knife 10		25
	bought for orphan Kenan one hat	1	00

The orphans of Wm McCrary dec'd to the Estate Dr.
To one half quire of paper
pd. Pryor Wright 25¢ for crying a negro 11
William Durden for the midwife
William Durding Bartley McCrary admr

Fig. 7-38. Hiring record of William McCrary's Negro slaves.

HIRING DAY

Of all the groups of McCrary family slaves, the nine slaves of William McCrary received the worst fate. They had no place to call home, not even a single plantation. They were the most unsettled of all the McCrary slaves following their slave master's death. (William died c.1819 in Wilkinson County, Georgia).

William McCrary's nine slaves: Peter, Ned, Lucy, Sam, Bazel, Jude, John, Patience and Ben were first uprooted from Wilkinson County, Georgia and brought to Baldwin County where their slave master's father, Bartley McCrary lived. After Bartley died, (c.1826) they were then taken to Talbot County, Georgia to William's brother, Matthew McCrary. There they were "hired out" year after year from one planter to another. Matthew McCrary preserved their movements in the Talbot County Returns. Matthew was the last guardian of his deceased brother William's minor children, Johnathan, Martha, Kinian, Tabitha and William (Jr.). My sad experience of finding their hiring Returns, prompted me to read about the practice of "hiring out" slaves. Lincoln's Emancipation Proclamation became effective on New Year's Day. History books make little or no reference to Lincoln's selection of New Years Day. But that day each year in the lives of slaves brought wrenching tears of sorrow. It was "hiring day."

M. W. Starling, in <u>The Slave Narrative, Its Place in American History</u>, Washington, D.C., Howard University Pr., 1988, references works describing the daily lives of slave women.[7] An original copy of *Incidents in the Life of a Slave Girl,* a slave narrative by Linda Brent published in Boston in 1861 is in the rare books section of the Schomburg Center for Research in Black Culture. Linda Brent, a former slave, described "hiring day."

> "Hiring day at the south takes place on the 1st of January. On the 2d, the slaves are expected to go to their new masters. On a farm, they work until the corn and cotton are laid. They then have two holidays. Some masters give them a good dinner under the trees. This over, they work until Christmas eve. If no heavy charges are meantime brought against them, they are given four or five holidays.

> Then comes New Year's eve; and they gather together their little alls, or more properly speaking, their little nothings, and wait anxiously for the dawning of day. At the appointed hour, the grounds are thronged with men, women and children, waiting like criminals, to hear their doom pronounced. The slave is sure to know who is the most humane, or cruel master, within forty miles of him.
>
> It is easy to find out, on that day, who clothes and feeds his slaves well; for he is surrounded by a crowd, begging, "Please, massa, hire me this year. I will work *very* hard massa."
>
> If a slave is unwilling to go with his new master, he is whipped, or locked up in jail, until he consents to go, and promises not to run away during the year...
>
> But to the slave mother, New Year's day comes laden with peculiar sorrows. She sits on her cold cabin floor watching the children who may all be torn from her the next morning; and often does she wish that she and they might die before the day dawns. She may be an ignorant creature, degraded by the system that has brutalized her from childhood; but she has a mother's instincts, and is capable of feeling a mother's agonies." p.3

The slave mothers on Bartley McCrary's Inventory shared the same bitter experience. The young girl Mary suffered a "mother's agonies." The cruel lot fell upon her. Mistress Jenny Poindexter died and Mary's two small children were torn away and sold. The evil deed touched "Lovenia and her 4 children." Grandma Lovenia, my ancestor suffered the sting of the slave "mother's agonies." Her child Ned, forced to leave with Bartly McCrary, Jr., left her. Her child Josh, wrenched away, left with Jenny Poindexter and she, recorded as "Vicey and child and Sindy" departed with David Moses. Those mothers, like countless others, sobbed bitterly over their loss during the dreary years of slavery. It was a sad and peculiar fate.

The recorded date was four days after the 1st of January 1827. Abraham Lincoln issued the Emancipation Proclamation the 1st of January 1863, 38 years later.

RECORD
GROUP 6

[handwritten:]
A Return of the sale of the negroes belonging to the minor children of Matthew McCrary sold on the first Tuesday in March 1846 one half payable 1st January 1827 the other 1st of March thereafter

Daniel a man bought by William McCrary $400.00
Fanny a girl "   " Henry H McCrary 339.00
*   739.00*

Matthew McCrary
Guardian

Recorded May 28th 1846
Chas. H. Stillwell O.C.O.

Fig. 7-39   Return. Matthew McCrary, dec'd. c. 1846
               Talbot Co., GA. Sale of two Negro slaves to support
               his minor children. Matthew McCrary (probably Jr.)
               Guardian.

RECORD GROUP   MATTHEW McCRARY. Estate Records. Deceased ca.
No. 6   1846. Talbot Co. Sales Book
  page
  424   Return of the sale of the Negroes belonging to
                 the minor children of Matthew McCrary.

                 Daniel, a man bought by William McCrary $400
                 Fanny, a girl   "   " Henry McCrary   339

The latter two records continue the trend of keeping the Negro slaves within the McCrary family. The proceeds from the sale of Negroes owned by the minor children were used for the support of the minors. This Matthew is brother of William.

I concluded from the McCrary research that my slave ancestors, "Lovenia and her 4 children" listed on Bartley McCrary's Hiring list in 1827, were probably separated but named somewhere within the vast number of McCrary estates. RECORD GROUP 7 unraveled the mystery.

SEPARATING "MAN" FROM "MARE"

As copies of documents were made for this text, the manuscript handwriting attracted attention. As I looked for names of people, I discovered names of "mares" were often the same as people. Information given in *How to Read the Handwriting and Records of Early America* by E. Kay Kirkham, (Salt Lake City, Utah, Deseret Book Co., 1965) served as a key to reading the handwriting. Repetition of the same letters in other words helped with interpretation. Kirkham's book gave samples (starred) of letters and numbers I found difficult to decipher in many of the documents in the text.

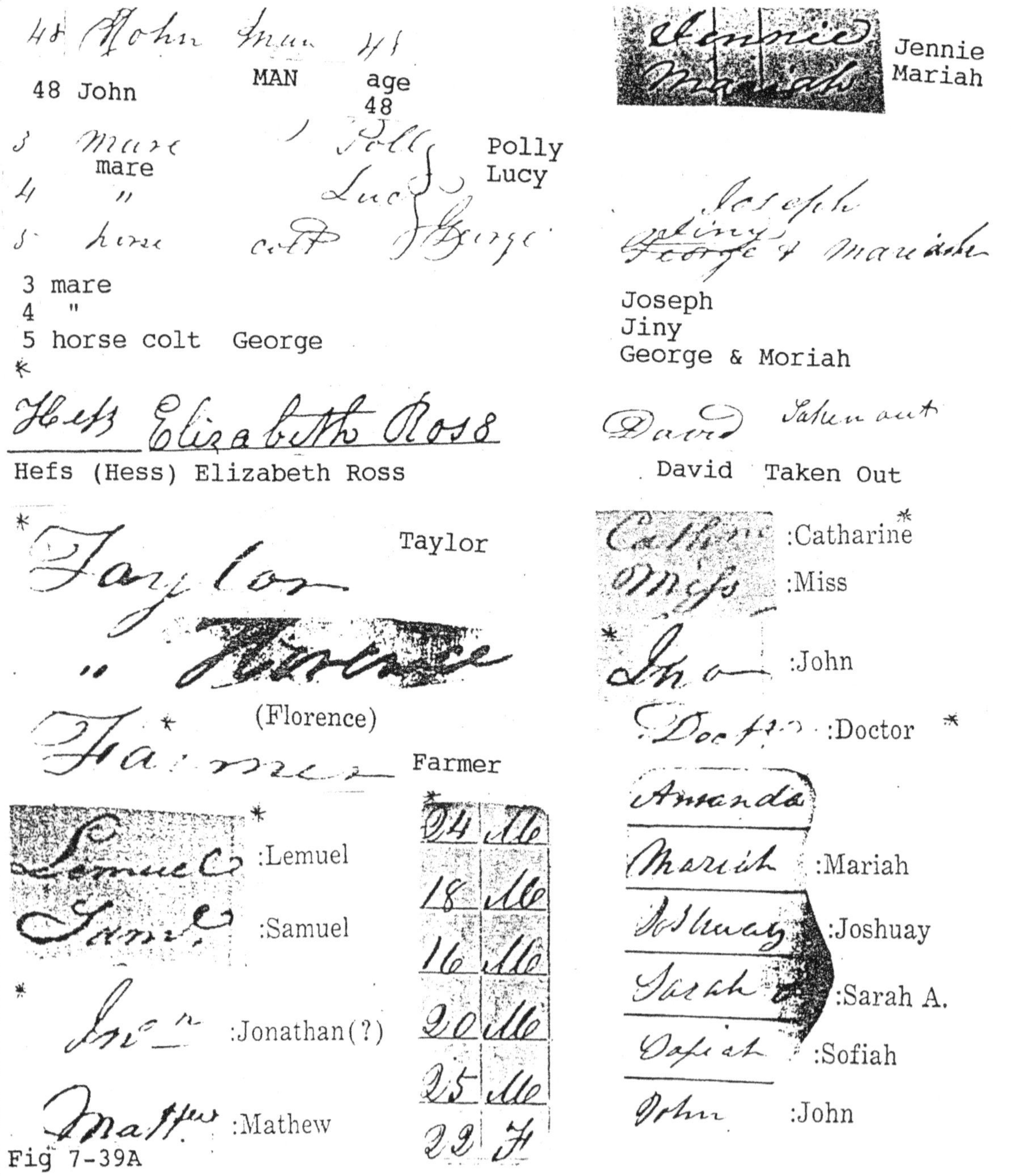

48 John   MAN   age 48

3 mare
4 "
5 horse colt   George

Polly
Lucy

Hefs (Hess) Elizabeth Ross

Taylor

(Florence)

Farmer

:Lemuel
:Samuel
:Jonathan(?)
:Mathew

Jennie Mariah

Joseph
Jiny
George & Moriah

David   Taken Out

:Catharine
:Miss
:John
:Doctor

:Mariah
:Joshuay
:Sarah A.
:Sofiah
:John

Fig 7-39A

John McCrary

Georgia Taylor County

Inventory and appraisement of the estate of John McCrary late of said County decd taken this 25th day of December 1854

1	negro man	Drake	valued	1600	00
1	"	"	Stephen	"	900	00
1	"	"	Joe	"	900	00
1	"	"	Hamp	"	1000	00
1	"	"	Hosea	"	1000	00
1	"	"	Lee	"	1000	00
1	"	"	Madison	"	1000	00
1	"	"	Isaac	"	1000	00
1	"	"	Will	"	1000	00
1	"	boy	Peter	"	900	00
1	"	"	Allen	"	900	00
1	"	"	William	"	900	00
1	"	"	Tom	"	900	00
1	"	Woman	Judy	"	800	00
1	"	"	Creasy & Child	1000	00
1	"	"	Phebe & 3 children	1500	00
2	"	Boys	Gus & Reuben	1100	00
1	"	"	Horace	450	00
1	"	Woman Sally & her 2 children	1500	00
1	"	" Malinda & Becky & Frank	1500	00
1	"	" Silla & Margaret & child	1400	00
1	"	Girl Frances	900	00
1	"	Woman Venus	100	00
1	"	" Lucy & Monk	100	00
1	"	Woman Casey	100	00
1	"	Negro man Peter	1100	00
1	Mare Colt Valued at	150	00
1	Gray Mare & Colt	85	00
1	Bay Horse named James	125	00
1	" mule Allen	75	00

Fig. 7-40. Inventory and Appraisement. John McCrary, dec'd. 1854. Taylor Co. GA.

1	Bay horse mule Dick	85	00
1	Black " " Jane	125	00
1	" " " Billy	140	00
1	Bay " " Jack	140	00
1	Bay mare " Beck	140	00
2000	Bushels Corn more or Valued at 80 cts pr Bus		
2000	lbs fodder 50 cts pr cwt		
78	Porke Hoggs at $6 00 Gross		
62	Head Hanson Cattle at 4.00 pr Head	248	00
1	yoke Oxen Brush &	50	00
1	" Old "	55	00
60	head Stock Cattle Pullen Stock	180	00
50	Bushels Oats at 65 cts pr Bush		
3000	lbs Sheaf Oats 65 cts pr cwt		
1	four horse Waggon	40	00
1	two Horse Waggon	45	00
1	Ox cart	25	00
1	pr Ox Cart Wheels	15	00
1	4 horse Waggon & Harness	130	00
15	Bush Cotton 7 cts pr lb		
1	lot Lead	10	00
1	" " for planting	15	00
	Stock Hogs	150	00
58	head Sheep 1 pr Same	58	00
75	Bushels Potatoes 30 cts pr	23	00
9	Sides Leather 1.25 pr hide	11	25
30	Bush Peas	30	00
	lot spun yarn lot wool	3	25
	Box & Barrels	1	00
1	Cross Cut Saw	3	00

Fig. 7-40. Inventory and Appraisements, John McCrary, deceased, c.1854. Taylor Co., GA.

1	Carry all	50	00
7	Seven ??		
1	lot Barrels	1	00
8	Sacks & Juggs		
1	lot Barrels Tubs &c	3	00
1	par Large Stillards	2	50
1	" Small "		25
1	lot Kitchen furniture	5	00
1	Loom	3	00
1	lot Blacksmith Tools	10	00
1	Lot ?? & Sheep Shears	3	00
1	farming tools &c	15	00
1	Grind Stone & Crank	1	25
1	lot Juggs & Barrels	2	50
3	Sythes & Cradles	5	00
1	lot Shucks	25	00
1	four Shot Gun Small Bu	25	00
2	Single Barrel Shot Gun	8	00
3	Spinning Wheels	2	00

Georgia } We the undersigned appraisers do
Taylor County } certify that the above & foregoing are
a true appraisement & Valuation of the Estate of John
McRary decd as presented to us by Bailey McRary
Administrator on said Estate to the best of our
knowledge & understanding this 25th day of
December 1854

Andrew J Colbert
C H ??
E S Butt
J C McCants

Georgia }
Taylor County } I certify that the above Appraisers
were duly qualified by me to perform their duty as
appraisers on the Estate of John McRary decd according to
law this dec 25th 1854

J?as McNully

Recd March 25th 1855

JOHN McCRARY   RECORD
                                                GROUP 7

Inventory and appraisment of the Estate of John McCrary
late of said county dec'd. taken this 25th day of December 1854.

1 Negro man	Dick	valued	$1600.00
1 " "	Stephen	"	900.00
1 " "	Joe	"	1000.00
1 " "	Hamp	"	1000.00
1 " "	*(F)lousury	"	1000.00
1 " "	Ned	"	1000.00
1 " "	Madison	"	1000.00
1 " "	Isaac	"	1000.00
1 " "	Will	"	1000.00
1 " boy	Peter	"	900.00
1 " "	Allen	"	900.00
1 " "	William	"	900.00
1 " "	Tom	"	900.00
1 " woman	Cady	"	800.00
1 " "	Creasy & child		1000.00
1 " "	Philice & 3 child		1500.00
2 " boys	Gus and Ruben		1100.00
1 " "	Horasine		450.00
1 " woman	Sally & her 2 children		1500.00
1 " "	*Matilda & Becky & Zussui		1500.00
1 " "	Litty & Margaret her child		1400.00
1 " girl	Frances		900.00
1 " woman	Veny		100.00
1 " "	Dicey a man Dick		100.00
1 " "	Casey		100.00
1 " Negro man	Peter		1500.00
1 Mare Colt valued at			150.00
1 Gray mare & Colt			85.00
1 bay horse named Jane			125.00
1 grey horse mule Allen			75.00
1 " " " Georgie			75.00
1 mare " Gim			75.00

*Writing is not clear.

Fig. 7-40. Partial Inventory of John McCrary, Bartley McCrary, Administrator. Appraisers: Andrew J. Colbert, C. H. Hickler, E. C. Butler and J. C. McCants.

Slave Ancestral Research

RECORD GROUP No. 7

JOHN McCRARY, Estate Records. Deceased ca. 1854 Taylor Co. <u>Inventories and Appraisements</u>

page 55

This Inventory, dated 25 Dec. 1854 listed "Veny" my seventh generation ancestor! She is valued at $100. The small value indicated a very old woman. Listed above "Veny" are my ancestors "Matilda, Becky and Zussre." Matilda is my great, great, great grandmother. I was drawn to conclude John McCrary was the slave owner of my slave ancestors because four of their names appeared on his "Inventory" in Taylor County. My ancestors were in Taylor County in 1870. By reading Davidson's book, *Rockaway in Talbot*, I learned that the McCrary family moved from Baldwin County to Talbot in the early 1830's.

Fig.7-40.

Talbot Co. 1850 Slave Schedule, page 367

In the Talbot County 1850 Slave Schedule, John McCrary had 33 slaves. The oldest female was 60. See Fig. 7-41

Taylor County 1870 Census Page 12

In Taylor County 1870 Census, Lovinia's age is stated as 90. Few ex-slaves knew their exact ages. Fig. 7-2.

Below is the record of John McCrary's family. Date of Census enumeration 1 March 1850

	Name	Age	Sex	Occupation	Property Value	Birth
Talbot Co 1850 Population Schedule page 294	McCrary, John	61	M	Farmer	$70,000	S.C.
	Bartly	23	M			Ga.
	Jane	21	M			Ga.
	Johnathan	17	M			Ga.
	John	17	M			Ga.
	Henry	16	M			Ga.

District 24 of Talbot County, Carsonville, became Taylor County in 1852. John McCrary is deceased in Taylor County in 1854.

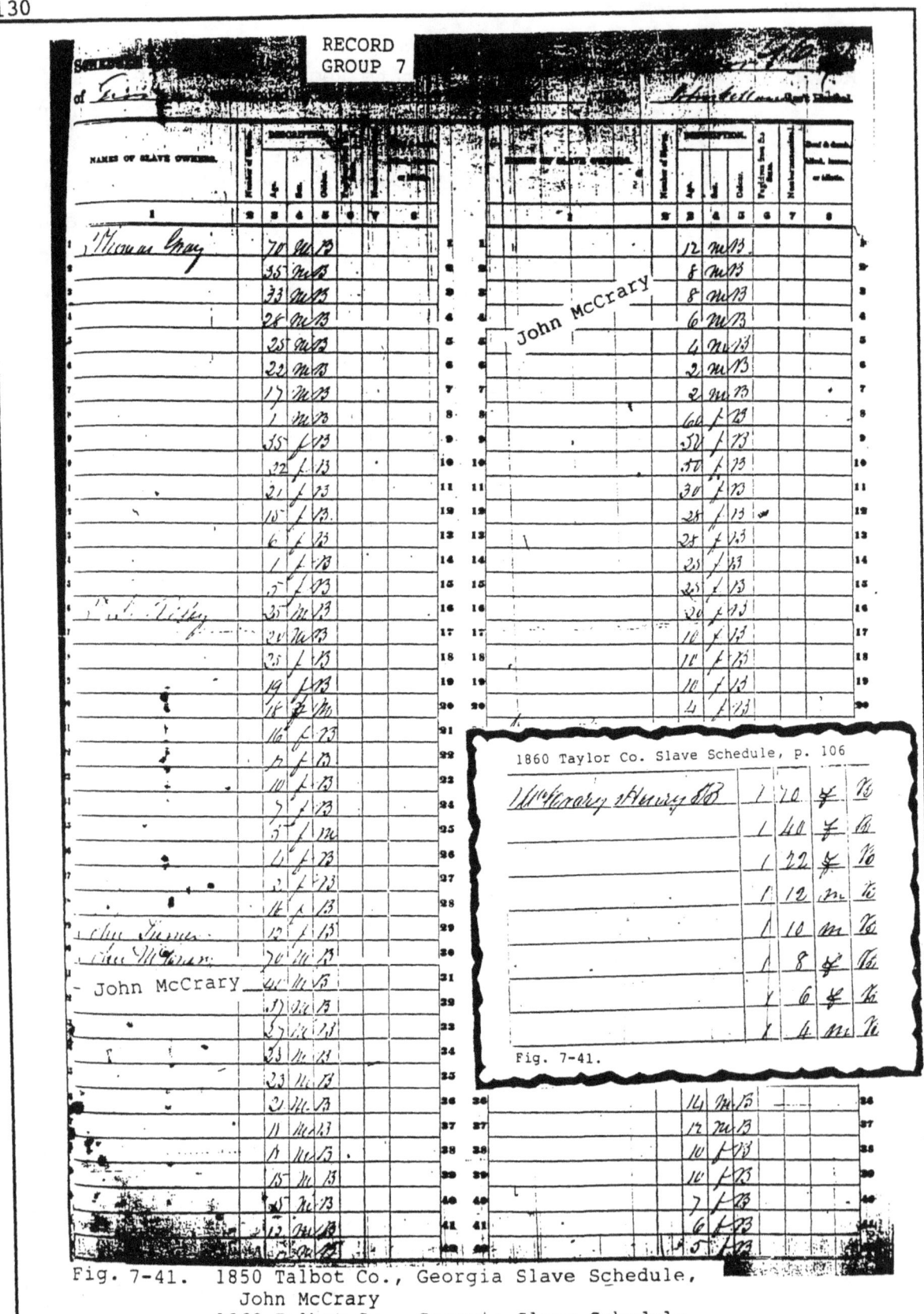

Fig. 7-41. 1850 Talbot Co., Georgia Slave Schedule, John McCrary
1860 Talbot Co., Georgia Slave Schedule, Henry McCrary

Slave Ancestral Research   131

Taylor Co. John McCrary's son, Henry age 16 in 1850,
1860 Slave was not listed a slave owner in Talbot County.
Schedule   In the 1860 Taylor County Slave Schedule, Henry
page 29   has become owner of eight slaves. The oldest
            female is 70, who I believe is "Veny." Henry
            received her, I believe, from his father, John
Fig. 7-41. McCrary's estate.

RECORD GROUP John McCrary's "Sale of Perishable Property"
No. 7   dated 28 Dec. 1854, did not include his slaves.
pages 33-38   However, the sale itemized in detail the
              products of their labor. This is a partial list
              of the "Sale." John's son Bartley served as
              Administrator of the Estate. Much of the
              property was sold to members of the McCants and
Fig. 7-43.   McCrary families.

              As I looked at the list of property sold, I
page 33   wondered which of John McCrary's female slaves
              used the "1 Spinning Wheel" sold for $1.30 to G.
              McCrary; and worked at the other two spinning
              wheels and loom; Which of the males had the
              skill to use the Blacksmith tools which sold for
              $7.00?

              G. McCrary bought 7 plow hoes for $1.00; 8 plow
              hoes for $1.60; 6 plow hoes for $1.20 and 7 more
              for .62. Lots of hoes and axes were sold to H.
              B. McCrary and A. McCants. Male and female
              slaves used each plow hoe at one time or
              another, not one hoe a treasured choice.

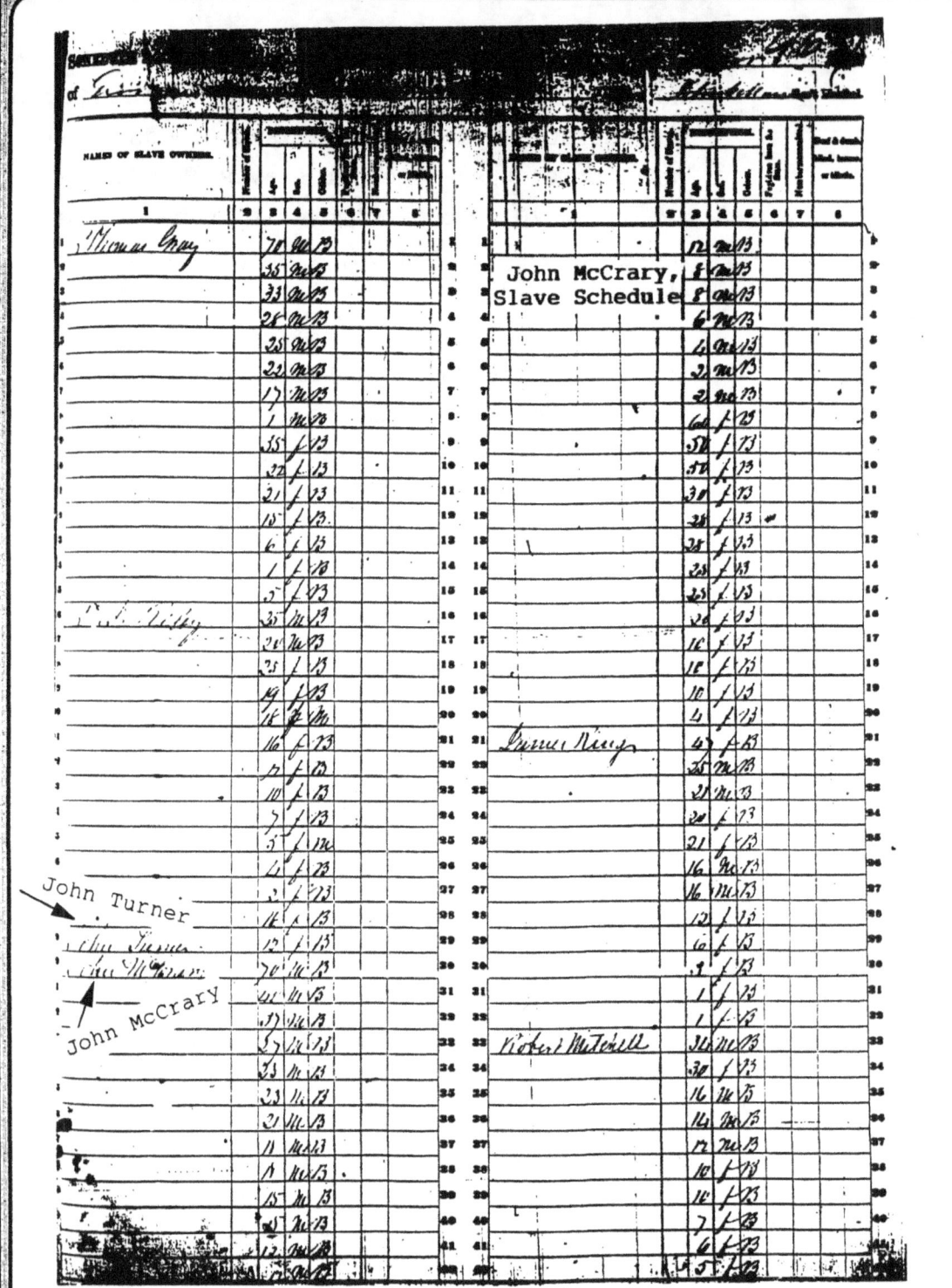

Fig. 7-41. 1850 Talbot Co., Georgia Slave Schedule. John McCrary has 33 slaves. The oldest male is 70; the oldest female is 60 and two females are 50.

Slave Ancestral Research

RECORD GROUP No. 7	JOHN McCRARY. Some of his slaves were children in Bartley McCrary's estate and are listed in John's Inventory as "Negro men." See Record Group No. 1.
Fig. 7-40.	John McCrary seemed to have received Joicy's child, Hamp; Vicey's child, Ned; and Patience's child, Peter. (Unless these were other slaves with the same names) A study of these records revealed increasingly the appearance of slave names in more than one record.
Taylor Co. 1870 Census	A few of the John McCrary slaves as "freedmen" in the Taylor County 1870 Census are listed. I observed that both names, McCants and McCrary, were adopted as surnames, as they were in my family living in the same household in 1870: Simon and Matilda were McCants, and Lovinia, a McCrary. In these 1870 Census records, names were repeated. Ned has a Hampton and Sylvia has
Fig. 7-42.	a Missouri. My ancestor Matilda McCants also had a daughter, Missoury. From observing the naming patterns of the slaves, a researcher may conclude that they were in some way related since they were owned by the same two families of slave masters and were transferred among them.

An Afterthought

Slave ancestral research is not an exact science. Once names of ancestors are discovered, one cannot be sure, without question. The researcher records what "seems to be;" for all that is consistent in the research is perpetual "inconsistencies."

134 Slave Ancestral Research

RECORD GROUP NO. 7		JOHN McCRARY. A few of his exslaves in the 1870 Taylor Co. Population Census.				
		Name	AGE	Sex	Color	Names on John McCrary's Inventory
page	340	McCrary, Harriet	18	F	M	
		Joseph	70	M	B	"Joe"
		Prudence	65	F	B	
	334	McCants, Hampton	45	M	B	"Hamp"
		Sillie	44	F	B	
		...	8	F	B	
	310	McCrary, Rheuben	26	M	B	"Rueben"
	311B	McCants, Isaac	34	M	B	"Isaac"
		Mary	40	F	B	
	323	McCrary, William	39	M	B	"Will"
	338	McCrary, Flurnoy	19	M	B	"Flousury"
	339	McCrary, Albert	34	M	B	"Allen"
	339	McCrary, Peter	48	M	B	"Peter"
		Susan	32	F	B	
		...				
		Lucy	50	F	B	
	319	^McCants, Charles	34	M	B	In "Inventory" of ^Andrew McCants
		Phillis	31	F	B	"Philice"
		...				
	312	McCrary, Ned	38	M	B	"Ned"
		Sallie	40	F	B	"Sally"
		Robert	19	M	B	
		Hampton	10	M	B	
	310	*McCants, Matilda	45	F	B	"Matilda"
	311	*McCrary, Lovinia	90	F	B	"Veny"
	311	*McCants, Simon	50	M	B	
		*Johnson, Missouri	18	F	B	"Zussre"
		...				
	315	McCants, Sylvia	35	F	B	
		Wright	20	M	B	
		...				
		Missouri	11	F	B	

*My slave ancestors.

Fig. 7-42. 1870 Taylor County, Georgia Census, Excerpts ("Freedmen").

Sale of the Perishable property of
John McCrary dec'd Dec 28th 1854

Buyer / Item	Amount
Gilly McCrary 5 Jars	1.60
J. L. Gray 3 Jars	1.00
B McCrary 3 "	1.25
Mr Mangham 1 lot Jugs	.15
J L Gray 1 Tin can & churn	.55
" " 1 lot Glass	.40
Mr Berry 2 pr Stilyards	.85
G McCrary 1 lot barrels	.45
" " 2 hogsheads	.60
B McCrary 2 "	1.00
G McCrary 1 Spinning Wheel	1.30
Mr Mangham 1 lot tallow	.85
" French 1 Spinning wheel	.50
A McCants 1 lot Jugs & do	1.00
G McCrary 1 lot Crockery	1.50
" " Blacksmith tools	7.00
Mr Mangham 4 Jugs	.30
G McCrary 7 plow Hoes	1.00
H Mangham 1 lot dog letters	.55
G McCrary 8 plow hoes	1.60
" " 6 " "	1.20
A McCants 8 " "	3.00
G McCrary 7 " "	.62
H B McCrary 1 lot Hoes	1.10
" " 1 " Axes	2.00
" " 6 " G Hoes	2.30
J L Gray 3 Barrels	.10
G McCrary 1 Grindstone	1.55
B Pope 1 lot Jarware	2.25
J B McCrary 3 Axes	2.00

Fig. 7-43.

Sale of the Perishable property of John McCrary, dec'd. 1854.

John McBary Continued

G McBary 3 plowstocks	2	75
A McCants 2 " "	5	50
J P McBary " "	2	70
A J Colbert 1 lot Scythe cradles	1	00
G McBary 1 " " "	1	25
W V W Mitchell 1 " " "		50
G McBary 1 " " "	1	00
" " 1 lot Potatoes 50		55
" " 1 " " 50	18	57
L McBary 1 " " 36		
J P McBary 1 Tray		25
" " " 1 loom	3	50
B McBary 1 tatto side board	1	50
J Peage 1 lot pot ware	5	75
Wm Berry 1 Carry all	50	00
A Moulfort 6 cowhides	7	15
J Berry 1 Mule	50	00
A Wilson 1 "	75	00
B McBary 1 "	65	00
A J Colbert "	175	00
" " 1 "	175	00
J P McBary 1 "	155	00
" " " 1 "	175	00
J Berry 1 "	134	00
J A McBary 1 bay mare colt	150	00
G McBary 1 Gray Mare	100	00
H B McBary 1 Bay Horse	85	00
J G N Lockhart 5 Meat hogs 8½	125	00
Dr Walker 5 - 1358 at 8¼	112	03
A J Colbert 5 - 1316 at 8¼	108	57
J W Dixon 5 " 964 at 8¼	87	36
Dr Walker 5 " 1250 8¼	103	12

Fig. 7-43.

John McGary Continued — RECORD GROUP 7

Julius Turner 1 ox cart	2	50
C W Wade 1 two horse wagon	50	00
H H Maugham 1 Road waggon	30	00
Wm P Hitchcock 1 log chain	1	55
B Monfort 10 bushels oats	8	40
" " 10 " "	8	40
J H McGary 10 " "	7	60
John T Gray 10 " "	7	80
G H McGary 12 " "	8	60
B Pyfar 1 sole leather	1	00
J T Gray 1 " "	1	30
H H Maugham 1 " "	1	80
Lucy McGary 1 " "	1	15
J H McGary 1 " "	1	00
H H Maugham 1 " "	1	62½
B Pyfar 1 sole leather	1	99
Julius Turner 1 " "	2	00
A J Willey 2 " "		41
J T Gray 1 X cut saw	4	85
A J Colbert 1 lot boxes & soil	4	20
A McCary 5 bushels pears	5	25
" " " 5 " "	5	51
" " " 5 " "	5	36
L Walker 5 " "	5	56
J T Gray 5 " "	5	57
B Monfort 5 " "	5	41
J L Parker 1 pr ox wheels	15	25
J T Gray 2 old tires		50
H B McGary 1 Road Waggon	100	00
B McGary two 9 bushel bales 7½	60	00
" " " 9 " 7½	60	00
A J Colbert 1 pr cotton cards	10	50
H B McGary 1 cot. planter	21	00

Fig. 7-43.

John McRary Continued

Description	Amount	
J McRary 100 Head Cows	100	00
" " 100 " "	100	00
" " 100 " "	100	00
L McRary 100 " "	100	00
J A McRary 100 " "	100	00
" " 100 " "	100	00
A J Colbert 100 " "	100	00
J A J McRary 100 " "	100	00
L McRary 100 " "	100	00
A J Colbert 100 " "	100	00
" " 100 " "	100	00
" " 100 " "	100	00
" " 100 " "	100	00
C Wade 100 " "	95	00
H B McRary 100 " "	95	00
" " " 100 " "	97	50
David Sawyer 100 "	96	00
D B Ferrel 100 " "	95	00
J H Preaster 100 "	97	00
J A McRary 50 Mules $95 pr	1495	00
J T Gray 1000 Sheep Oats		
J Lawson 1000 " "		
H B McRary 500 fodder	50	00
L McRary 500 "	50	00
H B McRary 500 "	50	00
C W Wade " "	50	00
J T Gray 1 Grain Fan	50	
A McCan 635 Head Cattle	105	00
" " 60 " "	180	00
A McCan 1 pen sheep	3	
" " " " "	3	
" " " " "	12	
W J M Mitchel 54 head sheep		

Fig. 7-43.

Fig. 7-43.

John McCary [?]	
G. F. McCary [?]	
A. J. Colbert [?]	
Willis [?]	
J. A. J. McCary 60 Stock Cattle	195 00
G. F. McCary 1 × [?]	
Bartley McCary House furniture	46 40
Dr Walker 5 Head Meat hogs	98 76
L. McCary 5 " "	95 44
A. J. Colbert 5 "	105 71
" " " 5 " " "	91 40
" " " 5 " " "	76 88
" " " 5 " " "	75 28
" " " 5 " " "	85 44
" " " 5 " " "	105 40
Dr Walker 7 " "	169 62
J. Berry 1 Cow & Calf	10 00
J. P. McCary 1 " "	8 00
J. Berry 1 " "	6 00
" " 1 " "	9 25
" " 1 Cow "	8 00
" " 1 " "	9 00
John W. Owen 1 " "	6 25
John H. Graves 1 " "	11 00
J. Berry 1 " "	10 00
Samuel H. Hughey 1 " "	10 00
J. A. J. McCary 1 " "	17 00
Jos Wilcher 1 " "	29 00
A. Averitt 7 yoke Work Steers	36 00
Julius Herrin 1 " " "	50 50
A. J. Colbert 1 Male Hog	5 00
W. G. Boleman 1 Blacksmith	
Peter Montfort 1 [?]	

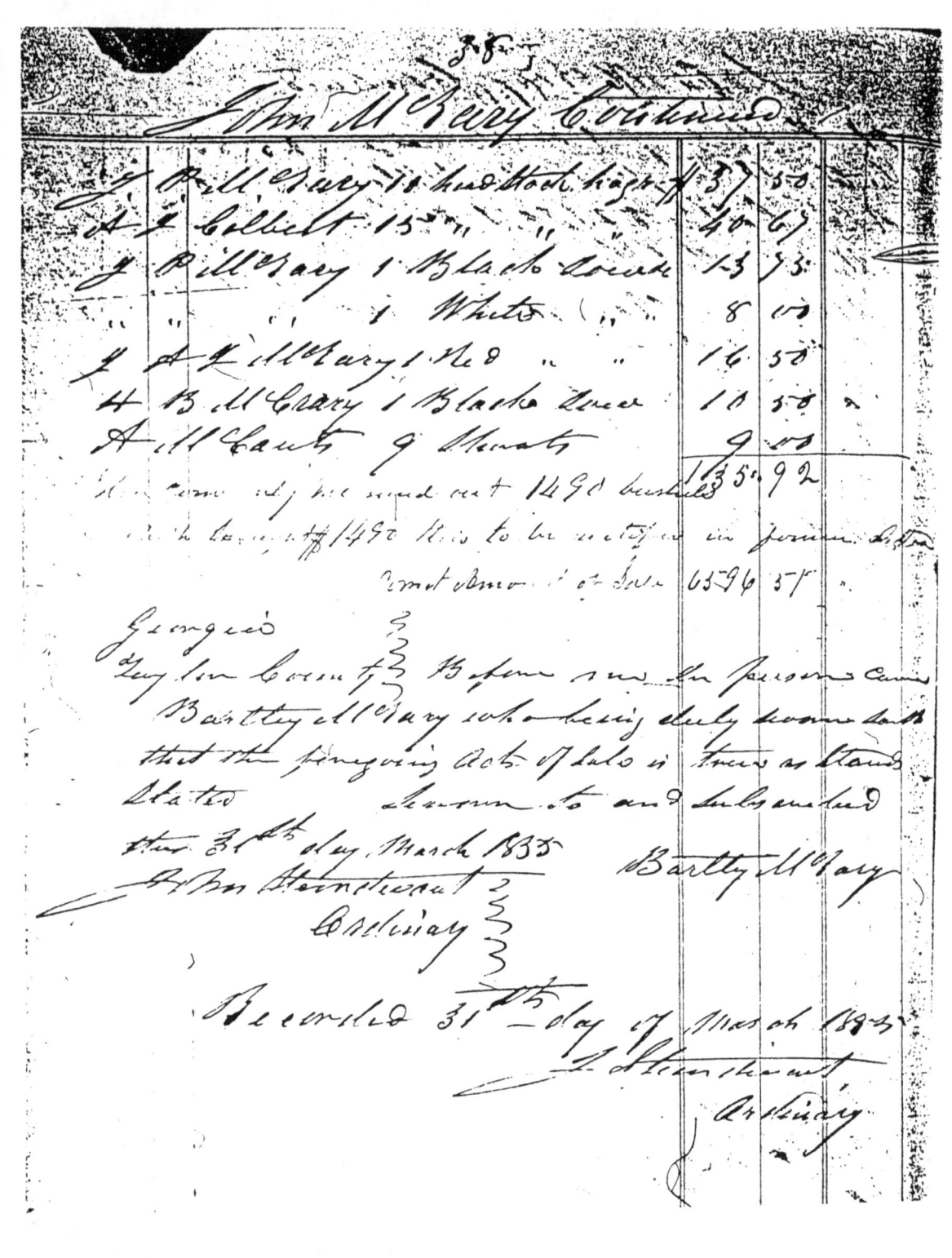

Fig. 7-43.

Slave Ancestral Research

RECORD GROUP No. 7 Inventory page 55	The selection of names for the mare colts and horses were the same as slave names: a bay horse named Sam; gray mule, Allen; a mule, Georgie; a mare, Gim; a bay mule, Dick; ... a bay mare Beck, but they were not valued as highly as a slave. A slave with the value of a horse, $125, would be very old and may be called "worthless." But my folks worked with those same mules and horses in Taylor County on the McCrary farm.
Fig. 7-40.	Four slaves named on John McCrary's Inventory were my ancestors. They helped to grow the products listed in his Inventory and later sold. They toiled to help yield "2000 bushels of corn" sold at $100 for each 100 bushels to mostly family members. Slaves stacked bushel-barrels of corn for buyers; fed 78 hogs, tended to 60 head stock cattle; picked 18 bales of cotton; tended to 38 head of sheep; dug up and bagged 75 bushels of potatoes; picked 30 bushels of peas; pushed and pulled wagons, and plows; cooked, cleaned, washed, ironed, wove and spinned. --all for nothing.
"Sale" page 38	The total "Amount of the Sale, $6596.51." These records revealed the "fruits of slave laborers," those who worked long, hard hours for the McCrary family in Taylor County and they were my folks,
Fig. 7-43.	Lovinia, Matilda, Missouri and Isabella.

Chapter Eleven

A NAME, A NAME, WHAT NAME SHALL I TAKE?

A number of the former slaves of John McCrary, shown in Fig. 7-42. in Record Group No. 7, kept the surname McCrary. However, after listing all of the record groups of McCrary slaves and studying their movement from one owner to another, I wondered, "What surnames did the others take?"

One unusual name in Bartley McCrary's Estate Division was "Orrange." (See Record Group No. 1.) In 1827, as a boy, he was passed down to Jenny, who had the surname, "Poindexter." Curiosity forced me to see what happened to him. He lived until freedom remaining in Baldwin County until 1870. There he was: "Orange" McCrary, 63 years old in the Baldwin County Ga. Census, page 199, living with Louisa, age 55, who was perhaps his wife. (Notice the spelling of "Orange.")

All their lives, the McCrary slaves were known only by their given names and referred to as "a Negro woman, a Negro man, a fellow, boy, girl, or child" in the McCrary estate records. As outgrown clothing of older brothers and sisters become "hand-me-downs" to their younger siblings, the slaves became "hand-me-downs" as their owners died and they were passed down to minor and married children.

When a minor child, as an heir, received ownership of a slave, the court appointed a guardian, which was most often a McCrary relative--perhaps the minor child's uncle, aunt or grandparent. Thus, the slaves were listed in the "Inventory" of the minor child's guardian. These were still in a McCrary surname household.

144 Slave Ancestral Research

The question, "What name shall I take?" compelled an answer for the "hand-me-down" McCrary slaves passed to married daughters. Did each one keep the McCrary surname, as Orange McCrary, or adopt the surname of the married daughter?

After the McCrary slaves were free in 1865, they had the pleasure of telling their last names which they had kept secret. Researchers who studied slave naming practices in Herbert G. Gutman's, *The Black Family in Slavery and Freedom 1750-1925*, (Random House, 1976, p. 190) reported that "the naming of children for their fathers was a particular slave naming practice..." In the records studied of slave naming practices of the "late eighteenth and nineteenth century men and women who lived in Virginia, North and South Carolina and Louisiana...A son often had his father's name, but it nearly never happened that a daughter had her mother's name." pp. 188-189.

The McCrary "hand-me-down" slaves had common Anglo-American given names. They may have retained their original name McCrary or taken either of the surnames from McCrary marriages.

I compiled from several sources McCrary family marriages. By using PERSI, (PERiodical Souce Index), I was referred to printed Bible records and genealogical journals containing early marriage records performed in the counties of my research: Baldwin, Warren, Talbot and Taylor.

Early Georgia marriages were listed in books and on the IGI microfische from the Family History Library of the Church of Jesus Christ of Latter-day Saints. (The IGI, International Genealogical Index is an index of millions of names of deceased persons worldwide. It lists marriages, births, and deaths extracted from vital records dated from the early 1500s to 1875. Names continue to be added to the index by church members. The IGI is available for research at associated Family History Centers like the one I used in Lake Mary, Florida.)

Some of the McCrary slaves passed down may have chosen surnames from persons who married into the McCrary family. To aid further research, I listed some of the surnames from the McCrary Estate Distributions with other family marriages.

Slave Ancestral Research

BALDWIN COUNTY MARRIAGES

Bateman, Bryant	married	Charity McCrary	21 Jan. 1808
Beckham, Albert G.	"	Mary McCrary	7 Apr. 1825
Calton or Caulter, Sary		Widow	
Chapman, John	married	Missouri H. McCrary	3 Oct. 1849
Colbert, William	"	Lettice McCrary	?
Durdon, William	"	Mary McCrary	11 Mar. 1822
Herrington, Able		Unknown	
Jourdan, Matthew	"	Sarah McCrary	25 Aug. 1830
McCrary, Andrew	"	Mary S. McWhorter	22 Dec. 1856
McCrary, Bartley, Sr	"	Rebecca McCrany	13 Apr. 1813
McCrary, Isaac	"	Hannah Hay	4 Aug. 1813
McCrary, Isaac	"	Martha F. Robinson	14 June 1865
McCrary, James	"	Jane McCrary	8 Jan. 1822
McCrary, James	"	Martha Elizabeth Jenkins	16 Nov. 1837
McCrary, John	"	Jenny McCrary	12 Mar. 1813
McCrary, Wiley	"	Polly Colbert	24 Dec. 1820
Moses, David	"	Martha (Patsey) McCrary	30 Nov. 1826
Poindexter, Jenny		Widow	
Riddle, Wiley	married	Unknown	
Salter, Richard	"	Elizabeth McCrary	16 Jan. 1823
Scurlock, John	"	Gracey McCrary	23 Apr. 1829

TALBOT COUNTY MARRIAGES

Berry, James F. (or Falkenberry)	married	Mary McCrary	4 July 1838
McCants, Andrew	"	Elizabeth McCrary	14 Jan. 1844
McCants, Jeremiah	"	Tabitha McCrary	5 June 1832

TALBOT COUNTY MARRIAGES

McCrary, Isaac	"	Ardna Cosby	9 Jan. 1840
McCrary Jonathan B.	"	Catherine L. Jamieson	5 May 1842
McCrary, Matthew	"	2nd wife, Nancy Eason	25 Jan. 1838

The above list does *not* represent all of the McCrary family marriages. The dates varied in some sources. It is the surname that is important.

I observed throughout my research that many of the surnames appeared in McCrary estate sales. I learned when trying to trail the Negro property, the importance of knowing about family marriages. Often slave names appeared in an estate "Inventory" but were missing in the final "Distribution." In some instances, the Negro property was in the heirs' possession, loaned for their use, but ownership had not passed legally to the sons or daughters.

I did not attempt to determine the surnames selected by all McCrary slaves, only those of John McCrary, deceased in 1854.

Chapter Twelve

WHERE TO GO FROM HERE

Up to this point, my research had not followed a chronological continuum. This narrative account of the search for my slave ancestors began in Taylor County, Ga. with the 1900 and 1870 Taylor County Population Census Schedules.

From Taylor County, I traced the possible slave owners to Talbot County and searched the 1850-1860 records. After a trip to the LaGrange Archives, I learned that the possible slave owners were originally from Laurens, South Carolina and settled in Baldwin County, Ga.; participated in the 1805 Georgia Land Lottery and were listed in the Baldwin County 1810 Tax Digest.

My attention changed to focus on Baldwin County records. By 1830, the possible owners had moved and were listed in the 1830 Talbot County Census. The Talbot County district in which they settled became Taylor County in 1852.

The order of my research was as follows:

1st	2nd	3rd
Orlando Pub. Lib.	Ga. Trip	Georgia Archives-1st Visit
Taylor Co.	Taylor & Talbot Co.	Baldwin Co.
1870 records ...	LaGrange Archives...	1800-1829 records ...
& all census ...	1830-1860 records	
schedules		

4th &	5th	6th
Lake Mary Family History Ctr.		Georgia Archives-2nd Visit
Talbot Co.	Taylor Co.	
1830-1852 records ...	1854-1870 records	Taylor Co. Probate
		Records of John
		McCrary, deceased 1854

148   Slave Ancestral Research

I had collected dozens of slaveholder's lists in Taylor, Talbot and Baldwin Counties. I had placed the McCrary records into seven groups and observed the transference of slaves among them, but I did not know their family relationships until many months later when I visited the DAR Library in Washington, DC. Then I "ADDED" information in the RECORD GROUPS Nos. 1-7 in a different type font. However, before the DAR Library visit, I made one final visit to the Georgia Archives. A significant date was July 7, 1993.

JULY 7, 1993, A DAY REMEMBERED

"Momma, here it is. I found it!" The words were spoken by my daughter, Julie L. Anderson. She was rejoicing as she stared at the microfilm image of a page dated November 22, 1854 in an issue of the "Georgia Journal and Messenger," published in Macon, Ga. 139 years before. We both read the article submitted by Bartley McCrary, Administrator of John McCrary's Estate, advertising the "Sale of all perishable property of John McCrary at his residence."

"They didn't include any slaves in the sale, thank goodness for that." I said. Before Julie copied the page, we read other articles about "Negroes for Sale," "Wanted to Hire...prime Negro men to work on the South Western Railroad" and F. P. Holcomb's "offer to sell his plantation situated on Flint River in Macon Co...I will also sell if desired the Negroes, thirty in all, with the place, together with stock and implements of all kinds." I explained to Julie, "When the Negroes are hired, their owners receive the money for their work." Other advertisements included sales of everything from fruit to whiskey, marriage and death announcements and a $100 reward for the "recovery of my boy, Christopher Columbus Deloach...14 yrs. old with bluish gray eyes, very white skin, freckled face, light curly hair..." I said, "I wonder if H. J. Nicholes ever recovered *his* "boy." See Fig. 7-44. "It was unusual that a surname was given for Christopher."

On Saturday, July 3, 1993, I had traveled to Atlanta with my daughter, Julie, a 36-year old Investment Officer for Nations Securities. We had planned a mother and daughter joint vacation for one week. Julie spent her days becoming familiar with her new job

ADMINISTRATOR'S SALE.—By the consent of all the parties concerned, will be sold at the late residence of John McCrary, of Taylor County deceased, all the perishable property belonging to the estate of said deceased, consisting of horses, mules, cattle, pork and stock hogs, sheep, corn, fodder and oats, a set of blacksmith tools, wagons, and ox cart, together with the household and kitchen furniture, and in fact every article generally used on a large plantation. Sale to continue from day to day until all is sold. Terms on the day of sale.

BARTLEY McCRARY, Adm'r.

Nov. 22

Fig. 7-44. Georgia Journal and Messenger, Nov. 22, 1854. Advertisement for Sale of Personal Property at residence of John McCrary, dec'd, 1854.

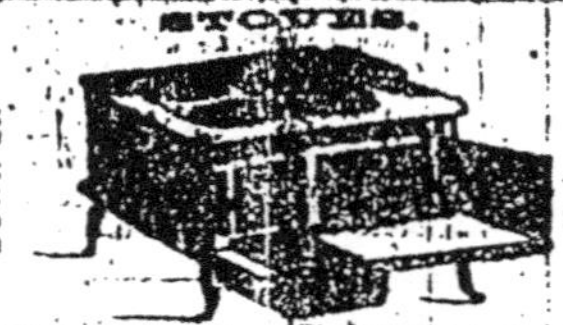

ADMINISTRATOR'S SALE.—Will be sold at the Court house in Oglethorpe, Macon county, on the first Tuesday in January, 1855, fifteen likely negroes, consisting of men, women, and children, according to an order by the Honorable Ordinary of said county. Sold as the property of Joseph and Mahala Edwards, deceased. Terms, a credit of twelve months for notes with approved security, and if not punctually paid, with interest from date.

DAVIS GAMAGE, Adm'r.
of Mahala Edwards, and Adm'r. of Joseph Edwards, de lonis non, with the will annexed.

nov 22 34-40d

EXECUTOR'S SALE.—By virtue of an order of the Honorable Court of Ordinary, of Pulaski county, will be sold before the Court house door in the town of Hawkinsville, on the first Tuesday in January next, two negroes to-wit: Bill and Preston. Sold as the property of Turquill McNair, deceased, for the purpose of distribution, according to the terms of said will.—Terms cash.
P. F. D. SCARBOROUGH, } Ex'rs.
DANIEL RAWLS,
nov 22

EXECUTOR'S SALE.—Will be sold on Wednesday, the 6th of December, at the plantation belonging to the estate of James Pope, deceased, and whereon Jas. S. Pope now resides, in Houston county, the crop of corn and fodder, four mules, two wagons, buggy, &c., together with farming implements, gin, cotton seed, and some articles of household and kitchen furniture. Terms on the day.
nov 22 34-tds   ALEX. EVERETT, Ex'r.

EXECUTOR'S SALE.—Will be sold on Thursday, 21st of December, at the plantation in Dooly county, belonging to the estate of Jas. Pope, the crop of corn and fodder, with the entire stock of mules, cattle and hogs, including 90 or 100 pork hogs, and some valuable milch cows, oxen and cart, wagon, a good family carriage, blacksmith tools, with all the plantation implements and household and kitchen furniture. Sale to continue from day to day until all is sold.
nov 22 34-tds   ALEX. EVERETT, Ex'r.
☞ Telegraph Macon, please copy.

TRUSTEE'S SALE.—Agreeably to an order of the Court of Chancery, will be sold, on the first Tuesday in January next, between the usual hours of sale, at the court house door in the town of Starkville, Lee county, the following property, to wit: ten negroes, and the plantation, consisting of about five hundred acres, being the place on which the late James Chastain resided, in said county, and the negroes are those upon said plantation. Said property sold for the purpose of a division among the heirs of said deceased.
nov 22 34-4tds   JOHN M. CHASTAIN, Trustee.

EXECUTOR'S SALE.—Will be sold, on the first Tuesday in January next, at the court house in Starkville, Lee county, Lots No. 232 and 233, in the second district of said county—sold as the property of Joseph A. White, deceased, late of Bibb county.
nov 22 34tds   ROBERT F. BALDWIN, Ex'r.

GEORGIA, Bibb County.—Ordinary's Office, November 22d, 1854.
Whereas, Elijah L. D. Riggins applies for letters of guardianship over the person and property of Sarah A. L. Riggins, the orphan and minor daughter of Stephen E. Riggins, late of Sumter county, deceased;
These are to cite all persons interested to appear at the expiration of 30 days from this date, at my office in Macon, and show cause, if any, why said letters should not issue.   P. TRACY, Ordinary.
nov 22 34-1m

ADMINISTRATOR'S SALE.—By the consent of all the parties concerned, will be sold at the late residence of John McCrary, of Taylor county deceased, all the perishable property belonging to the estate of said deceased, consisting of horses, mules, cattle, pork and stock hogs, sheep, corn, fodder and oats, a set of blacksmith tools, wagons, and ox carts, together with the household and kitchen furniture, and in fact every article generally used on a large plantation. Sale to continue from day to day until all is sold. Terms on the day of sale.   BARTLEY McCRARY, Adm'r.
nov 22   34-tds

---

assortment of PIANO FORTES, of Chickering & Sons', Nunn & Clark's, and A. H. Gale & Co's manufacture, just opened in the large and elegant Ware Rooms immediately over our store.
Also, Guitars, Violins, Accordeons, Flutinas and Flutes, Guitar and Violin Strings, &c.
Watches and Jewelry neatly repaired at short notice, and warranted.
nov 15 33tf   E. J. JOHNSTON & CO.

THE PULASKI HOUSE,
FRESH PAINTED AND RENOVATED
THROUGHOUT,
WILL BE RE-OPENED THIS DAY.
W. H. WILTBERGER & CO.
Savannah, Ga., Nov. 1, 1854.

CHAPPELL & LAMAR,
ATTORNEYS AT LAW,
MACON, GEORGIA.
A. H. CHAPPELL,   L. Q. C. LAMAR.
nov 15   33-tf

ONE SECOND HAND SERAPHINE for sale low by
Nov. 15 33-tf   E. J. JOHNSTON & CO.

A DISCOVERY.
SILVER and Copper has recently been discovered in the county of Wilkinson, in the State of Georgia. A discovery made by the American Captain Levi Simpson. These minerals are on the top of the earth.
Nov. 15 1854.

CO-PARTNERSHIP NOTICE.
THE undersigned, successors of the late firm of JOSEPH H. BURROUGHS & SON, have entered into a Co-partnership for the transaction of a GENERAL COMMISSION AND PRODUCE BUSINESS, under the firm of WILLIAM H. & RICHARD BURROUGHS. They will occupy the counting room, and continue the business of the late firm of Joseph H. Burroughs & Son, and will be prepared to make advances on produce sent to them.
W. H. BURROUGHS,
nov 15-tf   RICHARD BURROUGHS.

STRAY COW.
STRAYED from the Subscriber about the 29th Sept., a nohorned cow, mostly white, with dark brown head and neck, and spoted on the fore parts, middle size, ears marked with a cross off the right ear, and a split in the left. Any information will be thankfully received. All reasonable charges will be paid.
nov 15 35-6t   FREDRICK PLYLER.

Wanted to Hire.
TO work on repairs of the South-Western Rail Road for the next year (1855,) sixty prime negro men; contracts will be made by Mr. J. M. Walden, Supervisor, Fort Valley, or the undersigned Macon.
GEO. W. ADAMS,
Macon, Nov. 15, 33-6t   Superintendent.

NOTICE.
FROM and after this date, all persons making accounts par J. S. Graybill, will be considered as cash, and expected whenever the bills are presented.
15   33 tf

NEGROES FOR SALE.
WILL be sold before the Court House door in Oglethorpe, Macon county, on the first Tuesday in January next, by virtue of an order of the Court of Ordinary of said county, the negroes belonging to the estate of Edmund Brooks, late of said county deceased, about 35 negroes consisting of men women and children.
Terms on day of sale.
Nov. 15 33-tds   JOHN F. WILLIAMS, Adm'r.

TO RENT.
AGREEABLY to an order of the Honorable the Court of Ordinary of Macon County, will be rented before the Court House door in the town of Oglethorpe, on the 25th December, 1854, the Plantation in said county,

---

house, as well as those of Tilden, complimented by the Nation
oct 15   FITZGER.

QUININE, Piperine, Morphine by Hydrogen, Ca Nitrate of Silver, Hydriodaphorus, and other Chemicals, unsurpassed purity.
oct 18   FITZGER.

CASTOR OIL, Spirits of Snake Root, Ginger, Canna, Manna, Cream of Tart Medicines used in domestic
oct 18   FITZGER.

WHITELEAD, LINSEED and Putty.
oct 18   FITZGER.

BURNING FLUID, Camphene Oil, for sale by
oct 18   FITZGER.

FARINA, CORNSTARCH ders, Cooper's Gelatine, Moss, &c.   FITZGER.
oct 18

FLAVORING EXTRACT la, Strawberry, Pine-apple
oct 18   FITZGER.

BRUSHES.—Hair, Nail, Shoe, Paint and Varnish
oct 18   FITZGER.

FOR THE HAIR.—Hair Macassar Oil, Ox Marrow and Hair Dye.
oct 18   FITZGER.

PERFUMERY —The Best our own make; Florida Water; Musk, Otto of Rose, Poncine, Rose, Palm, Brown other Soaps.   FITZGER.
oct 18

H. N.
MACON,........

Has opened his Eating Saloon
C. A. ELL
On Mulberry Street, one Hall, or just opposite the L. luxuries of the Seaboard w style at all hours of the day, til 12 o'clock at night.
All orders from the country ters by keg or gallon; Fish be supplied at shortest notice.
ORANGES, LEMONS and all other Fruits by the hand,
GROCERIES AND PROVISIONS, Retail.
BRANDIES, WINES, SOKEY, of the best quality; a ly kept in a Family Grocery.
CIGARS.—A fine lot of equal to any kept in the South, CANDIES, PRESERVES FIGS, RAISINS, TEAS, & nary purposes.
OIL, CAMPHINE, and F LAMPS, always on hand.
Oys
I have also made my arrangements of hand opened single Oysters in the country.
She
In their Season, will be ready for City and Country supply.
Nov. 8

P. McEVOY has paid assortment of WARE, at L ular Block, to They compri of new and r

---

Fig. Georgia Journal and Messenger, Nov. 22, 1854.
7-44. Advertisement for Sale of Personal Property at residence of John McCrary, dec'd., 1854.

location and I spent my days in research at the Georgia Archives. On Wednesday, July 7, as we left our hotel and stepped into her black leased 1993 Probe, Julie said, "Momma, I'll go with you today to the Archives to help you look." A brisk walk from the parking lot and we were at the door when it opened.

As I handed her the roll of microfilm, I said, "Look for this article on John McCrary. It should be interesting to read a newspaper so old." Julie had assisted me in the research before in Florida. Neither of us had the slightest feeling that the copy she made of that article reproduced here, would be her last contribution to this research. We did not think that her final illness from a nine-year bout with cancer would allow her only a few weeks to work at Nations Securities. She would never return home again. I returned and spent the last week in her hospital room. Julie died on Saturday morning, October 2, 1993, twelve weeks after July 7 in Northside Hospital in Atlanta.

How did I learn about the article? Two months before our trip to Atlanta, on May 6, I went to the Family History Center at Lake Mary to view several rolls of microfilm ordered from the LDS Library. I made copies of the Administrator, Bartley McCrary's 14-page record of the settlement of John McCrary's Estate from a microfilm of Vouchers for Taylor County. An entry for Voucher 5 stated "To Rose & Co. 1854 to advertising in Georgia & Messenger Nov 22, Sale of Personal property 40 days $3.50... Bartley McCrary." (See V. 5 in John McCrary's Estate Papers, Fig. 7-46.) The Georgia Archives had early issues of that newspaper on microfilm.

When I began looking at the microfilm of Vouchers, I had no idea about the kind of records I would find. This is the reason that I have always maintained, there's "Divine Guidance" in this project." Within those Vouchers, I discovered answers to two questions that burned in my mind throughout my years of research: Who was the overseer? What happened to my slave ancestors, Veny, Matilda, Bucky and Zussure (Missoury) after John McCrary died in 1854 until 1870, when they are free and their names appear in the 1870 Taylor County Census?" The Vouchers revealed the answers. John McCrary Estate Papers, containing the vouchers are in the next chapter.

Chapter Thirteen

THE DAY I FOUND MY FOLKS

No one could have predicted that on May 6, 1993, one year and a day after the death of my mother, and thirteen years from August, 1980, when I began my roots search, I would learn what happened to Veny, Matilda, and the rest of my folks after the death of John McCrary in 1854. My research had progressed through 13 years in notches. There were inactive intervening periods of grief due to family deaths. Those who would have enjoyed most knowing my discovery were gone, my daughter Julie, my mom and dad, Sylvester and Jewell Moore Jackson.

When I set out for the Family History Center, a one-hour drive from my home, few smiles crossed my face. It was a bright morning, warm, sky-blue and cloudless. The road to the LDS Family History Center passed an exit which spun off to Sanford, my home town. I never passed it without thinking about my mom and visits home during her illness and especially on the first anniversary of her death. I had always stopped by home to show Momma whatever I found after leaving the Center.

By the time I reached Lake Mary, I managed to shift my thoughts. I planned to view two rolls of microfilm: "Vouchers" and "Returns" of Taylor County in search of a record of the final distribution of John McCrary's Estate. Two years before I had found a copy of his Estate Inventory (see Record Group No. 7).

John McCrary's Inventory listed my kinfolks Matilda, Becky, Zussre/Missouri and Veny. I yearned to know what happened to them after his death. The roll of Vouchers dated 1852-1858 was not indexed. I read page by page until finally, at the top of page 180, I saw, "The Estate of John McCrary, deceased...Bartley McCrary, Administrator from 1st December 1855 to the day 5th March 1856."

Quickly, my eyes sprinted down the page, up and down the next page, raced up, down, eleven pages of Vouchers, scanning through statements of amounts paid to county officials for various services, like taxes on the estate, travel expenses of the administrator and on and on for various expenditures--17 Vouchers. Alas, page 191, a list in lots numbered 1-8, naming the Negro slaves. My eyes fell on "No. 3...Matilda Ralia Bucky & Missouri ($) 1500." I blurted out, "I've found my folks!" Where's Veny? My fingers slid down the remaining list of slaves imaged on the screen. "There she is in No. 7 with Ned, Peter, Sal, Robert and Caroline... Old Visues, $25. She's valued at only twenty-five dollars for a whole life of slavery." The librarian bent over my shoulder, I pointed out the names. She hugged me, sharing a tender moment. When I regained my composure, I moved the roll of film from the machine. I said, "Copy the Estate records. They will go in my book." After 13 years of research, on that day, May 6, 1993, I found my folks.

In a second glance at the Estate Distribution, I noticed "Ralia" was not named in John McCrary's Inventory. I observed the name "Bucky" had appeared as "Becky" in John McCrary's Inventory. "Buck" was a name commonly given to male slaves and many changed their names after freedom. "Bucky" is believed to be Simon, Matilda's husband. Fortunately, he and his family were distributed together to Andrew McCants. They were listed as Simon McCants and Matilda McCants in the 1870 Taylor County, Georgia. Census. They took the name of the last owner before freedom.

At last, I was certain, I had indeed found my folks.

JOHN McCRARY
(1789-1854)
ESTATE PAPERS

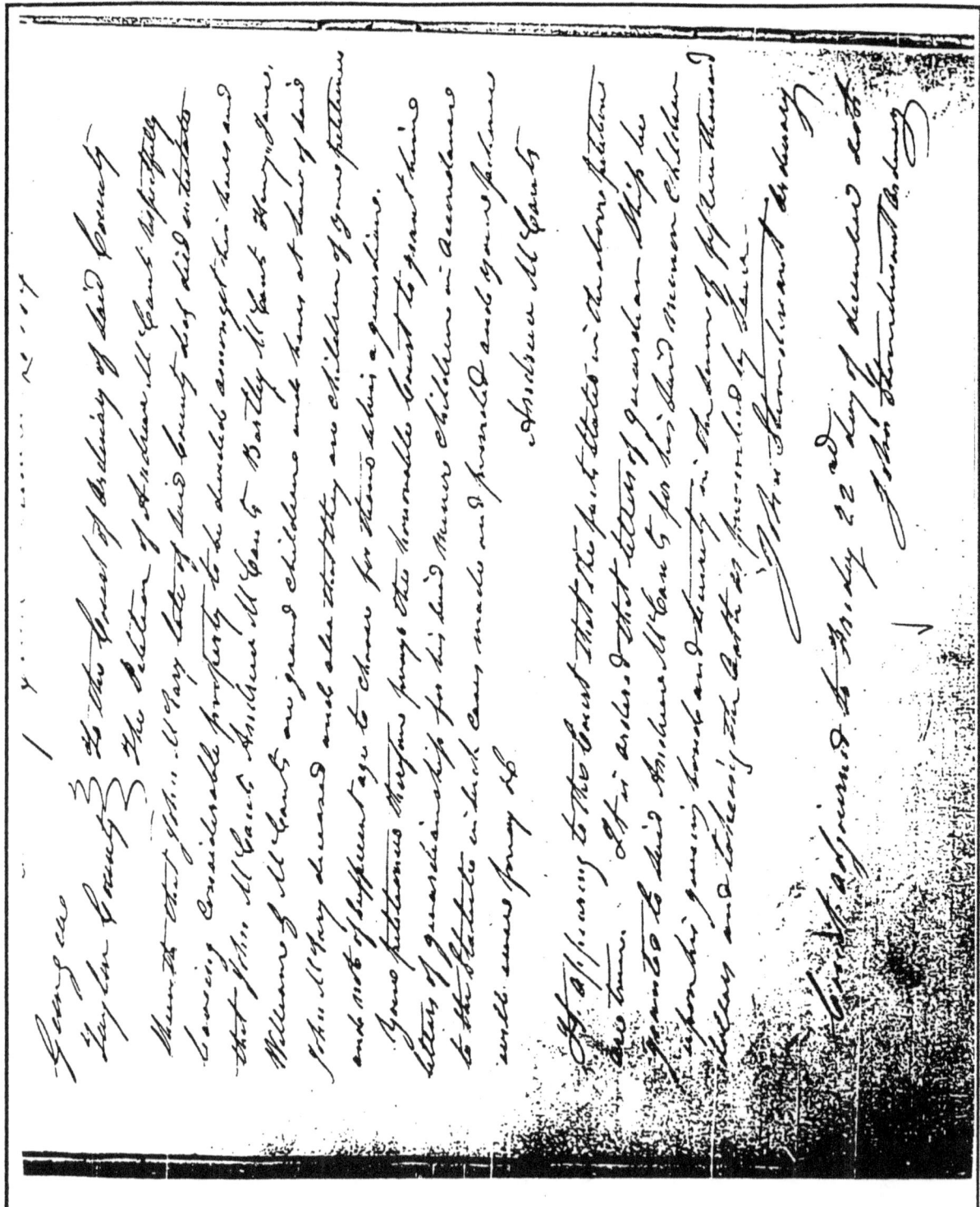

Fig. 7-45. Petition and issue of Letters of Guardianship to Andrew McCants as Guardian of his children, who are the grandchildren of John McCrary, deceased 1854. A bond as security in the sum of $15,000 is asked along with taking of an Oath.

Ordinary Court December Twenty 1854

Georgia

Taylor To the Court of Ordinary of said County

The Petition of Andrew McCants respectfully herewith that John McCrary late of said County dec'd died intestate having considerable property to be divided amongst his heirs and that John McCants Andrew McCants Bartley McCants Henry, Jane, William G. McCants are grandchildren and heirs at law of said John McCrary deceased and also that they are children of your petitioners and note of sufficient age to choose for themselves a guardian.

Your petitioners therefore pray and these honorable court to grant him letters of guardianship for his miner children in accordance to the statue in such cases made and provided and your patience will serve...

Andrew McCants

It appearing to this court that this fact stated in the above petition are true. It is ordered that letters of guardianship be granted to said Andrew McCants for his said minor children upon his giving bonds and security in the sum of fifteen thousand dollars and taking the Oath as provided by law.

John Sturdivant, Ordinary

Court adjourned to Friday 22nd day December 20th

John Sturdivant Ordinary

Fig. 7-45 Petition and issue of Letters of Guardianship to Andrew McCants as Guardian of his children, who are the grandchildren of John McCrary, deceased 1854. A bond as security in the sum of $15,000 is asked along with the taking of an Oath.

1854
The Estate of John McCrary deceased in acct with
Bartley McCrary Administrator from 1st September
1855 to the day 5th March 1856 —

Paid To Thomas Ragland Acpt No 1			63.95
March 1st J.A. & F.S. Rucker " " 2			31.30
Tax 1854 " 3			78.61
" " 1855 " 4			48.17
April 5th Paid J. Rose & Co. 5			8.57
Dec. 22/54 John Sturdivant 6 "			15.00
Feb 20/55 Crane & Levy 7 "			25.79
May 5th W.I. & I.A. Hamilton 8 "			11.44
11= Sam H Cissye 9 "			225.00
March 3. 1856. Dr Runnels Acpt 10 "			63.00
" Drs Dyane & Matthews 11			8.00
" Dr. Ropers Acpt 12 —			27.00
Dr. Bells do— 13			12.00
4 " Dr Hillmans do. 14 "			28.80
For running well on plantation 15			
Paid for walling graveyard 16 "			48.50
Feb 19th B H Keen attorney &c — 17 =			25.00
			718.86
Jany 20th 1855 Paid Dr Andrews			28.00
Paid J.P. McCrary in cash			520.00
John McCrary "			520.00
L H McCrary "			520.00
D C McCrary			520.00
Henry McCrary			520.00
J A Berry			520.00
Andrew McCants			520.00

Nothing collected but what is
charged in the Sale Bill and
Inventory already returned & but a
of that

Fig. 7-46. Estate Papers of John McCrary, dec'd. 1854.
Bartley McCrary, his son, is Administrator
of the Estate.

1855   180

The Estate of John McCrary, deceased ... with Bartley McCrary,
Administrator from 1st December 1855 to the day 5th March 1856-

					$	c
	Paid To Thomas Ragland	Ac_t	Vo. 1		53	95
March 1st	" J.A. & F.S. Rucker	"	" 2		31	20
	Tax 1854	"	3		78	61
	1855"		4		48	07
April 5th	Paid S. Rose & Co.		5		8	50
Dec. 22/54	John Sturdivant					
			6	"	15	00
Feb 20/55	Crone & Levy		7	"	25	79
May 5th	W. J. & J. A. Hamilton		8	"	11	44
11=	Sam W. Visage		9	"	225	00
March 3. 1856	Dr- _____		10	"	63	00
	Dr. Drane & Matthew		11		8	00
	Dr. Ropers Ac-t		12		27	00
	Dr. Bells do		13		12	00
4	Dr Hillsman do		14		22	80
	... Dump Well on Plantation					15
	Paid for swelling graveyard		16		40	50
Feb 19th	B F Rease attorny for		17	=	25	00
					718	86
Jany 20th 1855 paid Dr Andrews					28	00
	Paid J P. McCrary in cash				520	00
	John McCrary				520	00
	G F McCrary				520	00
	L Q C McCrary				520	00
	Henry McCrary				520	00
	J. F. Berry				520	00
	Andrew McCants				520	00

Nothing collected but what is $4358.96
charged in the sale Bill and   Commiss- $21,1794.35
Inventory-already returned & but a small amount of that.

Fig. 7-46.

Fig. 7-46

Recapitulation

Amount Paid Out. $4588.86
Commissions on Same 217.94
Dr Estate &c $4576.88
                 28.00
Be taken from Inventory & Sale Bill $404.30

Georgia   } Personally came Bartley McCrary
Taylor County } Who being duly sworn deposith
& sayeth the above return is true to the
Best of his belief – this 5th day of March
1856.   Bartley McCrary
John Sturdivant Ordinary }

N. 1st
Butler Georgia 1854 –
B McCrary Admr of John McCrary Sr
96 yds Bagging 16.80 = 122 lbs Rope 17.35 – $34.15
Nails 30 – Salt 2.25 – flour 2.50 – Whis 2.00 Sold 9.00 –
   flour 2.50   18.75
   Whis 1.00   1.00
                                     $53.90
Bal on Draz Cr. 35.00 }
                Recd Payment
                      J. Ragland

N. 2nd
Bartley McCrary Admr of John McCrary
To I. A. & F. S. Rucher
Pr Order Nov 14th 25 pr russet shoes 120 $30.00
1 pr   do 120   1.20
                                          $31.20

N. 3.
Estate of John McCrary – 78 dollars 61 cents 3 mills
Tax for the year 1854 L. A. Lloyd T.C.

181
Recapitulation

Amount paid out	c $4358.86
Commissions on same	217-94
Dr. Estate & so	$4576.80
	28-00
Be taken from Inventory & sale Bill	$4604.80

Georgia   Personally came Bartley McCrary
Taylor County   Who being duly sworn deposith and payth the above return is true to the Best of his belief-this 5th day of Mach 1856

                          Bartley McCrary

John Sturdivant Ordinary

V' 1st

Butler Georgia 1854-
B McCrary, Admr of John McCrary-Dr   c

96 yds Bagging 16.80=122 ... Rope 1735 - "$34.15
nails 30 - Salt 225 flour 250 - whis. 2 00 sold 900
    flour 2.50   18.75
      Whis   100   1 00
                                                     53:90

Bal on dr... cr. 35.00
         Recd Paymt
                            G. Ragland

V. 2nd

Bartley McCrary , Admr of John McCrary
   To.J.A. & F.S. Rucker
                                                   c

Pr order * Nov. 14th 25pr russet Shoes $1.20 $30.00
1 pr   do 1 20   1.20
                                                                      $31.20

V. 3.

Recd of John McCrary-78 Dollars 61 cents 8 mils
for his tax for the year 1854 C . A. Lloyd _C

Fig. 7-46.*Purchase of 25 prs. of shoes for the Negro slaves.

Continued

N. 4.
Rec'd of Bartly McCrary, Admr. on the Estate of
John McCrary L. $45.17 8
for his Tax for the year 1855 & Alleys X 6.

N. 5.
Bartly McCrary --- Admr. of John McCrary
To J. Rose & Co.   Dr
1854 To of advertising in Georgia & Messenger
Nov 22. Sale of personal property 40 days $3.50
Dec 20 Printing 800 notes.   5.00
                                                        ─────
                                                        8.50
Rec'd of B. McCrary, Eight dollars --
and 50 cts. in full of the above account Jan
6th 1855.   J. Rose & Co.

N. 6
Bartly McCrary Admr. J. John McCrary
Deceased —
1854 To John Sturdivant Ordinary Dr
       For permant letters Admr on said
Estate $9.25
       for two orders   2.00
                                                      ──────
                                                      $11.25
For Temporary letters   3.75
Rec'd of Bartly McCrary Administr   15.00
tor of John McCrary dec'd sixteen dollars the
Amount of the above account this 22 Dec 1857
                              John Sturdivant

Fig. 7-46.

Continued   182
                        V.4.
Recd of Bartley McCrary Admr. of the Estate of
John McCrary L $4847. 8
    for his tax for the year 1855-6 & _____

                        V.5.
Bartley McCrary--Admr - of John McCrary -
To S Rose & Co.   Dr
1854   To advertising in Georgia & Messenger
Nov 22. Sale of Personal property 40 days $3.50
Dec. 20   Printing   800 notes   5.00
Recd of B McCrary   Eight dollars -   8.50
and 50 cts in full of the above account Dec
6th   1855.   S Rose & Co.-

                        V.6.

Bartley McCrary   Admr of John McCrary -
Deceased-
1854   To John Sturdivant Ordinary   Dr
    For ... Letters Admr on said
Estate: $ 9.25
    For Two orders.   2.00
                                                        $11.25

For temporary letters   3.75
Recd of Bartley McCrary- Admistrator   15.00
of John McCrary -decd fifteen dollars the
amount of the above account this 22 Dec 1854
              John Sturdivant Ordinary

Fig. 7-46.

Fig. 7-46.

N. 7

Bart McCrary Estate Dr to Crane & Levy

Nov 11	8 yds Blk velvet 62½	$5.00
	12 " velvet Ribbon 20	2.40
	2 White do. 10	.20
	7 Jaconett 50	3.50
	5 y Bl. Homespun 18¾	1.04
	1 Pr. White gloves	.50
	1 " Socks	.25
	3 Spools thread 5	.15
	1 Paper needles	.05
	13 yds. Irish Linen 75	9.75
	1 yd. Jaconett	.50
	2 papers Tacks 10	.20
	1 do. Brass Tacks	1.00
	5 yds. Blk. ribbon 10	.50
15	4 Bl Homespun 18¾	.75
		$25.79

Recd Paymt Feb 20th 1855
Crane & Levy

N. 8

1854 Bartlet McCrary for the Estate of
John McCrary to W.J. & J.H. Hamilton Dr

Nov 16th	To 35 yds Kersey 22			$7.70
28	17 do 22			3.74
				$11.44

Recd the within acct by cash
Jun 5, 1855
W.J. & J.H. Hamilton

V.7.

1854 McCrary Estate Dr to Crone & Levy -

Nov 11,	8	Yds Blk Velvet 62½		$ 5.00
	12	" velvet Ribbon 20		2.40
	2	White do. 10		.20-
	7	Jacconett 50		3.50
	5	Bl. Homespun - 18		1.04
	1	pr. White gloves		.50
	1	" Socks		25
	3	Spools Thread 5		15
	1	Paper Needles -		.05
	13	Yds. Irish Sinar 75		9.75
	1 yd.	Jaconett		.50
	2	paper Tacks. 10.		.20-
	1	do. Brass Tacks		1.00
	5.	yds- Blk. ribbon 10-		.50
15	4	Bl Homespun 18½		.75
	Rcd Paymt Feb 20th 1855			$25.79

                            Crane & Levy -

V.8

1854 Bartley McCrary for the Estate -of
     John McCrary to W.I. & J.A. Hamilton Dr

Nov 16th	To 35 yd Hersy 22-		$ 7.70
28	17. do 22-		3.74
Rcvd the within act by cash			$11.44
June 5	1855		

              W.J. & J.H. Hamilton

Fig. 7-46.

Fig. 7-46

V. 9.

Received of Bartly McCrary, Administrator of the Estate of John McCrary, deceased, the sum of Two hundred and twenty five dollars — for oversees Wages — for the year Eighteen hundred and fifty four. this Jan 11th 1855 — Samuel W. Visage

V. 10

John McCrary Dec'd To William Greene Dr

1854. Nov 27.	To visit 12 miles squills cloth and Laudanum for miss Jane & negro	$8.00
Dec 1	To visit via from Butler, Bot. Salts	3.25
3	to visit from Mrs Rileys tough meat Zig Spts nit 97	3.00
		$14.75
1854. Aug 30	to visit 5 miles — for self	7.00
	Morphine & Sugar Lead	1.00
28	visit from 15 miles	3.00
	Solution morphine Z oz	2.00
Oct 16	visit 12 miles — for self	7.00
	Solution morphine Z oz	2.00
	Astringent gargle	.50
26	visit 12 miles — for self	7.00
	Solution morphine Z oz	2.00
	Collyrium Z ii	.50
Nov 3	visit miles for self	7.00
	Solu morphine Z i, squills & cath.	1.75
14	visit 12 miles for self	7.00
	Solu morphine Z ij	1.50

Continued

V. 9

Received of Bartley McCrary Administrator of the
Estate of John McCrary deceased this sum of
Two hundred and twenty five dollars for overseers
wages for the year Eighteen hundred and
fifty four this June 11th 1855 Samuel W Visage

V. 10

John McCrary Dec'd to William Drane   Do

1854 Nov. 27	To visit 12 miles... and Land division for Mifs Jane & Negro	$8.00
Dec. 1	to visit via from Butler 1 Box pills cath	3.00
3	to visit from Mrs. Riley Bough mixed...Spts Nit gz	3.00
1854 Aug. 30	to visit 12 miles for self	7.00
	Morphine & sugar Lend	3.00
28	visit from Butler	3.00
	Solution morphine 3oz	2.00
Oct. 16	visit 12 miles for self	7.00
	Solution morphine 2oz	2.00
	Astrigent gargle	.50
26	visit 12 miles for self	7.00
	Solution Morphine	2.00
	Colly une	.50
Nov. 3	Visit miles for self	7.00
	Solu morphine to... & Cath	1.75
11	Visit 12 miles for self	7.00
	Solu morphine	.50

Fig. 7-46.

THE OVERSEER

> Questions that plagued my mind at the beginning of this research were: who was the overseer of my slave ancestors? Was he kind or cruel? I never expected to learn his name. Bartley McCrary, son of John McCrary and Administrator of his father's estate, recorded these records 140 years ago. They are the slim shadowed remains of my kinfolks. The records don't tell me how my kinfolks were treated, but I know the names of the ones who touched their lives severely and one important one, the overseer. Voucher No. 9 identified the overseer as Samuel W. Visage.

Fig. 7-46

N° 10

Georgia } Personally came before
Talbot County } me William Drane & after
being duly sworn saith that the above
account of sixty three dollars is just and
true as stands stated Sworn to &
Subscribed before me this 18th Decr 1854
Simeon Parker J.P.   Wm Drane

Recd sixty three dollars of Bartly McCrary
Admr of the Estate of John McCrary Decd
In full of the above acct this 3rd March 1856
                                William Drane

N° 11

John McCrary to Drane & Matthews Dr.
1854 Aug 4. to visit case of Syphilis pr negro child $6.00
1846 Aug 5. 4 men pills Mur. Hydr. camph tict   2.00
                                                      8.00

Georgia }
Talbot County } Personally came before me
William Drane one of the former firm of
Drane & Matthews & after being duly sworn
saith that the above account of eight
dollars is just & true as stands stated
Sworn to and subscribed before me
this 18th of Dec 1854   William Drane
Simeon Parker J.P.

Recd eight dollars of Bartly McCrary
Admr on the Estate of John McCrary
Decd in full of the above acpt
This 3rd March 1856
                                Drane & Matthews

Continued

V. 10

Georgia   Personally came before me William Drane and after
Talbot County   Being duly sworn saith that the above account
of sixty three dollars is just and true as stands stated sworn to &
subscribed before me this 18th Dec. 1854-
Simeon Parker - J.P.   Wm. Drane
Recd sixty three dollars- of Bartley McCrary -
Admr. of the Estate of John McCrary - Decd
In full of the above act. this 3rd March 1856-
                       William Drane

V. 11

John McCrary to Drane & Matthews Dr. 1854 Aug 4 to
visit case of syphiles for Negro child $6.00
1846 Aug 5   Amen pils Mur. Hydr camph liot   2.00
                                                  8.00

Georgia   Personally came before me
Talbot County   William Drane one of the former firm of
Drane & Matthews & after being duly -Sworn Saith that the above
account of eight dollars is just and true as stands stated
sworn to and subscribed before me
This 18th of Dec. 1854
                       William Drane
Simeon Parker J P
Recd Eight Dollars - of Bartley McCrary
Admr on the Estate of John McCrary
Decd in full of the above acpt
    This 3rd March 1856-
                       Drane & Matthews

Fig. 7-46.

Continued

Fig. 7-46

1854   No. 12

~~Est. John McCrary~~ decd Dr to Jams E Roper

Oct 23	To mileage & visit	$4.70
	Pill & Alt Powders	1.25
	4 oz Liniment	.75
30"	mileage & visit	4.75
	Linament	1.00
	Cathartic pows & Pills	1.00
Nov 10	Mileage visit & Medicine	6.00
		$19.50

Georgia } Personally came before
Taylor County } J. H. Wallace a Justice
of the Peace in and for said County Jams
E Roper who being duly sworn saith the
above account of nine & 50/100 dollars — is
just & true Sworn to and subscribed
to before me this the 20th day of January
1855.

1855   John Wallace J.P.   }   James E Roper

Est of John McCrary — decd Dr to Jams E Roper

Feb 13	to mileage & visit	$5.25
	Liniment & Bitters	1.75
13"	1 Box Escent. Powders	.50
		7.50

Georgia } Personally came before me J. H.
Taylor County } Wallace a Justice Peace
In and for said Jams E Roper who being
Duly sworn saith the above account
seven 67/100 — is just & true sworn to
Subscribed to before me this 20th day
Jan. 1855
John H Wallace J.P.   }   James E Roper

Continued
1854   V. 12

Est John McCrary Dec'd   Dr to James E. Roper

October 23 to mileage & visit	$4.75
Pills & Alt Powders	1.25
4 oz Liniment	.75
30 mileage and visit	4.75
linament	1.00
Diashortic pous & pills	1.00
Nov. 10 mileage visit & medican	6.00

Georgia   Personally came before
Taylor County J. H. Wallace a Justice
of the peace in and for said county James
E. Roper who being duly sworn saith the
above account of nine do/100 dollars is
just and true sworn to and subscribed
To before me this the 20th day of January
1855
1854   John Wallace J P   James E. Roper

Est of John McCrary -Decd Dr to James E. Roper

Feb 13 to mileage and visit	$5.25
Liniment & Bitters	1.75
15 1 Box Escut Powders	.50

Georgia   Personally came before me J. H.
Taylor County Wallace a Justice Peace
in and for said James E. Roper who being
duly sworn saith the above account
Seven 50/100 is just and true sworn to and
subscribed to before me this 20th day of
June 1855
John H. Wallace   James E. Roper

Fig. 7-46.

Rec'd Bartly McCrary Adm'r of [McCrary]
Dec'd payment in full for the within acc't
March 3rd 1856 —   James E. Roper

Rec'd of Bartly McCrary Administrator of
John McCrary. Dec'd Payment in full for the
within acc't March 5th 1856
                                James E. Roper

                    № 13 —
1854 John McCrary to J.D. Beall Dr
March 13. to visit Girl Emaline Blisters & meds $ 3.50
      14. to visit Emoline & medicine   3.00
      15. to visit   do   do   3.00
      Do to tonic Bitters for Emaline   .50
                                                 ─────
                                                 $10.50

Georgia —   Personally came before me
Taylor County   C. B. Dixon a acting Justice
of the peace in and for said County, J.
J. D. Beall who being duly sworn deposeth
And saith, that the above account is just
And true as it stands stated to the best
of his knowledge and belief sworn
To and subscribed to before me this
Dec 26th 1854. C. B. Dickson J.P. —
Rec'd Payment by Bartly McCrary —
March 5th 1856 —
                            J. D. Beall —

Continued

187

Rec'd Bartley McCrary Admr of John McCrary
Decd payment in full for the within acct
March 3rd 1856   James E. Roper
Rec'd of Bartley McCrary Administrator of
John McCrary Dec'd payment in full for this
within acpt March 3rd 1856
                      James E. Roper
                V 13-
1854 John McCrary to J. L. Beall   Dr
March 13 to vist Girl Emoline Blisters & Meden $3.50
       14 to visit Emoline and Medican   3.00
       15 to visit   "   "   3.00
       30 tonic Bitters for Emoline   .50
                                               $10.50

Georgia   Personally came before me
Taylor County C. B. Dixon acting Justice of the Peace
in and for said county I J D Beall who being duly sworn
deposith and saith that the above account is just and
true as it stands stated to the best
of his knowledge and belief sworn To and
subscribed before me this Dec 26th 1854
C B Dickson J P
Recd Payment by Bartley McCrary
March 22 1856
                      J D Beall

Fig. 7-46.

A most interesting Voucher is No. 13. It recorded the account for doctor visits to a Negro girl owned by John McCrary. Bartley McCrary paid the account two years after the death of John McCrary. Emoline was ill. Doctor visits for three days implied kindness and concern by her master, John McCrary. The name, Emoline, does not appear in John McCrary's "Inventory" list of slaves nor "Estate Division." She may have died, was sold or transferred to a family member. I found no records of slave deaths. See endnotes.[8]

Fig. 7-46.

Est. John McCrary to Josiah Hillman

May 27	to visit & medicine for self	$5.00
27	Call visit from Geo	3.50
June 3.	Visit & medicine for self	5.00
13.	Visit & medicine	5.00
July 12.	Visit & medicine	5.00
Aug 7.	Visit & medicine	5.00
		28.50

Georgia
Crawford County

Personally Appeared Before me Thos Rains a Justice Peace in and for said County Joseph Hillman who being duly sworn reposeth & saith that the above acpt is just & true as stands above stated. Sworn to & subscribed Before me this January 22nd 1855

Thomas Rains J.P.   Josiah Hillman

Recd of Bartly McCrary, administrator of John McCrary, deceased Twenty Eight 50/100 Dollars — in full of the within acpt March 4th 1856 — Josiah Hillman
 By John T. Gray

$11.17

Recd of Bartly McCrary Admr Estate of John McCrary, deceased Dollars — for professional services 19th Feby 1856 — Benj. A. [?]

Continued

```
                        V.14
1854   John McCrary to Josiah Hillsman   Cr
    May 24  To visit & medican for self    $6.00
        27  Call visit from Geas            2.50
    June 3  Visit & medican                 5.00
        13  visit & medican                 5.00
    July 13  visit & medican                5.00
    Aug  7  visit & medican                 5.00
                                           28.50
```

Georgia   Personally appeared
Crawford County   Before me Thos Rains
a Justice Peace in and for said
Joseph Hillsman who being Duly
sworn reporeth and saith that the
above acpt is just and true as stands
above stated sworn to & subscribed
Before me this January 22nd 1855
Thomas Rains J P   Joseph Hillsman
Recd of Bartley McCrary Administrator
of John McCrary deceased twenty Eight
50/100 Dollars in full of the within acpts
March 4th 1856   Joseph Hillsman
                   by John T. Gray
                        V.17
Recd of Bartley McCrary Admr on this
Estate of John McCrary deceased thirty
dollars for profeffsional (professional) sirvis (service) this
19th Feb 1856   Benj F. Rease
Fig. 7-46.

John McCrary was ill a few months before his death in 1854. His son, Bartley, paid $28.50 to Josiah Hillsman of Crawford County, Ga. for visits and medicine between May 27 and Aug. 7, 1854. Bartley was attentive to his father. He traveled 12 miles roundtrip from his home to Butler often during the months of August through November. He purchased many bottles of morphine and astringent gargle and paid William Drane, a physician, $63.00.

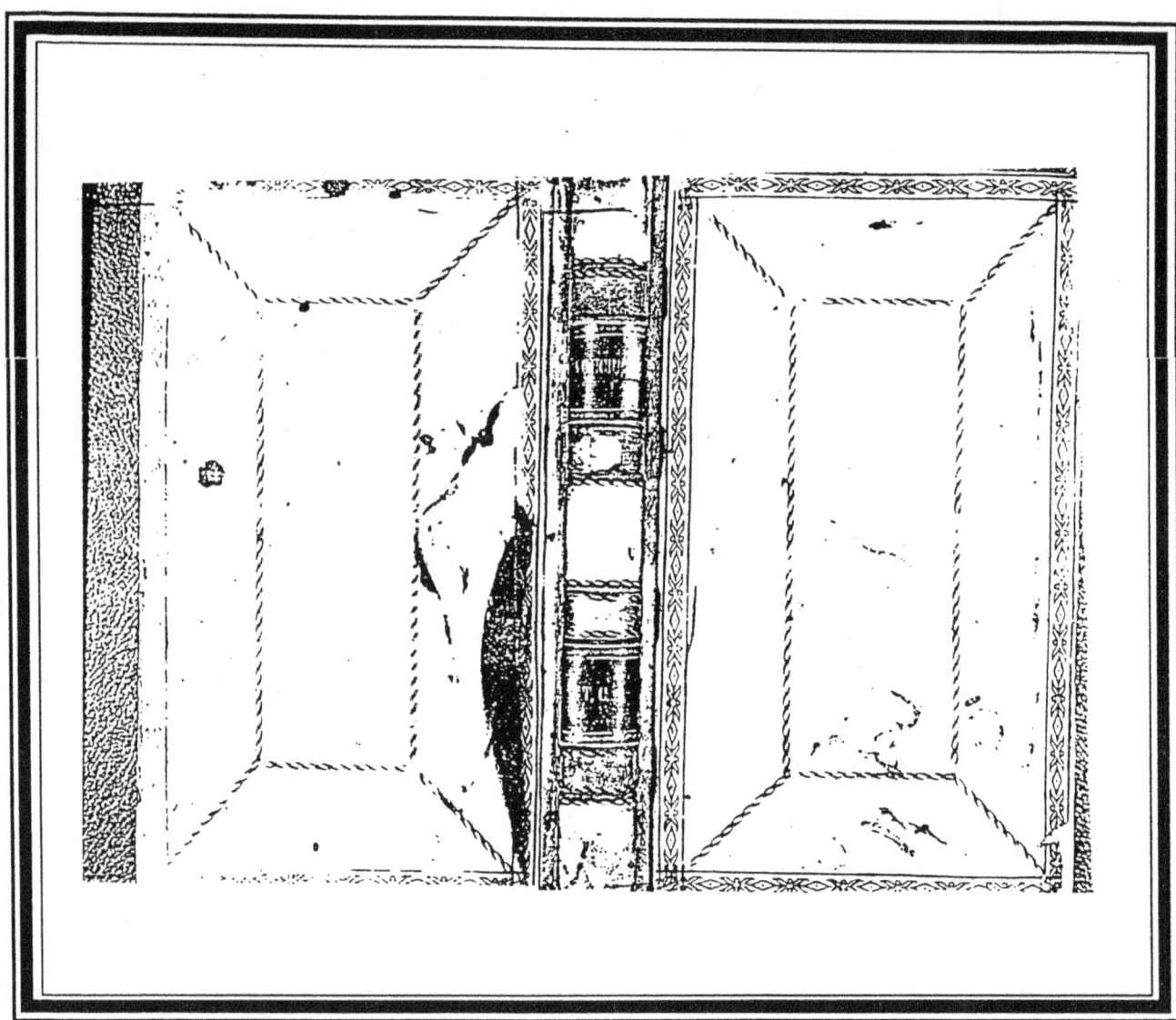

Fig. 7-46. Book of Vouchers

    Within the covers of this book, Bartley McCrary, Administrator, and John Sturdivant, Taylor County, Georgia Ordinary, recorded the Estate Division of John McCrary. In this book, the names of my slave ancestors were recorded 140 years ago. The next three documents are copies of pages 191, 192 and 297. These pages revealed McCrary family members who received my kinfolks, Veny, Matilda, Missouri, and two other children of Matilda.

    The microfilm copy of the book did not include an index. The Estate records of John McCrary were recorded on pages 180-193, 365-368 and page 297. This meant that each page of the entire roll(#321101) of film had to be read to find all of the records. The microfilm rolls of Taylor County Probate Records were ordered at the Lake Mary Family History Center, an affiliate of the LDS Library, Salt Lake City, Utah.

B. F. GRIFFIN,

MACON, GA.,

BOOK AND JOB PRINTER

AND

BOOK-BINDER,

Has in operation a very superior Job Printing Press, which enables him to execute Printing with great dispatch, and upon the most reasonable terms. He also has every facility for Printing and Binding books of all kinds. Blank Books ruled to any pattern and bound in the most substantial manner. ☞ OFFICE No. 10, *Cotton Avenue.*

Copy of printer's imprint found on the front inside cover of the Book of Vouchers, Taylor County, Court of Ordinary 1852-1858.

191

Georgia
Taylor County

By virtue of an order of the Honorable Court of Ordinary of said County on 2d day of December Instant to us Directed authorising & requiring us to make distribution of the Estate of the late John McCrary among the distributees intitled to said Estate we Proceded this day to the performance of that duty. There were Eight distributees to wit Bartly McCrary, Gilley F McCrary, Jonathan P McCrary, John A J McCrary, Jas. G McCrary, Andrew McCants As guardian for his minor children & grand Children of said dec'd to wit John McCants, Andrew McCants, Bartly McCants, Henry, Sarah & Weldon C McCants and James F Berry in the right of his wife Mary Berry formerly Mary McCrary. Henry McCrary said Henry Being represented by Bartly McCrary. The Shears were numbered 1) (2) (3) (4) (5) (6) 7) (8) And carefully placed in a hat each Shear having the number of negros and their valuations placed on said Shear As well as their names — the distributees Then proceeded to draw untill all the Tickets were drawn the following is the Result No. 1. Bartly McCrary –
No 2. Gilley McCrary –
No 3. Andrew McCants Guardian
No 4 Jonathan McCrary –
No 5 James F Berry
No 6 Henry McCrary –
No 7 James G McCrary
No 8 John A J McCrary

Fig. 7-47. Estate Division. John McCrary, dec'd. 1854. Taylor Co., Ga.

The following is a typed copy of the final division and "Distribution" of John McCrary's Negro property from his estate.

191

State of Georgia	By virture of an order from the
Taylor County	Honorable Court of Ordinary of said

County on 22 day of December Instant to us--
Directed orthorising & requiring us to make distri-
bution of the Estate of the late John McCrary among
the distributees intitled to said Estate we
proceded this day to the performance of that duty
There were Eight distributees to wit Bartley McCrary
Gilley F. McCrary Jonathan P. McCrary- John
A. J. McCrary Jane G. McCrary Andrew McCants,
As guardian for his minor children & grand
children of said decd to wit   John McCants
-Andrew McCants
Bartley McCants Henry
Sarah J. Weldon   G. McCants and James F Berry-
in the right of his wife Mary Berry formerly--
Mary McCrary, Henry McCrary, said Henry-
Being represented by Bartley McCrary, the
shears were numbered 1) -(2) (3) (4) (5) (6)
7) (8) And carefully placed in a hat each
shear having the nuber (number) of Negros-and
There valuations placed on said shear
As well as there names--the distributees
Then proceded to Draw untill all the
Tickets were drawn the following is the
Result   no. 1   Bartley McCrary
           no. 2   Gilly McCrary
           no. 3   Andrew McCants Guardian
           no. 4   Jonathan McCrary
           no. 5   James F. Berry
           no. 6   Henry McCrary
           no. 7   Jane G. McCrary
           no. 8   John A. I. McCrary

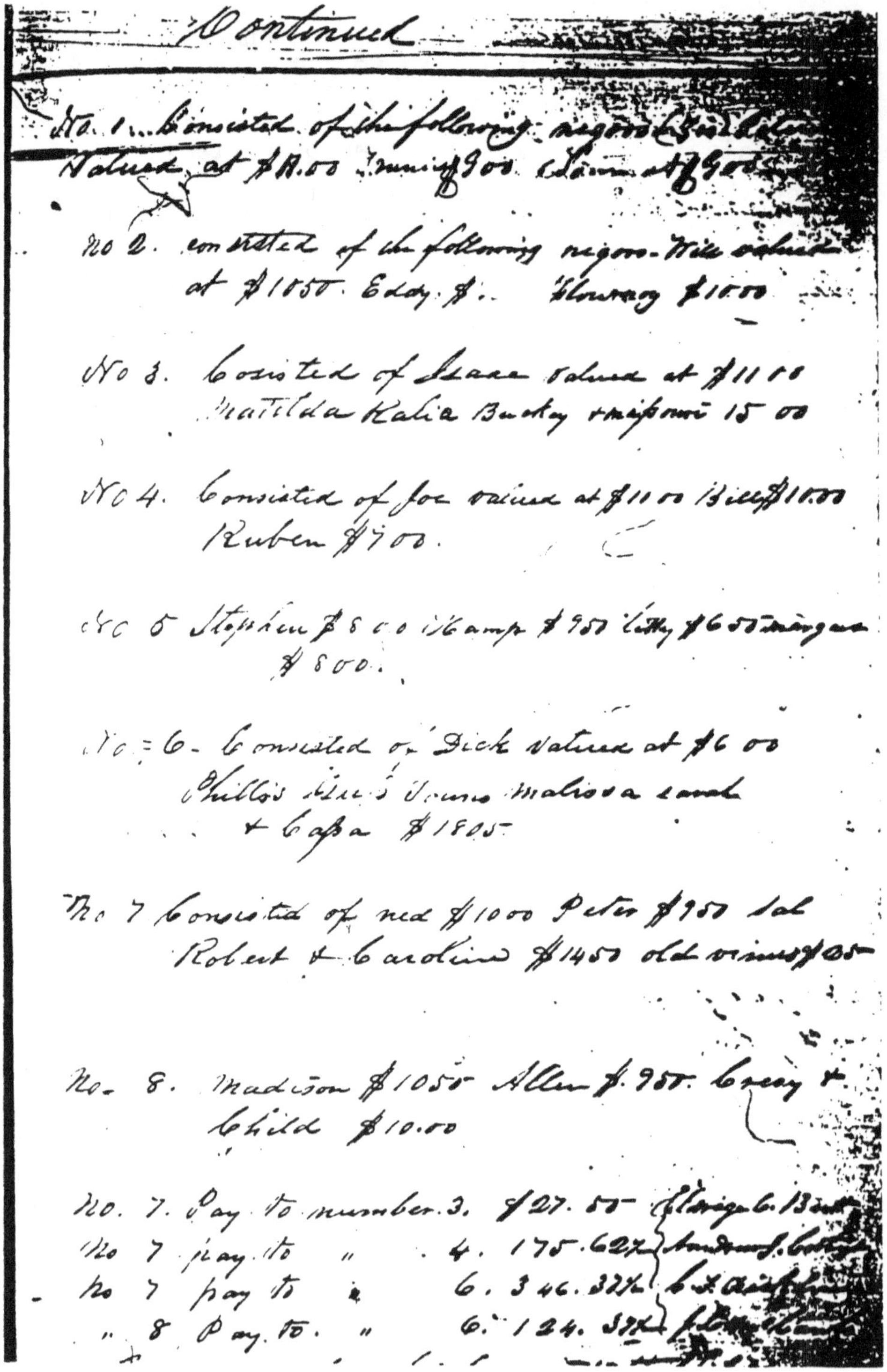

Continued

No. 1. Consisted of the following negros [illegible]
Valued at $8.00 [illegible] 900 [illegible] $900

No 2. consisted of the following negros. Will valued
at $1050. Eddy $ [illegible]. Howrey $1050

No 3. Consisted of Isaac valued at $1100
Matilda Kalia Busky & infant 15 00

No 4. Consisted of Joe valued at $1100 Bill $1000
Ruben $700.

No 5 Stephen $800 Kamp $950 Letty $650 [illegible]
$800.

No. 6. Consisted of Dick valued at $600
Phillis [illegible] Malissa [illegible]
& Cassa $1805

No 7 Consisted of Ned $1000 Peter $950 Sal
Robert & Caroline $1450 old [illegible] $25

No. 8. Madison $1050 Allen $950 Crecy &
Child $10.00

No. 7. Pay to number 3. $27.50 [illegible]
No 7 pay to "   4. 175.62½ [illegible]
No 7 pay to "   6. 346.37½ [illegible]
 " 8 Pay to. "   6. 124.37½ [illegible]

Fig. 7-47. Estate Division. John McCrary, dec'd. 1854.
Taylor Co., GA.
The Final Transfer before Freedom.

No. 7....Old Visues $25.00
for a whole life of work, transferred to
Jane G. McCrary in 1856.

Continued

No. 1. Consisted of the following negros (Vis) Peter
valued at $1100 Frances $900 Tom at $900

No. 2. consisted of the following negros- Will valued
at $1050. Eddy $725. Floursury $1000

No. 3 Cosisted of Isaac valued at $1100
Matilda Ralia Buckey & Missouri 1500

No. 4 Consisted of Joe valued at $1000 Bill $10.00
Ruben $700.

No. 5 Stephen $800 Hamp $950 Litty $650 Margaret
$800

No. 6 Consisted of Dick valued at $600
Phillis's Gus Touns Malissa Sarah
& Cafsa (Cassa) $1805

No. 7 Consisted of Ned $1000 Peter $950 Sal
Robert & Caroline $1450 old Visues $25

No. 8 Madison $1050 Allen $950. Cresy &
Child $10.00

No. 7	Pay to number	3	$27.50	Eldrige C. Butt
No. 7	Pay to "	4	175.62 1/2	Andrew J. Colbert
No. 7	Pay to "	6	346.37 1/2	C. F. Ficklin
" 8	Pay to "	6	124.37 1/2	J. C. McCants

Georgia   I do herby certify that Eldridge C. Butt
Taylor County   J. McCants Colbert C. F. Ficklin & Jeremiah C.
McCants - commissioners appointed to divide this Estate of
John McCrary Decd were duly sworn to the performance of there
duty-given under my hand & official signature this 25th day of
Dec, 1854   Issac Mukey - J.I.C.
Recorded May 15th 1856   John Sturdivant Ordinary

Fig. 7-47

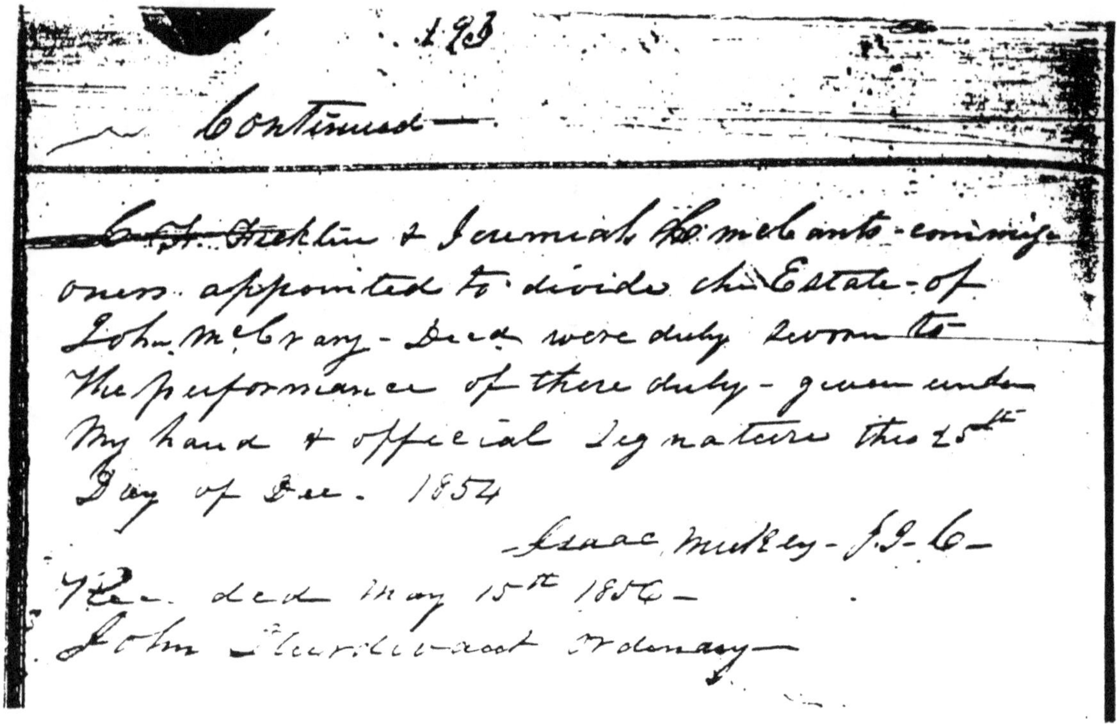

> 193
>
> ~ Continued ~
>
> Capt. Ficklin & Jeremiah McCants commissioners appointed to divide the Estate of John McCrary - Dec'd were duly sworn to the performance of there duty - given under my hand & official signature this 25th Day of Dec. 1854
>
> Isaac Mickley - J.I.C -
>
> Rec. ded May 15th 1856 -
> John Sturdivant Ordinary

Fig. 7-47. Estate Division. John McCrary, dec'd. 1854. Taylor Co., GA.

Continued

C. F. Ficklin & Jeremiah H. McCants
Commifsoners appointed to divide the Estate of
John McCrary Decd were duly sworn to
the performance of there duty given under
my hand & official signature this 25th Day
of December 1854

          Isaac Murkey I D C_

Recorded May 15th 1856
John Sturdivant Ordinary
Fig. 7-47

 The foregoing Division records of John McCrary, dec'd 1854, transferred my ancestors to Andrew McCants, his son-in-law and Jane, his daughter.(Fig.7-47, pp. 191-192) Was this the final transfer before freedom in 1865? Chapter Fourteen answers that question.

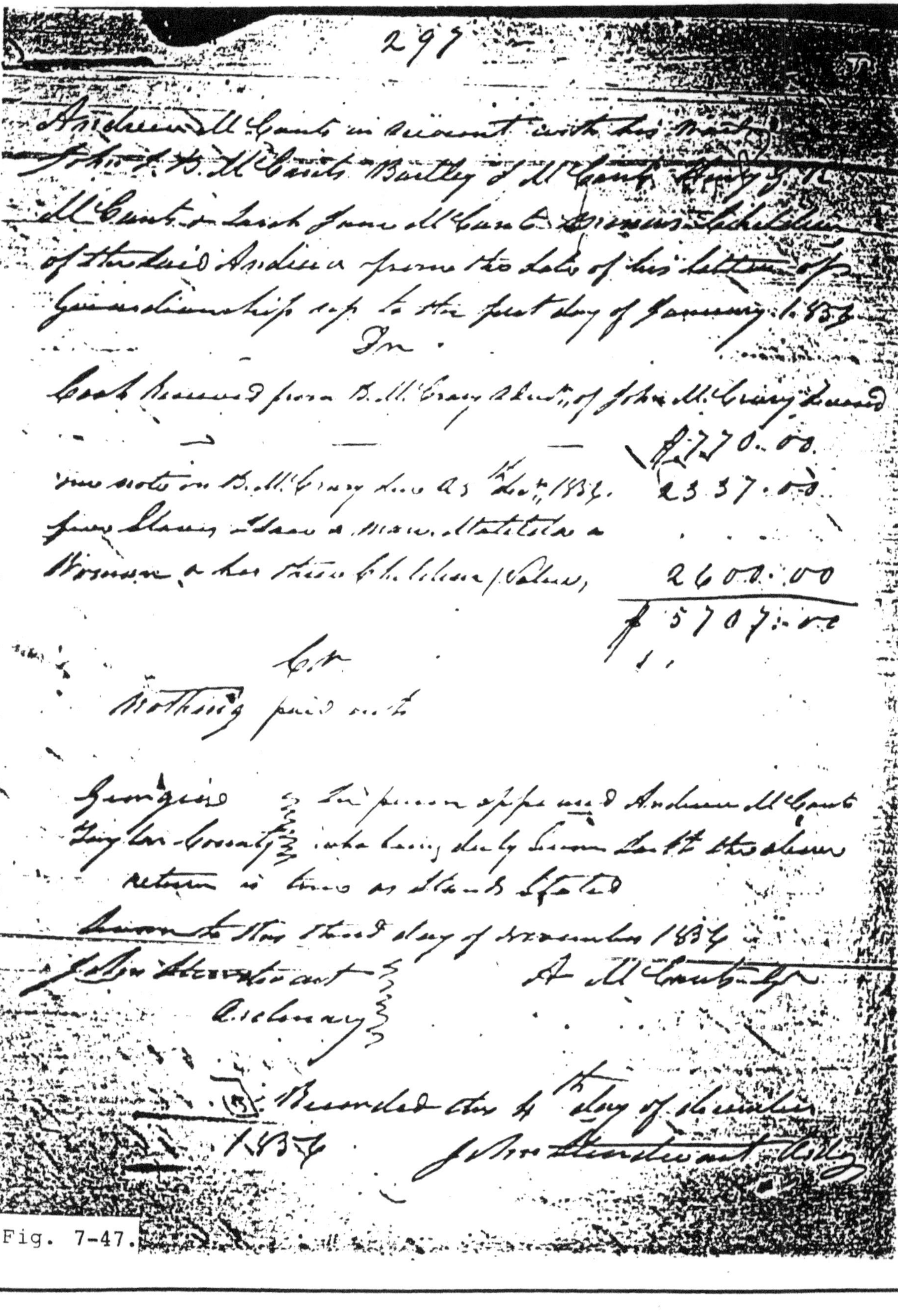

297

Andrew McGant in account with his ward
John H. McGants Bartley McGant [illegible]
McGant Sarah Jane McGant & [illegible] children
of the said Andrew from the date of his letters of
Guardianship up to the first day of January 1837

Dr.

Cash Received from B. McCrary admr. of John McCrary deceased $770.00

His note on B. McCrary due 25th Dec. 1837   2337.00

[illegible] Slaves Isaac & Mary, Matilda &
Wonson & her three Children, Values,   2600.00
                                                                 ─────────
                                                                  $5707.00

Cr.
Nothing paid out

Georgia   } In person appeared Andrew McGant
Taylor County} who being duly sworn saith the above
             return is true as stands stated
Sworn to this third day of November 1837
John Stewart   A. McGant
  Ordinary

Recorded this 4th day of December
1837   John Stewart Ordy

Fig. 7-47.

Andrew McCants in account with his wards
John L. B. McCants, Bartley L. McCants, Henry G. B.
McCants Sarah Jane McCants miners children
of the said Andrew from the date of his letters of
guardianship up to the first day of January 1856

Dr

Cash received from B McCrary Admr of John McCrary deceased
$770.00
One note on B McCrary due as 1st Dec 1856   2337.00
five slaves Isaac a man Matilda a woman & her
three children/value   2600.00
$5707.00

Cr

Nothing paid out

Georgia   In person appeared Andrew McCants
Taylor County who being duly sworn saith the above
return is true as stands stated
Sworn to this third day of November 1856

                              A McCants Gr

John Sturdivant
Ordinary
Recorded this 4th day of November
1856   John Sturdivant

Fig. 7-47.

> I found this record during the first week of November 1994. I thought that I had copied all of John McCrary's Estate records when I returned to the Lake Mary family History Center to recheck the roll of Vouchers. As I read the above document and saw my great great great grandmother Matilda "and her three children" with their names omitted, I screamed, "Why didn't he write their names?" I was excited and happy to have found this additional record but so disappointed not to see the names of Matilda's children. That is the "something else" in slave ancestral research.

Fig. 7-47A. 1860 Taylor Co., GA Slave Schedule of John McCrary's Estate distributees:

		Age of oldest female slave
1.	JOHN A. McCRARY	no females
2.	ANDREW J. McCANTS,	45 yrs.
3.	GILLAH F. McCRARY	35 yrs.
4.	BARTLEY McCRARY, Jr.,	60 yrs.
5.	HENRY B. McCRARY,	70 yrs.

> **1860 Slave Schedules of the Distributees (heirs) of John McCrary's Estate Division.** Two of the eight heirs, JOHN McCRARY and JAMES F. BERRY, were not in the 1860 Taylor Co. Slave Schedule.
>
> My slave ancestors: "Old Visues," Matilda, Buckey/Simon and Missouri are represented only by their gender and ages in one or more of these lists.

Fig. 7-47A.

> JANE G. McCRARY received "Old Visues." LUCIOUS C. McCRARY, her husband, is listed in the 1860 Taylor Co. Slave Schedule.

Fig. 7-47A Continued

6. LUCIOUS C. McCRARY, 1860 Taylor Co., GA Slave Schedule, p.104
   His oldest female slave is 48 yrs. old.

7. JAMES F. BERRY, not in 1860 Taylor Co. Slave Schedule.
   The 1850 Muscogee Co., GA. Census, p. 389, lists:

	Age	Sex		Birthplace
Falkenberry, James	44	M	Laborer	Richmond Co., GA.
Mary	25	F		Baldwin Co., GA.
John James	11	m		Talbot Co., GA.

8. JOHN McCRARY (son of John McCrary, deceased, c.1854) is not in 1860 Taylor Co. Slave Schedule.

   John B. McCrary, a relative is in 1850 and 1860 Slave Schedules. (See Fig.7-6, for 1850.)

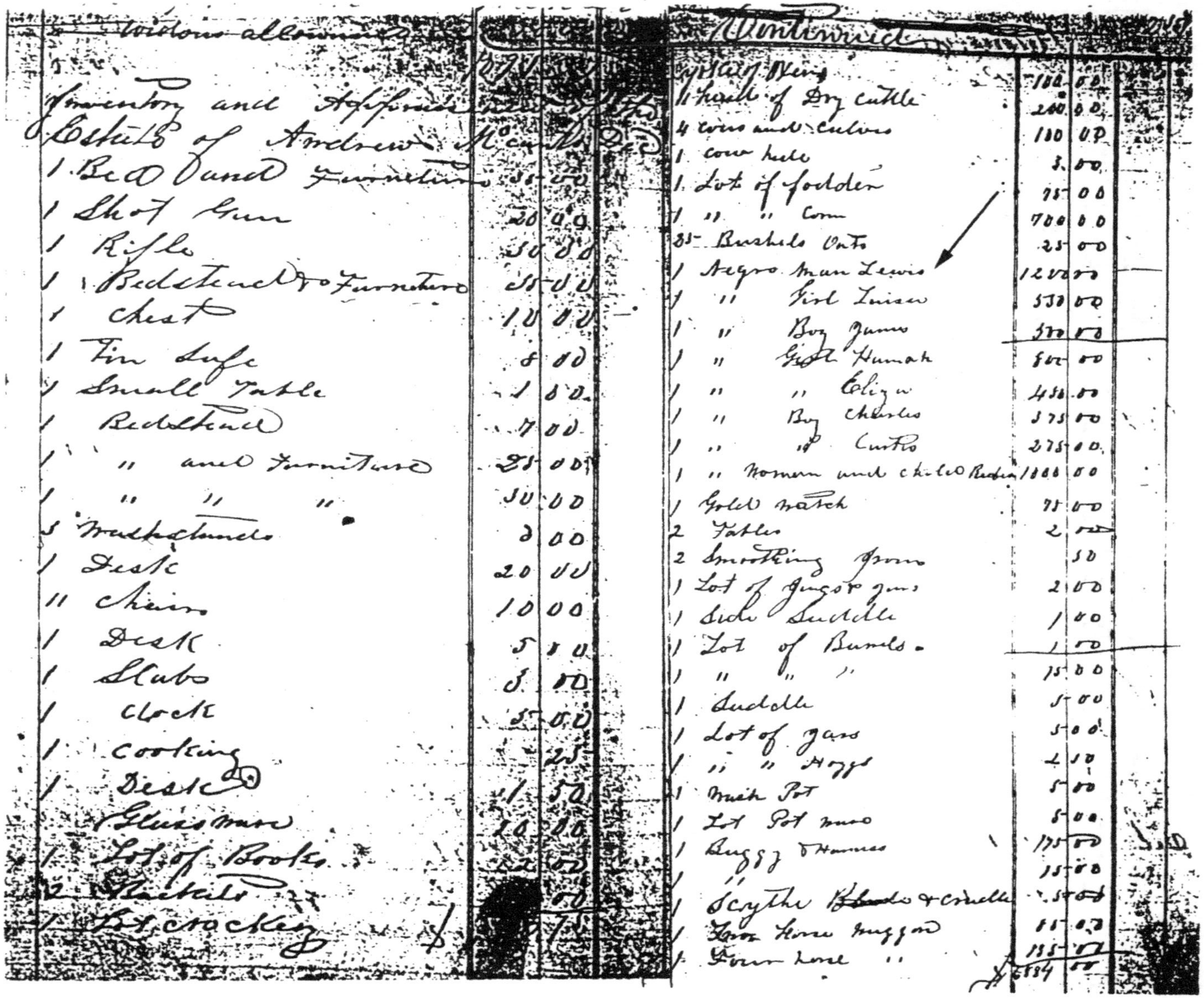

Fig. 7-47B.

Chapter Fourteen

THE DIVISION AND WHEREABOUTS OF "OLD VISUES"

In John McCrary's Estate Distribution, "Old Visues," valued at $25.00, was given to John McCrary's daughter, Jane McCrary. A "Return" (See Fig. 7-48.) filed by Andrew McCants, Administrator, read:

Paid Lucious Q. C. McCrary, who married Jane G. McCrary	
in Negroes as per division	$ 3425.50
from his notes as share this Estate	677.00
from the Sale of Land	2500.00
	6602.04
Taken from it his share	5933.90
Due Adm. from him	$ 688.03

Jane's father died before December 1854. She married Lucious 4 January 1855. The Estate Division was in December, 1856. Jane received in the "drawing": Old Viseus, Ned, Peter, Sal and her two children, Robert and Caroline. Apparently, my ancestor, called by so many names, Veny, Luesa, "Old Visues," did not spend her last days as a slave for Lucious and Jane McCrary. The age of "Old Visues," listed as Louisa in the 1870 Taylor County Census, was 90. In 1860, she would be about 80 years old.

Slave schedules listed only husbands and widows as slaveholders. In the Taylor Co. 1860 Slave Schedule, Lucious Q. C. McCrary had 16 slaves. The oldest female in his slave list was 48 years old (see Fig.7-47). Perhaps the old woman was not wanted by the young bride and Old Visues remained on the plantation with John McCrary's youngest son, Henry B. McCrary.

In 1850, Henry B. McCrary was not listed as a slave owner. However, after the death of his father in 1854, his name appeared in the 1860 Taylor Co. Slave Schedule with eight Negro slaves. The first one listed thus:

	Number	Age	Sex	Color	
McCrary, Henry B.	1	70	F	B	*She* may be Viseus.

Among the eight distributees named in John McCrary's "Distribution, "Henry B. McCrary had the oldest female slave in the 1860 Taylor County Slave Schedule (See Fig. 7-47A.) However, the 70 year old female slave could have been "Cassa" because Henry received a slave valued (the same as Veny/Viseus) at $100 from John McCrary's Inventory. There was no way to determine if the 70 year old female slave was Veny/Viseus or Cassa since names were omitted in slave schedules.

A TRIBUTE TO "OLD VISUES"

"OLD VISUES" my seventh generation slave ancestor, although old and valued at a mere $25.00, wherever she was during her last days before freedom, I pray that her master kept the advice given by a minister in 1859, quoted by James O. Breeden on pages 289-290 in <u>Advice Among Masters, The Ideal in Slave Management in the Old South</u>.

> Old and grayheaded servants are the heirlooms of the house. It is a pleasing thing to see an old family servant cherished....Let him talk on and enjoy the evening of life, and repose upon the fruits of labor past. Cast him not off, now that his once active limbs are stiff and his strong frame bowed...Beyond the sowing and the reaping He will be soon."...He bore your father in his arms and went afield with your grandfather when he was starting in life, and with those worn hands helped to lay the broad foundation of that estate which is yours today...indulge him...treat him with mingled tenderness and respect, and see to it that others treat him likewise...

Slave Ancestral Research

My kinfolks, Matilda, Buckey and Missouri were distributed to the minor children of Andrew McCants in John McCrary's Estate Distribution. But, did they move to their households? Andrew McCants, son-in-law of John McCrary, was married to John's daughter, Elizabeth, 14 Jan. 1844. Andrew, as guardian of John's grandchildren, was in charge of Matilda, Buckey and Misssouri. Buckey, I believe was the name given to Simon, husband of Matilda. A male slave called "Buck," changed it after freedom.

Slave Schedules of Andrew McCants before and after the
Estate Division of John McCrary in 1856

	1850 Slave Schedule Talbot Co.				1860 Slave Schedule Taylor Co.			
Slave Owner	Number	Age	Sex	Color	Number	Age	Sex	Color
ANDREW McCANTS	1	45	F	B	1	45	F	B
	1	16	M	B	1	25	F	B
	1	15	F	B	1	24	M	B
					1	24	M	B
					1	23	F	B
					1	14	M	B
					1	13	F	B
					1	6	F	B
					1	5	*F	B
					1	5	*F	B
					1	5	*M	B
					1	2	*M	B
					1	1 3/12	*M	B

Note:

Even though my ancestors were listed in lot No. 3 and distributed to Andrew McCants,(recorded 15 May 1856) Matilda does not appear to be in Andrew's 1860 slave list. Her age in 1860 was more than 25. If Andrew kept the 1850 slaves, he should have a 55 year old female. Perhaps precise age records were not kept.

Slave houses ..3
*Children born and added after John McCrary's death

Andrew J. McCants is deceased in 1862. His Inventory listed no slaves from John McCrary. He had one man, Lewis; three girls, Luisa, Hannah and Eliza; three boys, James, Charles and Curtis; a woman and child Rubin. (See Fig. 7-47B.)

> Jeremiah C. McCants Guardian in account current
> with Mary C. E. McCants & Sarah E. McCants Minors
>   Dr. to Minors
> To amount received from Andrew McCants Administrator
> of George R. McCants for Sarah E. McCants $4...
> To 2 negroes Mahaley a woman 17 years of age
> and Nash a boy 3 years old Received from Andrew
> McCants Administrator of George R. McCants
>   Sarah E. McCants
> To amount received from Andrew McCants A.
> of George R. McCants for Mary C. E. McCants $52
> To 2 negroes received of Andrew McCants Adm.
> of George R. McCants for Mary C. E. McCants namd
> a girl 6 or 7 years old & Eddy a girl 8 or 9 years old
> recd from J. B. McCants Estate in division January 22nd 1864 $721
> Georgia } In Person appeared before me Ordinary in
> Taylor County } and for said County Jeremiah C. McCants
> who being duly sworn says that the above return
> is just and true as it stands stated. J.C.M.
> Sworn to and subscribed before me March 2nd 1861
>   J. J. Huff Ordinary
> Recorded March 25 - 1861
>   J. J. Huff Ordinary

Fig. 7-47C. Record of transfer of two slaves, Jane, a girl 6 or 7 yrs. and Eddy, a girl 8 or 9 yrs. (The name "Jane" is readable on the microfilm copy of the original record.)

Note. "Mahaley, a woman 17 years of age..." above may be the "Ralia/Halia" listed in John McCrary's Estate Division, given to Andrew McCants. (Fig. 7-47) The date of the above record is 1861, five years after John McCrary's Division. Andrew McCants had a son, George McCants, named in John McCrary's Division and Andrew is Administrator of this George R. McCants. Furthermore, Andrew's Inventory in 1862 (Fig. 7-47B) listed none of the slaves transferred to him from John McCrary's Estate. Since "Ralia or Halia" was listed in the same group with Matilda, Becky/Bucky and Zussre (Missoury) in John McCrary's Estate Division, Mahaley may be my ancestor, Matilda's child. (See Fig. 7-47.)

Another record (Fig.7-47C) indicates that the Negro slaves continued to move after the "Distribution."

    Jeremiah C. McCants, Guardian in account current with Mary C. E. McCants and Sarah L. McCants minors

                        Dr to Miners

To amount received from Andrew McCants -Administrator of George R. McCants for Sarah L. McCants $447.23

To 2 negroes Mahaley a woman 17 years of age and Wash a boy 3 years old Received from Andrew McCants Administrator of George R. McCants from

    Sarah L. McCants

To amount received from Andrew McCants Adminis of George R. McCants for Mary C. E. McCants- $824.54

To 2 negroes received of Andrew McCants Admr of George R. McCants for Mary C. E. McCants named JANE a girl 6 or 7 years old and Eddy a girl 8 or 9 years old to amount recd from J. B. McCants Estate in Division January 22 1864   721.32

Georgia   In person appeared before me Ordinary in

Taylor County   <u>and for Said County Jeremiah C. McCants</u>

who being duly Sworn Says that the above return is Just and true as it Stands stated J. C. McCants

Sworn to and subscribed before me March 2nd 1861

                        J. J. Huff Ordinary

Recorded March 25, 1861...

Fig. 7-47C.

Gilly McCrary had drawn EDDY in the "Distribution" in 1854 from John McCrary's Estate Division. The above "Return" transferred her to Mary C. E. McCants (or another slave girl named Eddy). The underlined entry appeared to have been added after 1861. JANE may be my ancestor, Matilda's child. Matilda's daughter, Missoury is listed with a sister, Jane Coleman in the 1920 Census of Bibb County, Georgia. See Fig. 7-14B.

Who is the mother of Mahaley? Is she Matilda? (See Fig. 7-47C.) Is she Phillis? (See Fig. 7-47D.) More research is needed to find the answer.

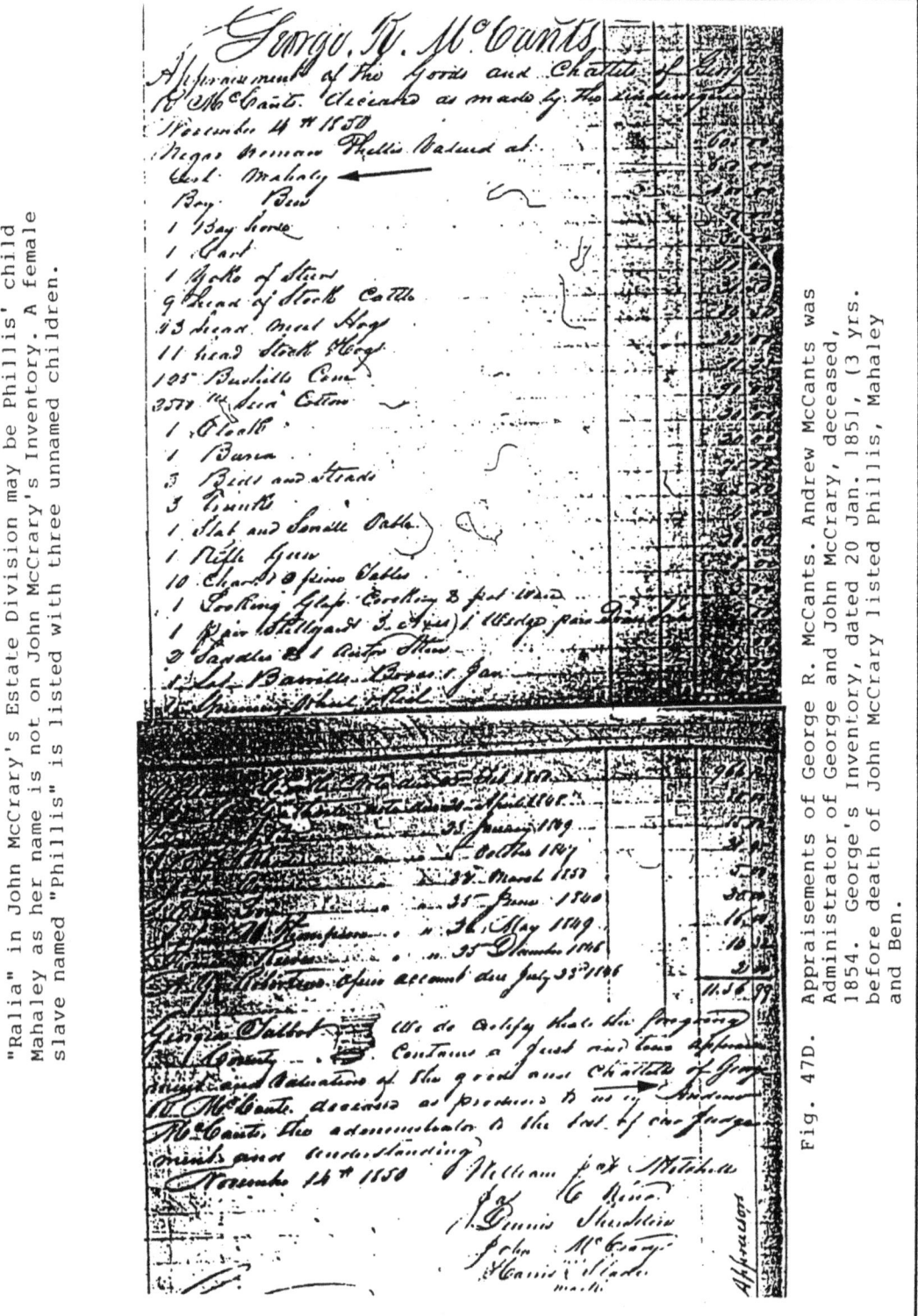

Fig. 47D. Appraisements of George R. McCants. Andrew McCants was Administrator of George and John McCrary, deceased, 1854. George's Inventory, dated 20 Jan. 1851, (3 yrs. before death of John McCrary listed Phillis, Mahaley and Ben.

"Ralia" in John McCrary's Estate Division may be Phillis' child Mahaley as her name is not on John McCrary's Inventory. A female slave named "Phillis" is listed with three unnamed children.

JOHN McCRARY

(1789-1854)

ESTATE DIVISION SUMMARY STATEMENTS

The estate of John McCrary dec'd in account
with Bart J. McCrary, Admr. from date
up to this date 2nd of June 1857
This return contains a full statement of a
full statement of the estate as came to hand as well
as the am't due each distributee & the amount
paid them

Amount Received
In Cash $4160.00
Am't Sale of Perishable property   6594.51
Negroes Valued at   23105.00
Lands Sold for   20000.00
Cash Collected on notes after inventory   116.00
Full am't of Estate $53975.51

To the Estate for amount paid out
Paid out as per past return   4404.80
Commissions on am't of Estate of $4744   1349.38
Paid attorneys fee   500.00
" Collecting fees   35.00
                                          $6304.18

After deducting the amount paid out for expenses
It leaves   8)47471.33
to be divided among 8 distributees $5933.91
which being done leaves to each the sum of

Paid to Gilly H. McCrary in negroes
    according to division   2775.00
    from Sale of Land   2900.00
    from Sale of Perishable property   349.00
                                          $6024.00
This am't of his share taken from the sum left
to the distribution $90.09

Fig. 7-48. Estate Division summary Statements. John McCrary dec'd. 1854. Taylor Co., GA.

The Estate of John McCrary Deceased in account
with Bartley McCrary admr from last ...
up to this date 2nd June 1857

This return contains a re cappitulation
of said full statement of the estate as ...
as the ... due each distributee and the amount paid them.

Amount Received

In cash	$4160.00
amt sales of Perishable property	6596.51
Negros valued at	23105.00
Land sold for	20000 00
Cash collected on notes after inventory	114.00
Full amt of Estate	$53975.51

Dr the Estate for amount paid out

Paid out as per first return	4604.80
Commission on acct of Estate	1349.38
Paid Attorney fee	500.00
Collected fees	35.00
	$6505.18

After deducting the amount paid out for expenses
it leaves   8)   47471.33
to be divided amoung 8 distributees $5933.91
which being done leaves to each the
sum of

paid to Gilly F McCrary in Negros according to division	2775.00
from sale of land	2900.00
from sale of perishable property	349.00

This amt of his shares taken from the leaves him
in debted to administrator $904.09

Fig. 7-48

[Paid ... McCray who was ...]
Paid [him in negroes as per division]   3[?]
[in the sale of land]   2[?]
from Amt. Sales in his own notes   2,9[?]
in Cash   50.[?]
                                                    6,147.[?]
The amt. of Shares taken from it   5,933.97
  Leaves due Administrator   113.10

Paid Lucius D. G. McCray who married [Sarah ...]
In negroes as per division   3,425.00
from his notes as due the estate   677.04
from the sale of Land   2,500.00
                                                    6,602.04
Taken from it his Share   5,933.91
due Admr. from him $ 668.13

Paid Jonathan P. McCray in negroes
as per division   2,700.00
paid him in his note due estate   765.03
Paid from sale land   2,500.00
                                                    5,965.03
                                                    5,935.91
Due from him to Estate   29.12

Paid John A.G. McCray in negroes   3,000.00
in his own notes due estate   813.72
from sale land   2,000.00
                                                    5,813.72
Takes off his part [...]
Admr. indebted to him   -$ 119.75

Fig. 7-48.

Paid James F. Berry was a distributee
    Paid him in negroes as per division   3200.00
      from sale of land   2500.00
      from amt sal in his own note   2900.50
      in cash   50.66
                                                                6047.00
This amt of share taken from it   5933.91
    Leaves due administrator   113.10

Paid Lucious C, McCrary who married Jane G. McCrary
    In Negroes as per division $3425.50
    From his note as due this estate   677.54
    From the sale of land   2500.00
                                                                6602.04
Taken from it his share   5933.91
    due admr from him   668.13

Paid Jonathan P McCrary in Negros
    as per division   2700.00
    paid him in his note due estate   763.03
    paid from Sale land   2500.00
                                                                5963.03
                                                                 5955.91

Due from him to admr   29.12
Paid John A.J. McCrary in Negros   3000.00
in his own notes due Estate   813.76
from sale Land   2000.00
Take of his part leaves   5813.76
Admr indebted to him   -$119.75

Fig. 7-48

Paid Henry Bell Trump

his Negros according to division	2933 ??
from Sale of Lands	1970 ??
Interest on notes due estate	649.??
	5954.??
take off his amount	5933.5?
Due from him	$20.77

Andrew McCants Guardian for his Children
paid him in Negros according to division 2600.??
from Sale of land   2500.00
from Sale of Perishable property   144.30
                                          $5244.31

Due him on final Settlement $689.24

This return includes the whole management of the estate

Georgia } Personally came Bartlett McLeary
Laurens County } who being duly sworn deposes and saith
that this return is correct and true to the
best of his knowledge and belief
Sworn to and subscribed before me   Bartley McLeary
this 6th day of July 1837
   John Thomas??? act Ordinary

Recorded this 21st day of August 1837
                John Thomas?????
                   Ordinary

Fig. 7-48.

367

Paid Henry B. McCrary
    in Negros according to division   2455.00
    from sale of land   2900.00
    Interest on notes due Estate   449.22
    Take off his amount   5954.22
        5933.51
  Due from him   20.71

Andrew McCants guardian for his Children
paid him in Negros according to division   2600.00
  from Sale of land   2500.00
  from Sale of Perishable property   144.30
        $5244.31

    Due him on final Settlement $689.26

This returnm includes ... management of
the <u>estate</u>

Georgia |Personally came Bartllet McCrary
Taylor County |who being duly sworn depose
and saith that this return is correct and true to the
best of my knowledge and belief
Sworn to and subscribed before me| Bartley McCrary
this 6th day of July 1857 |
  John Sturdivant Ordinary |

Recorded this 20th day of August 1857
        John Sturdivant
            Ordinary

Fig. 7-48

THE LAST MILE

There would be one final trip to end 14 years of research. That trip included visits to the National Archives and the DAR Library in Washington, D.C. while attending the Sixteenth Annual Conference of The Afro-American Historical and Genealogical Society, 29 April 1994 through 1 May 1994. This project began in August 1980.

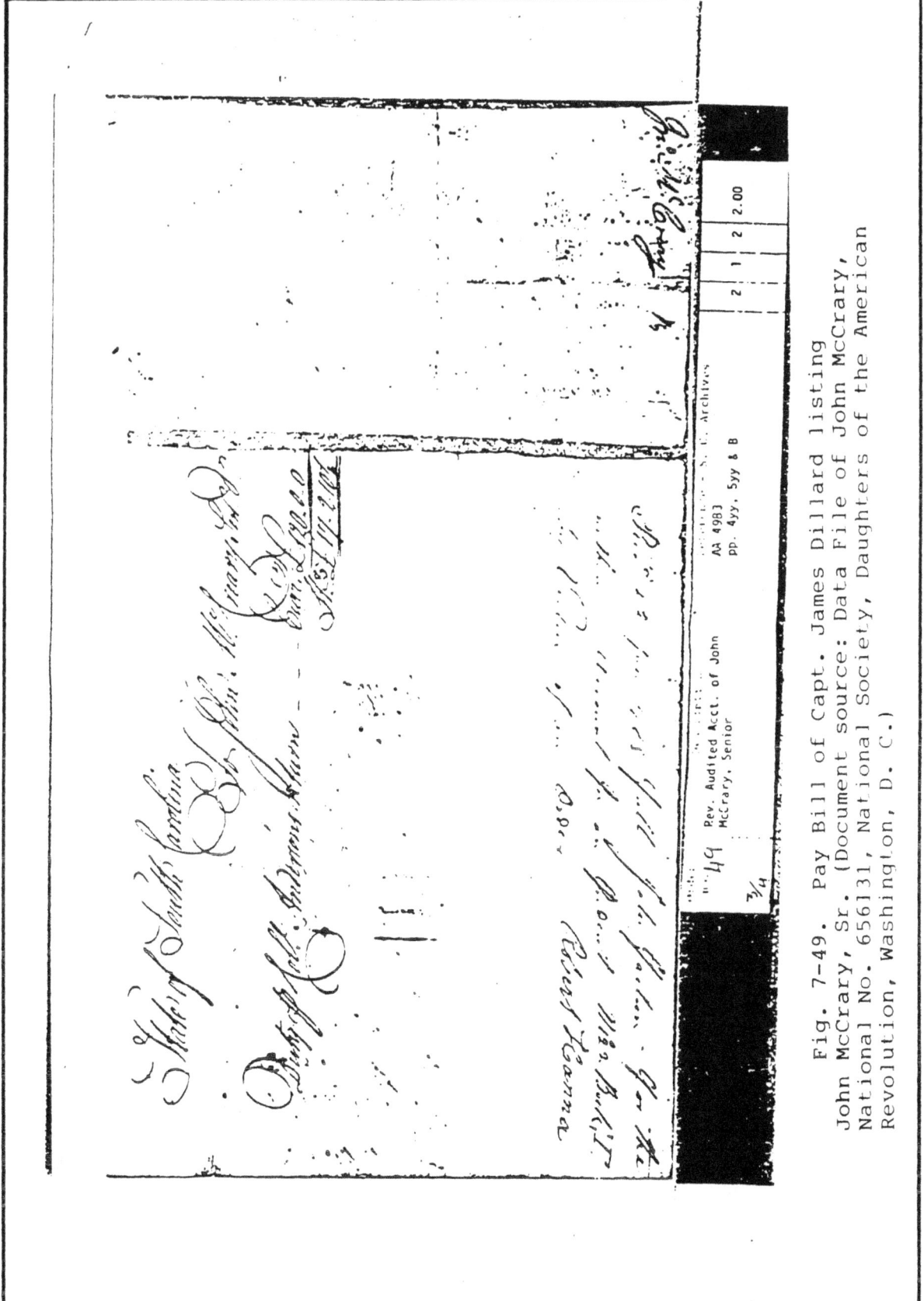

Fig. 7-49. Pay Bill of Capt. James Dillard listing John McCrary, Sr. (Document source: Data File of John McCrary, National No. 656131, National Society, Daughters of the American Revolution, Washington, D. C.)

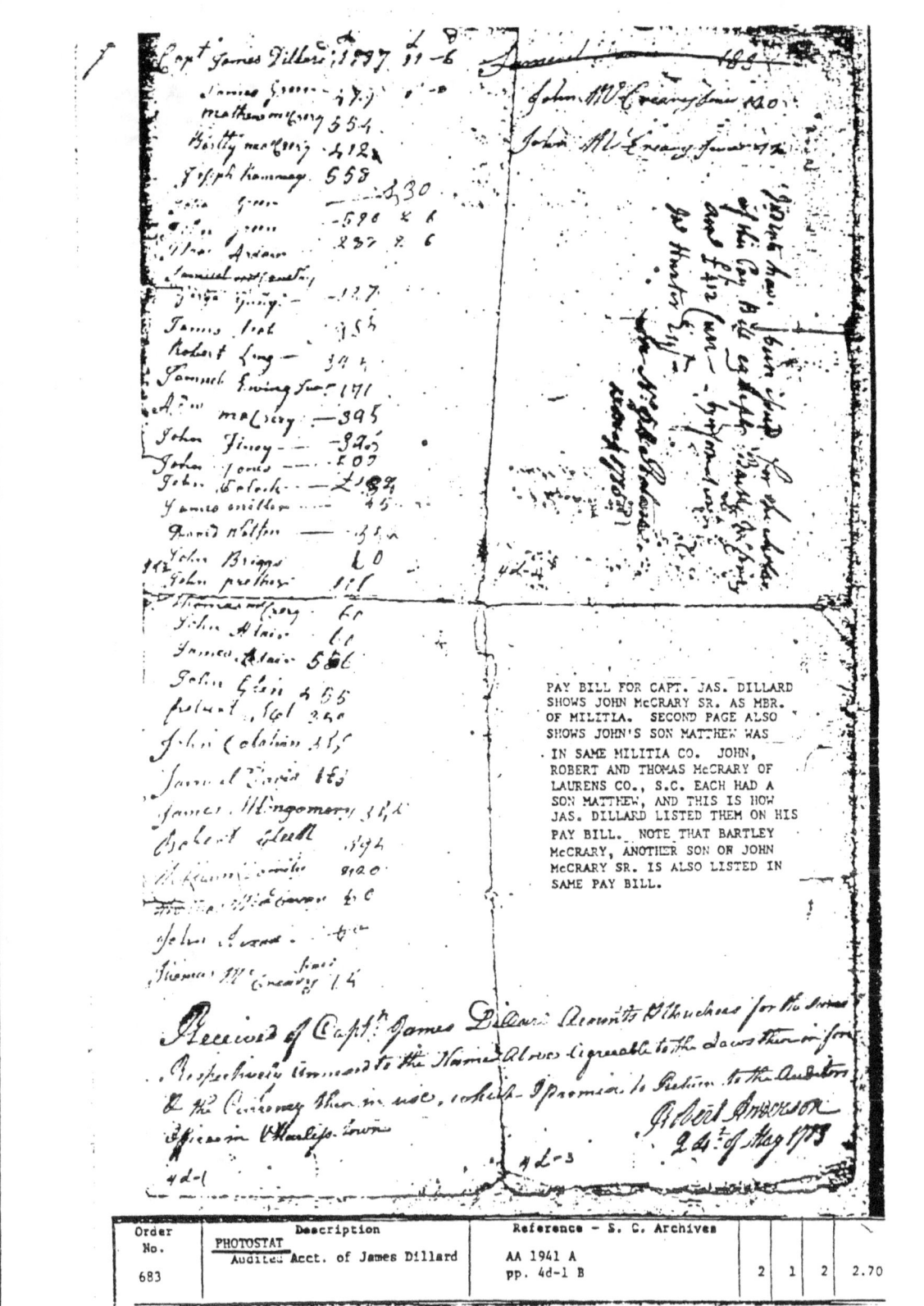

Fig. 7-49. Pay Bill of Capt. James Dillard. A Revolutionary War Record copied from DAR Records, Washington, D.C.

PROOF OF REV. SERVICE: NOTE THAT AMOUNT MATCHES THE SUM ON PAY BILL OF CAPT. JAS. DILLARD

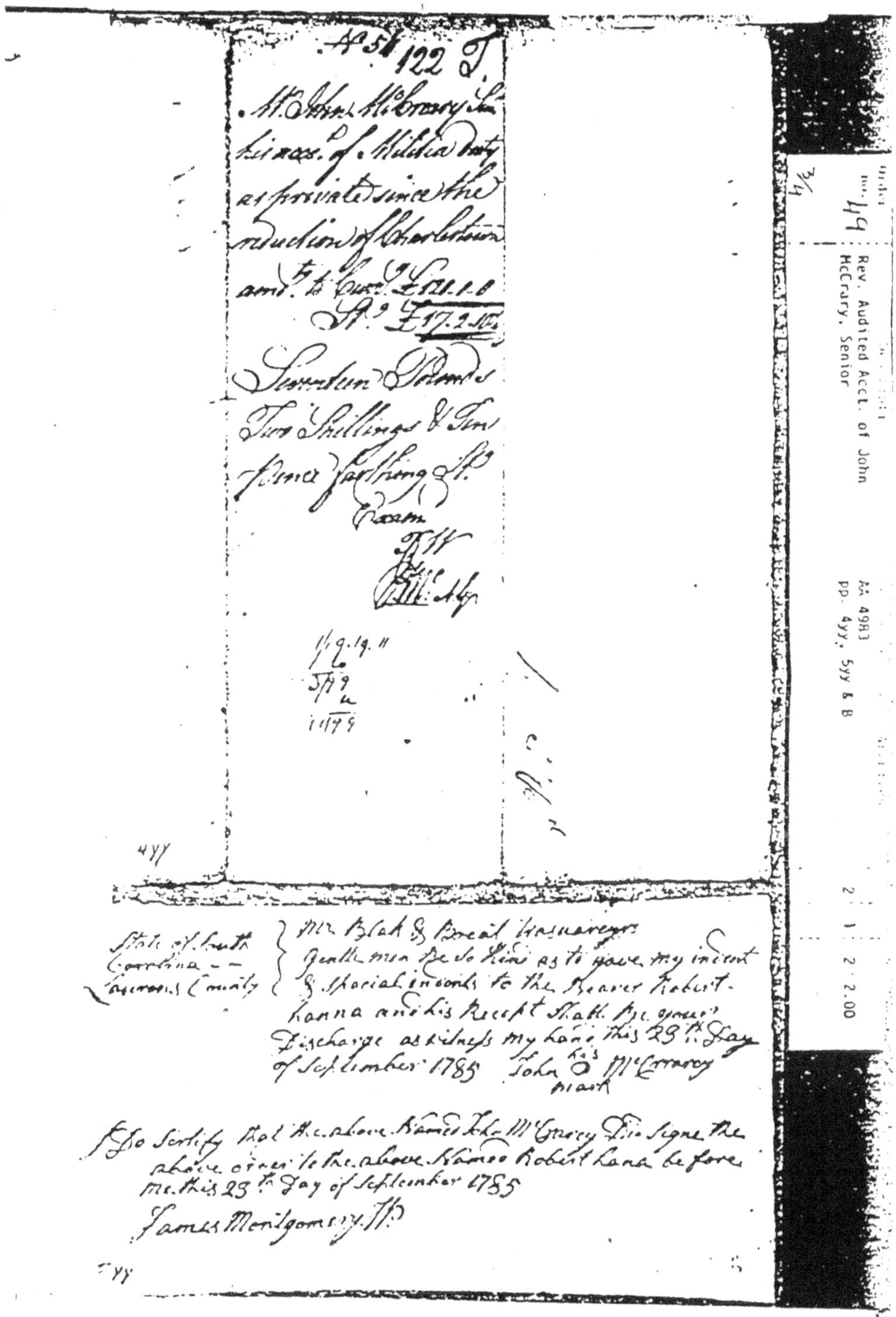

Fig. 7-49. Pay Bill of Capt. James Dillard. A Revolutionary War Record copied from DAR Records, Washington, D.C.

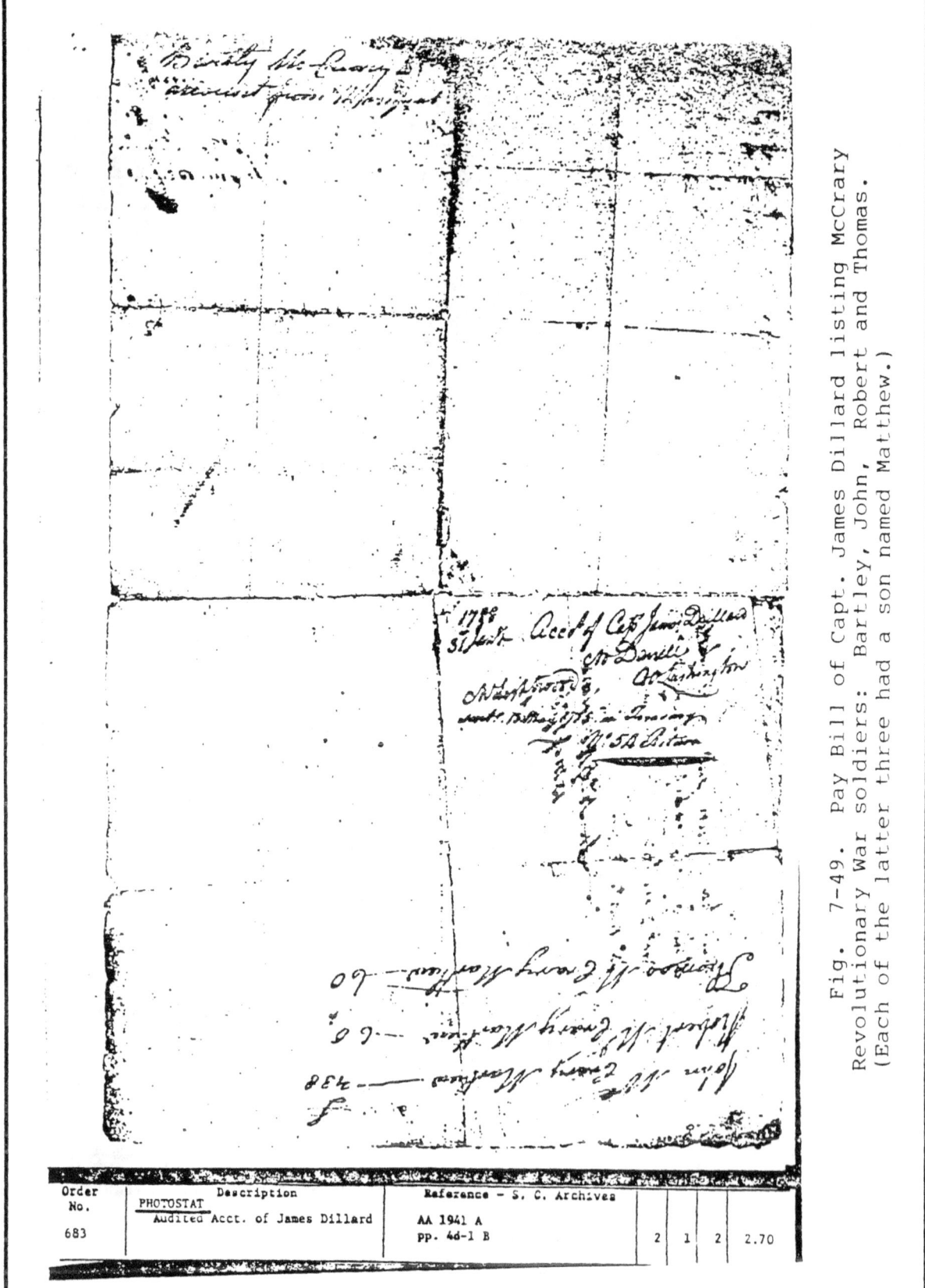

Fig. 7-49. Pay Bill of Capt. James Dillard listing McCrary Revolutionary War soldiers: Bartley, John, Robert and Thomas. (Each of the latter three had a son named Matthew.)

Chapter Fifteen

REVELATIONS FROM REVOLUTIONARY WAR RECORDS

I never dreamed that my research would lead to records at the Daughters of the American Revolution Library (DAR Library) in Washington, DC. However, it did.

Captain James Dillard had three McCrary Revolutionary War soldiers, believed brothers from Laurens County, SC in his Militia unit: John, Robert and Thomas McCrary and each had a son named Matthew. Figure 7-49 is a copy of the Pay Bill for James Dillard showing how he listed them. He also had two sons of John McCrary, Sr. in his Militia Co., a John McCrary, Jr. and a Bartley McCrary. The document is dated "24 of May 1783," six months before the last British soldiers were withdrawn from New York City. The Revolutionary War had ended.

This document (Pay Bill) was the beginning of my understanding of kin relationships within the McCrary family. By putting together information submitted by several applicants for membership in the DAR, I can relate the following story of the McCrary family and their relationship to my slave ancestors as they trekked from one McCrary household to the next.

THE BEGINNING

The McCrary men were American patriots. Both fathers and sons served with distinction and valor. Robert McCrary became a Colonel and served in St. Augustine, Fl. They had close family ties, adhered to a strict pattern of naming sons in each generation after fathers and grandfathers of previous generations. Daughters married cousins and sometimes two sisters married two brothers of the same family.

Daughters' names were repeated in generations. Uncles became guardians of nephews and nieces. McCrary sons and sons-in-law served as administrators of McCrary estates. McCrary family members received equal shares in " Estate Divisions" following the death of a McCrary member. Most made huge land purchases, were very wealthy successful planters and owned slaves.

The McCrary estate records listed my slave ancestors as they were transferred within the McCrary family. Data Files on the McCrary Revolutionary War soldiers enabled me to write the "Revelations" that follow and construct a Transfer Chart with notes on movements of the McCrary slaves with some understanding of McCrary family ties.

Along with the Data Files, early Georgia tax lists, Baldwin County court minutes and copies of McCrary estate records, I was finally able to narrate the McCrary family relationships with a clearer understanding of connections between the various types of records I had accumulated.

I had learned well. In order to adequately trace *my* slave ancestral routes, the research demanded that I locate records to *follow* the McCrary family move from South Carolina to four counties in Georgia; and secondly, acquire as many records as possible generated from within the slaveholding families, then study to understand the correlation between the records.

The chronology, "Revelations," illustrates this thread of correlation. McCrary names in repetition required conscientious study to understand family relationships and correlation of the McCrary documents I had accumulated.

Slave Ancestral Research

REVELATIONS
(From the DAR Data Files)

YEAR	
1783	Revolutionary War ended.

John McCrary, Sr., who served under Capt. Dillard, was born, c.1735. His wife Jane, predeceased him, perhaps in South Carolina.

LAURENS CO. SOUTH CAROLINA, McCrary Land Purchase

1786   "14 February 1786 - 16 January 1787 JOHN McCRARY and his wife, Jane, of Laurens District, sold to CHARLES HUTCHINGS, of same for 257 pounds sterling 300 acres located on Northside of Duncan's Creek, bounded all sides on vacant land when originally granted to DANIEL MOTE and recorded in Secretary State Office Book 3 BBB page 370 and from DANIEL MOTE, to JOHN McCRARY 2 August 1770. Wit: JAMES MONTGOMERY, GEORGE ROSS, ROBERT McCRARY. (from Laurens Co., SC Deed Bk. A., pp. 78-80)

1788   Georgia became a state. Between 1784 and 1820, thousands of Americans moved to Georgia. Many early settlers came from North and South Carolina and Virginia. Some came to Georgia directly from England and Scotland. Land was plentiful, cheap and available in Land Lotteries. The John McCrary, Sr. family from Laurens Co., SC joined in the influx. They qualified for drawings in the Georgia Land Lotteries by having served in the Revolutionary War.

McCRARY FAMILY MOVE TO GEORGIA

1788   From Wilkes County Deed Book DD, p. 221, dated 1 December 1788, Henry Townsend, Jonathan McCrary and Wadsworth are witnesses for the sale of 179 acres of land to Matthew McCrary. (This record placed the McCrary family in Georgia.) John McCrary, Sr., his four sons and daughter left South Carolina, exact date unknown.

1790   First Federal Census Taken - Georgia does not have a 1790 Census.

HANCOCK COUNTY, GA TAX RECORDS listed:
1794   Bartlett McCrary (Hancock Co. created in 1793.)
1796   John McCrary

REVELATIONS

WARREN COUNTY, GA. TAX LIST

1801 +Matthew McCrary

1803 Baldwin County, GA. created from Creek Indian land

1804 HANDCOCK CO., GA TAX RECORD listed:
- Bartley McCrary
- John McCrary
- Jonathan McCrary
- Robert McCrary

1805 Georgia Land Lottery participants:

	County
Bartley McCrary	Hancock
John McCrary	"
Jonathan McCrary	"
Isaac McCrary	Washington
+Mathew McCrary, Sr.	Warren
Mathew McCrary, Jr.	"
Robert McCrary	"

BALDWIN CO., GA TAX RECORDS listed:

1807 Bartley McCRARY
John McCrary

1808 Robert McCrary, had 2 slaves

BALDWIN CO., GA. INFERIOR COURT MINUTES
4th April 1808 p. 85

1808 Ordered: That the following hands work on the road from ...Bridge in Milledgeville to Pinch Gut viz: *JOHNATHAN McCRARY & hands, JOHN McCRARY, Richard Magriff, Thomas Lamar hands, Barrow & hands, BARTLEY McCRARY, Abel Woods, Elijah Smead, Tilman Buckner Wilder, --Tilly, David Chambers, Isaac Morgan and William Goode, and that Gillah Freeney be and he is hereby appointed overseer of the same.

This record placed *Johnathan, John and Bartley McCrary in Baldwin Co., Ga. in 1808. ("hands" referred to Johnathan's slaves.)

BALDWIN CO., GA, ESTATE RECORDS

1808 *Jonathan McCrary, died before December, 1808

BALDWIN CO., GA TAX RECORDS listed:

1809
Name	Slaves	Land
Bartley McCrary	15 slaves	15 acres land
John McCrary Sr.	7 slaves	
William McCrary	0 slaves	

WILKINSON CO., GA TAX RECORDS listed:

1809 Isaac McCrary   5 slaves)

Slave Ancestral Research

REVELATIONS

BALDWIN CO., GA TAX RECORDS listed:

1810
- Bartley McCrary — 14 slaves
- John McCrary, Sr. — 7 slaves
- John McCrary, Jr. — 0 slaves
- Isaac McCrary — 0 slaves
- James B. McCrary — 0 slaves

1814   John McCrary, Sr. died in Baldwin County

Although the 1810 Baldwin Co. Tax Digest listed a John McCrary, Jr.,this name does not appear in the Division of Estate record for John McCrary, Sr.

BALDWIN CO., GA TAX RECORD listed:

1818   John McCrary, Jr.   2 slaves
One slave was "Clary" received in 1815 from Jonathan McCrary's Estate Division. (See Record Group No. 3.)

WARREN COUNTY, GA ESTATE RECORDS

1809   Letty/Letitia McCrary, daughter of John McCrary, Sr., was married to the Matthew McCrary who died in 1809. He lived in Warren County, Ga. This Matthew was the son of Col. Robert McCrary, who served under Capt. Dillard. Letty married her cousin. Robert McCrary and John McCrary, Sr. were brothers. (See Record Group No.2)

1816   +Matthew McCrary(d.1816) and the Matthew McCrary(d.1809) both lived in Warren County at the same time. The latter Matthew was described as "the Lessor" as he was considerably much less wealthy than Matthew (d.1816), son of John McCrary, Sr.

BALDWIN CO., GA ESTATE RECORDS

1808   *Jonathan McCrary predeceased his father, John McCrary, Sr. In the estate division of Jonathan McCrary, my slave ancestor, Luveser is allotted to daughter Jane. (Jane is named after her grandmother Jane, stated above as having died in South Carolina.)

1813   A John McCrary married Jane McCrary in Baldwin County 12 March 1813, believed to be John McCrary, Jr., son of John McCrary, Sr., Revolutionary War soldier.

(Another John McCrary in Warren County married Amelia Milly Beall 27 Feb. 1808. This John McCrary is believed to be the son of Matthew McCrary, d.1809 in Warren County. This Warren County Matthew McCrary is the son of Col. Robert McCrary.)

REVELATIONS

1815   In Jonathan McCrary's Estate Division, John McCrary is given a slave, Clary. (See Record Group No.3.) William Grigg is named the guardian of Jonathan's minor children: Isaac, Rachel and Jane. Isaac McCrary died c.1820

1822   Jane, daughter of Jonathan McCrary, married James McCrary, (8 Jan. 1822, Baldwin Co.) her cousin and son of Bartley McCrary, Jonathan's brother.

James McCrary pays William Grigg for the slave Luveser. (See Record Group No.3.)

1823   Letty McCrary, daughter of John McCrary, Sr., died Warren Co., Ga.

1826   Bartley McCrary, who died in 1826, was the son of John McCrary, Sr. (d. 1814). Bartley had a son, William McCrary, (d.1816) Wilkinson Co. Ga.(See Record Group No.1.)

Bartley McCrary became the guardian of the minors of William McCrary. But after Bartley's death, his son, Bartley, Jr. was guardian for awhile until Bartley's son, Matthew became the guardian of William's minors.

After Bartley's son, Matthew, who lived in Talbot Co. Ga., became guardian of his brother, William's minor children, all of the records on William's slaves were transferred to Talbot County court records. Talbot County Returns showed the nine slaves were hired out yearly over many years. (See RECORD GROUP No. 6).

1826   ALBERT G. BECKHAM received a share in Bartley's Estate Division. Beckham was included in DAR Data File National Number 653-472. He was married to Bartley McCrary's daughter, Mary, 7 April 1825. Albert died in Elmore County, Ala. in c.1869.

TAYLOR COUNTY, GA. ESTATE RECORDS

1854   John McCrary, Jr. son of John McCrary (d.1814), died in Taylor County, Ga. He had four of my slave ancestors in his Estate Division:

Matilda, Becky/Bucky, Zussre/Missouri and an old woman named Veny, believed to be Luveser, who was first owned by Jonathan McCrary. (See Record Group No. 7.)

REVELATIONS

1855   John McCrary's (Jr.) Estate Division (son of John McCrary, Sr., Revolutionary War Soldier) transferred my ancestors to Andrew McCants, his son-in-law and to his daugher, Jane McCrary. Jane becomes the wife of Lucious Q. C. McCrary in 1855, one year after her father, John McCrary, Jr.'s death.

Although name repetition in the McCrary family was apparent, I was able to see McCrary family relationships and correlation between the numerous McCrary records I had, only after reading the Data Files at the DAR Library.

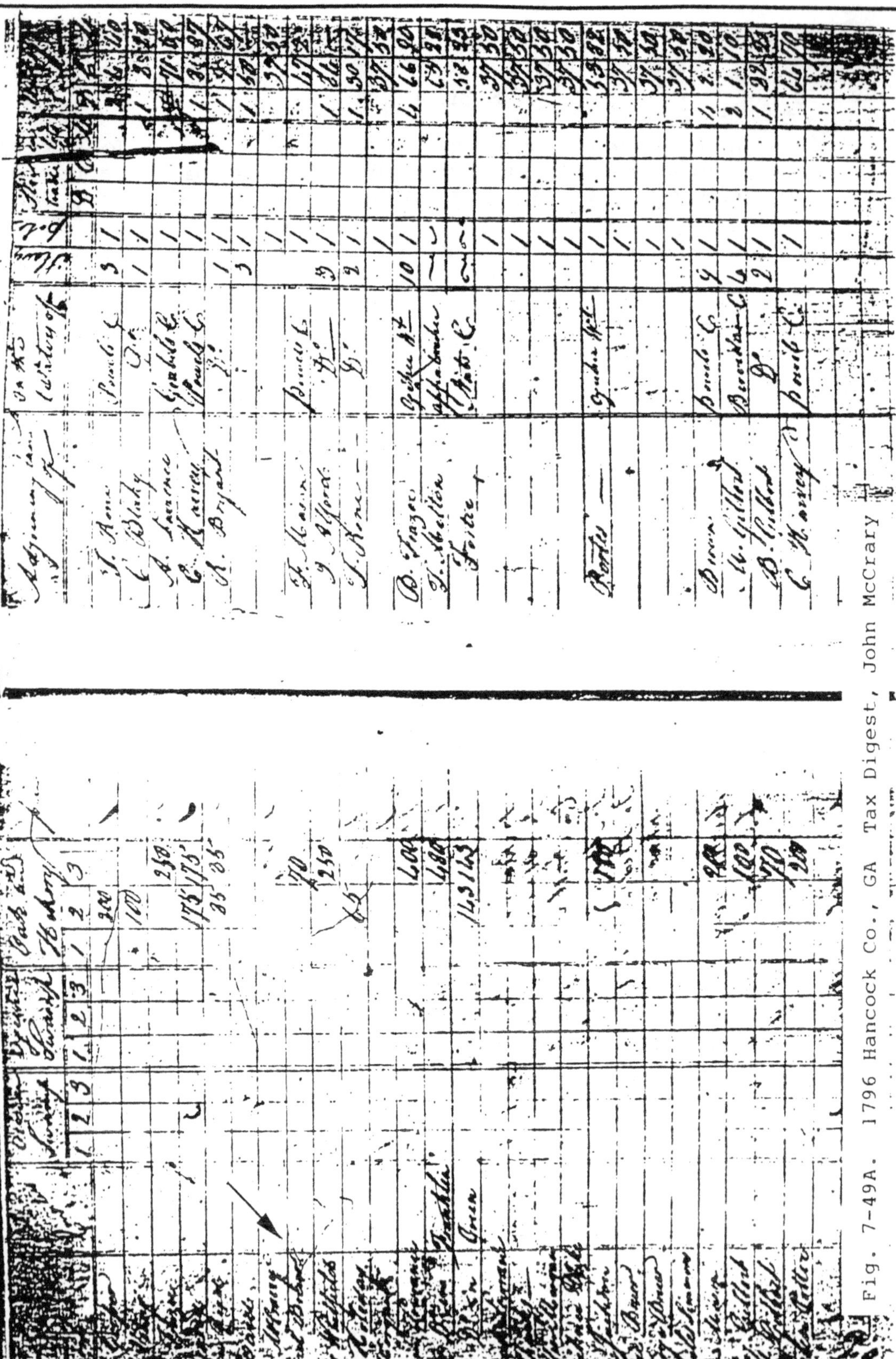

Fig. 7-49A. 1796 Hancock Co., GA Tax Digest, John McCrary

Chapter Sixteen

THE TRANSFER CHART

In order to trail the McCrary slaves during each transfer, I made a record of each family's children from their "Division of Estate Record" and noted marriages from many sources as indicated on previous pages of this text.

First, I placed the McCrary estate records in RECORD GROUPS Nos. 1-7. Revolutionary War records at the DAR Library led to additional McCrary estate records in Warren County, Georgia. Subsequently, I ended with Inventory, Sales and Division of Estate Records for most of John McCrary, Senior's family.

To distinguish persons with the same names, death dates and "son of" were used for identification. Information in the chart was taken from microfilmed probate records from several Georgia counties: Warren, Baldwin, Talbot and Taylor.

The "Key to Transfer Chart" which follows, serves to clarify the McCrary family relations in the "TRANSFER CHART" which graphically illustrates the movement of the McCrary Negro slaves.

KEY TO TRANSFER CHART

Death Date or Date of Record	NAME	Number of Slaves	RECORD GROUP
1808	^Jonathan McCrary (Son of John McCrary, Sr.)	7	No.3*
1814	John McCrary, Sr. (Father of Jonathan, Matthew, Isaac, Bartley and Letty)	12	No.2*
1816	^Matthew McCrary (Son of John McCrary, Sr.)	15	
1816	William McCrary (Son of Bartley McCrary)	9	No.6*
1817	^Isaac McCrary (Son of John McCrary, Sr.)	9	No.4*
1825	^Letty McCrary (Daughter of John McCrary, Sr.)	3	No.2*
1826	^Bartley McCrary (Son of John McCrary, Sr.)	32	No.1*
1827	Robert McCrary (Son of Bartley McCrary)	4	No.5*
1842	Jane McCrary/Jenny McCrary Poindexter, daughter of Bartley McCrary)	4	No.1*
1854	*John McCrary (Son of John McCrary, Sr. Revolutionary War Soldier)	33	No.7

^Sons and daughter of John McCrary, Sr. *See copies of the original lists in RECORD GROUPS Nos. 1-7.

The final Division of Estate and Sales records were used to chart the transfer of the Negro slaves. Slave names appear as in the original records.

A few names appeared in the "Estate Inventories" but were omitted in the "Division of the Estate" records. Also names appeared in the Division and not in the Inventory.

The research is endless. To find the missing names would require careful study of all county probate records, including marriage connections. It is possible that the slave/s died. Sometimes several years passed between the date of the estate inventory and final settlement.

McCrary slaves were transferred within their families to sons, daughters and others. Husbands of married daughters were recorded in the Estate Divisions as the new owners.

```
    1808                 1815
Baldwin Co. GA.    Estate Division
         JONATHAN McCRARY
      Negro Slaves Transferred To:
         VALUE
--------------------------------------

man    Rueben  $500   Isaac McCrary
                         (minor)

man    Jo      $550   Able Herrington

girl   Clary   $400   JOHN McCRARY

girl   Beck    $300   Wiley Riddle

child  *LUVESER $150  Jane
                        (minor)

boy    Jack    $150   Rachel McCrary
                         (minor)

woman  Winny   $425   Sary Calton


         Jonathan McCrary, owner
of **LUVESER, my Seventh Generation ancestor,
Great, great, great, great grandma Luveser.
```

```
1817                    1818
Baldwin Co., GA.      Estate Sale

       Isaac McCrary
Negro Slaves Sold to:
--------------------------------------
                 VALUE
man    Dick    $1015   John McCrary

woman  Dicey    706    John McCrary

boy    Stephen  333    John McCrary

girl   Betsey   350    John McCrary

boy    Lewis    200    John McCrary

woman  Jude     670    William McCrary

girl   Lucy     600    William McCrary

man    Peter   1003    William McCrary

man    Sam      755    Bartley McCrary

A family: Dick, Dicey, Stephen, Betsey &
          Lewis
Maybe a family: Jude, Lucy and Peter
```

Luveser

```
1846                     1847
Baldwin Co., GA.      Estate Sale

       JENNY POINDEXTER
   Negro Slaves Sold TO:
              VALUE

woman   *Mary
26 yrs.        and

child   Rhoda   $675    B. G. Morris
2 yrs.

girl
6 yrs.  Harriet $300    Jesse Thomas

boy     Hampton $300    Thomas Harris
3 yrs.
```

*Mary, a young mother, is sold away from two of her children. See RECORD GROUP NO. 1. for copies of the documents.

Jane Poindexter had received two boys: my ancestor, VICEY'S Josh, and a boy, Patrick from her father, Bartley McCrary, Sr. The boys' names do not appear in Jenny's Estate Inventory.

TRANSFER CHART

217

1814 — Baldwin Co. GA. — **1814 Estate Division**

JOHN McCRARY, Sr.
Negro Slaves Transferred To:
VALUE

fellow	**London	$450	Matthew McCrary
fellow	Dick	$500	Isaac McCrary
fellow	**Ceasar	$450	Matthew McCrary
fellow	Eaden	$475	Bartley McCrary
woman	**Cassey	$350	Letty McCrary
Dycea & two children Bill & Stephen		$575	Isaac McCrary
woman	Rachel	$360	Bartley McCrary
Wynney & child John		$500	Orphans of Jonathan McCrary
boy	**Dick	$160	Letty McCrary
woman	*Betty	$ 5	

*Listed in Inventory, omitted in Division. Small value of $5 meant very old.

**Slaves did not go to Warren Co. to live with John's son, Matthew and daughter, Letty. See Bartley McCrary (d.1826) and John McCrary, (d. 1854) in this chart.

Family: Dick, Dicy, Billy & Stephen

1854 — Taylor Co., GA. — **1856 Estate Division**

JOHN McCRARY, Jr.
Negro Slaves Transferred To:

		VALUE	THE FINAL TRANSFER BEFORE "FREEDOM"
man	Dick	$1600	
man	Stephen	$ 900	Bartley McCrary: Peter Francis Sam
man	Joe	$1000	
man	Hamp	$1000	Gilly McCrary: Will Eddy Flousury
man	Flousury	$1000	
man	Ned	$1000	Andrew McCants' guardians: Isaac
man	Madison	$1000	*Matilda Ralia *Buckey *Missouri
man	Isaac	$1000	
man	Will	$1000	
boy	Peter	$ 900	Jonathan McCrary: Joe Bill Ruben
boy	Allen	$ 900	
boy	William	$ 900	James F. Berry: Stephen Hamp Litty Margaret
boy	Tom	$ 900	
woman	Cady	$ 800	
woman	Creasy & child	$1000	Henry McCrary: Dick Phillis Gus Tom Malissa Sarah Cassa
woman	Philice & 3 children	$1500	Jane G. McCrary: Ned Peter Sal Robert Caroline *OLD VISUES valued $25
boys	Gus & Rueben	$1100	
boy	Horasine	$ 450	John A. T. McCrary: Madison Allen Cresy & child
woman	Sally & 2 children	$1500	
woman	Matilda Becky & Zussee	$1500	*"Old Visues" is my Seventh Generation slave ancestor.
woman	Litty & her child Margaret	$1400	*Matilda, daughter of "VISUES," Buckey/Becky and Missouri
girl	Frances	$ 900	
woman	*Vineys	$ 100	See the Chapter,
Dicey, man Dick		$ 100	"JOHN MCCRARY 1789-1854"
woman	Casey	$ 100	for copies of all of his
man	Peter	$1500	ESTATE RECORDS.

1825 — Warren Co., GA — **1825 Estate Division**

LETTY/LETTICE McCRARY
Negro Slaves Sold To:
VALUE

boy	Allen	$350	Simon Reese	
woman	Fillis* & Child	$600	Mariner Culpepper**	

*Name may be Phillis.

**Son-in-law of Lettice and Mathew McCrary (d.1809). Daughter Jenny married Mariner Culpepper, and daughter Martha married Benjamin Culpepper.

1816 — Wilkinson Co, Ga. — **1816-1847 "Hired Out"**

WILLIAM McCRARY
Negro Slaves Hired To:
*VALUE

man	John	$900
woman	Jude	$600
woman	Jude & child	$700
girl	Lucy	$400
boy	Ned	$450
boy	Bazzel	$300
boy	Benjamin	$200
man	Peter**	$800
boy	Samuel	$400

*Appraised "value" in "Inventory. William McCrary left minor children. The Negro slaves were "hired out" yearly for their support. William's brother, Matthew, was guardian and reared the children.

**John McCrary hired Peter often, and may be named on his list in 1854. See John McCrary (d.1854) on this chart.

1827 — Baldwin Co., GA. — **1827 Estate Sale**

ROBERT McCRARY
Negro Slaves Transferred To:
VALUE

boy	*Hardy	$365	Willie McCrary
man	*London	$300	Bartley McCrary (Jr.)
boys	**Alfred & Bird	$300	**James McCrary

*All were transferred from Robert's father, Bartley McCrary, Sr. to him one year before Robert's death.

**Alfred and Bird are brothers and their mother was Patience, who was transferred to Albert G. Beckham, along with another brother, Peter. The family was torn apart. Albert G. Beckham married Robert's sister, Mary McCrary.

**James McCrary is Robert McCrary's brother, both sons of Bartley McCrary, Sr.

James married Jane McCrary, daughter of Jonathan McCrary. Jane is the one who received my slave ancestor, LUVESER.

See RECORD GROUP NO.1 for other slave family separations in the Estate Division of Bartley McCrary, Sr.

1826 — Baldwin Co., GA. — **1827 Estate Division**

BARTLEY McCRARY, Sr.
Negro Slaves Transferred To:
VALUE

boy	*London	$250	Robert McCrary, $875 for: London Hardy Alfred Bird
man	Cesar	$400	
young	Sam	$500	
			Orphans of Wm. McCrary
man			Old Sam
man	Peter	$500	
man	Jo	$500	Bryant Batemen, $800 for: George Patsy Ellick
man	Arch	$400	
man	Ben	$500	Albert B. Beckham, $800 for: Patience Clark Peter
boy	Hardy	$300	
man	George	$500	James McCrary, $850 for: Young Dick Sam Hampton
Patience Alfred Bird & Peter		$900	
Joicy Hampton Ben & Jim		$700	Bartley McCrary (Jr.) $865 for: Cesat Balkus Ned
girl	Mary	$200	Jenny Poindexter, $875 for: Mary Patrick Joshua
boy	Patrick	$200	
boy	John	$200	William Colbert, $980 for: Ben Joicey Little Ben Jim
boy	Jimmie	$400	
Veney Josh Ned & Sindy		$700	David Moses, $885 for: *Vicey & Child and Sindy
boy	Dick	$300	
boy	Clark	$400	
girl	Balkas	$350	*This is my Seventh Generation slave ancestor, LUVESER, first owned by Jonathan McCrary and is owned by John McCrary in 1854. See details in Chapter "John McCrary (1789-1854)."
girl	Betsey	$250	
boy	Ellick	$150	
woman	*Winney	$100	
*Omitted in Division			

1816 — Warren Co, GA. — **1816 Estate Division**

MATTHEW McCRARY
Negro Slaves Transferred To:
VALUE

Names of Legatees*

man	Tom	$200	Fanny McCrary (widow) man $555, woman $312, girl $503, girl $451
woman	Jude	$200	
woman	Cloe	$300	Robert McCrary, man and wife boy
man	Peter	$700	
man	Eden	$650	Samuel McCrary, man
man	Joe	$500	Levi McCrary, man
man	George	$700	Mathew McCrary, young man
man	Bill	$750	Robert Beal, man
woman	Hagar	$500	Samuel Hall, woman & man
girl	Maria	$400	John McCrary, girl
girl	Hannah	$325	Catherine Brooks, girl
girl	Chaney	$250	
girl	Patsy	$250	The slaves transferred were recorded by "gender" and unnamed. Therefore, the names of the slaves cannot be identified with their new owners.
girl	Nancy	$300	
boy	Chapman		

*Legatees are legal heirs who received shares in the estate. John McCrary, son of this Matthew, as an administrator listed gender only, omitting names of the Negro slaves.

See Record Group No. 2, Warren Co. Records.

Values quoted are from the Estate Inventory. The "Sale" value to each Legatee was hundreds of dollars more as seen in the original record.

LEGEND

→→→ Trail of Luveser/Vicey/Lueser from Jonathan McCrary to John McCrary, Jr. (d.1854).

· · · · · Slaves transferred to John McCrary, Jr. (d.1854).

─ ─ ─ Transfer from John McCrary, Sr. to son, Isaac.

── ── Transfer from John McCrary, Sr. to Bartley.

──── Slaves transferred from Issac to: William, John McCrary, Jr. and Bartley, Sr.

xxxxxxx Slaves transferred from Bartley, Sr. to William McCrary.

Chart 2.

Chapter Seventeen

ALL THINGS WORK TOGETHER FOR GOOD

"All things work together for good" is a scripture I loved to quote from Romans 8:28. "There's Divine Guidance in this research," is a saying I repeated continuously as I progressed in the research. Just a few days before I boarded a plane for Washington, DC to attend a conference of the Afro-American Historical & Genealogical Society (AAHGS), a fellow researcher, Fanny Moore, who I met at a previous conference called. She mentioned the Daughters of the American Revolution Library (DAR) in Washington. I had little interest in visiting it as I was unaware of any relatives giving service in the Revolutionary War. However, after the call, I remembered the slave owner, Bartley McCrary of Baldwin County had served in the Revolutionary War.

Bartley McCrary's Estate papers had a slave woman named "Lovinia and 4 children" listed in his Inventory in 1826. I believed Lovinia was the 90-year old woman whose name was either Lovinia or Louisa, listed in the 1870 Taylor County Census. Lovinia/Louisa was listed with my great, great, great grandmother, Matilda McCants.

I reasoned, "If anyone had applied for membership in the DAR under Bartley McCrary's name, perhaps Bartley's family would be listed in the application and I could learn more about the slave owner's family." I called a local member of the DAR, Maurine Rankin, who explained where to go and what to ask for at the DAR Library.

A few days later, I arrived in Washington, DC for the conference, but I skipped the opening sessions and went directly to the DAR Library from the airport. My cousin LaVerne and her husband, kept my luggage in their car. At the DAR Library, I ordered copies of five applications of DAR members who applied under four McCrary names: Bartley, John, Thomas and Robert.

I discovered a "gold mine" in John McCrary's Data File! I had brought with me a Jonathan McCrary document found before this trip in the probate records of Baldwin County, Georgia. The record in my hand was on the son, of this Revolutionary War soldier, John McCrary! It was Jonathan McCrary's Division of Estate record. The Administrator of the son, Jonathan McCrary's Estate, gave "a slave girl "Luveser" to Jonathan's daughter Jane, his minor child. This girl "Luveser" was my slave ancestor. I had found the name of the father of the slave owner of Luveser, John McCrary, Sr. I was elated.

I did not have time to read John McCrary's file of 133 pages, so I had the whole file copied at twenty cents per page! The file was brim-full of information about the entire McCrary family! The applicant stated in the file, "He also fought in the Rev. War, together with his sons, Matthew, Bartley and Jonathan. After the war, this whole family moved to Georgia. John's wife was named Jane, but she predeceased him. His estate was administered in 1813 in Baldwin Co. Ga." The Bartley McCrary who had "Lovinia with 4 children" was John McCrary's son. What a find! (From DAR File National Number 737717)

Up to this time, I was never sure of the 90-year old woman's name in the Taylor County Census. Was it Lovinia or Louisa? Only a look at the original 1870 Taylor County Ga. Population Census preserved at the National Archives would answer that question. That was my next stop. The conference sessions would be missed again. "My, those census takers had heavy volumes to cart around," I thought as I opened the large volume containing the handwritten 1870 Georgia Census at the National Archives. I carefully turned the pages of this century-old brown-bound book. The pages were crisp and clean. The ink was a dark brown. There at the top of page 311 was the name of my great, great, great, great grand-mother, Louisa, the "s" was barely visible but clearly, her name was recorded as *Louisa*.

Slave Ancestral Research

A feeling of pride swept over me. I touched the writing saying aloud, "This is the exact page in the census taker's handwriting where my own dear kinfolks were recorded 123 years ago." I could see them standing wearily at their cabin door, fearfully giving the enumerator their names, and what they thought were their ages. One hundred twenty three years and seven generations later, I touched their names exactly where they were written! What a thrill! (Fig. 7-50A).

Soon after my return home from Washington, I read the 133 pages, and made a file for each of the McCrary Revolutionary War soldiers. Then I placed the McCrary documents I had gathered from my research in the probate records of both Baldwin and Talbot Counties in those files.

The name, John McCrary, was repeated in several records. It proved a challenge to distinguish one from the other. Likewise, to follow the slave girl "Luveser" through the metamorphosis of her name. A greater challenge was to trail her through the McCrary family until 1870 when her name appeared in the 1870 Taylor County Census. I had successfully followed her trail, yet there were a few missing links.

THE METAMORPHOSIS OF A NAME

Throughout my years of research, I was never sure of my great, great, great, great grandmother's name. She was listed as 90 years old in the 1870 Taylor County, Georgia Census. Her given name first appeared to me as LOUISA or LOVENIA McCRARY.

In various records the name varied in spelling:

Date	Name of Record	Her name
1815	Jonathan McCrary's Estate Division	L U V E S E R
1822	Jane McCrary's Return by Wm. Grigg	L O U E S A
1826	Bartley McCrary, Sr.'s Hiring List	L O V E N I A
1827	Bartley McCrary, Sr.'s Inventory	V I C E Y
1854	John McCrary's Inventory	V E N Y
1856	John McCrary's Estate Division	O L D V I S U E S
1870	Original record in 1870 Taylor County Georgia Census Book	L O U I S A

(See Fig. 7-50A.)

Slave Ancestral Research

The name of every person whose place of abode on the first day of June, 1870, was in this family.	DESCRIPTION.			Profession, Occupation, or Trade of each person, male or female.	VALUE
	Age at last birth-day. If under 1 year, give months in fractions, thus, 1/12.	Sex.—Males (M.), Females (F.)	Color.—White (W.), Black (B.), Mulatto (M.), Chinese (C.), Indian (I.)		Value of Real Estate.
3	4	5	6	7	8
Nede + ally Louisa	90	F	B	Keeps House	
— Matilda	6	F	B	at Home	
Johnson Abram	28	M	B	Works farm	✓
— Emsery	1	F	B	Cooks	✓
M Carla Simons Ella			B	works at Mill	✓
Sanderson Hal	27	M	W	Bailif	.10
— Mary T	45	F	W	Keeps House	

The census enumerator recorded the name of my seventh generation ancestor as L O U I S A. The name could be read as L O V I S A. I may never know the correct spelling. Based upon the continuous appearance of the letter "v" in her name as noted on page 222, I believe her name was "Luveser." In the Estate Division of John McCrary, one of her last owners, her name was recorded as "Old Visues." This study revealed that female names were passed down in several generations:

Generation
- 1st Luveser named a daughter Matilda.
- 2nd Matilda named a daughter *Emily*.
- 3rd *Emily* named a daughter Dorcas, who changed the name to Emma.
- 4th *Emma* named a daughter Irene.
- 5th Irene named a daughter, *Emma Lee*, another daughter, *Louise* and her oldest daughter, Jewell.
- 6th Jewell named a daughter, Mary *Louvenia*. (I am that daughter)
- 7th Mary *Louvenia* named her daughter Julie LaVera. (The similarity in Julie's name was coincidental. She was named years before this search began.)
  (See Chapter Twenty, Descendants of Luveser McCrary.)

Fig. 7-50A. National Archives copy of the Taylor County, Georgia Census Schedule, p.311.

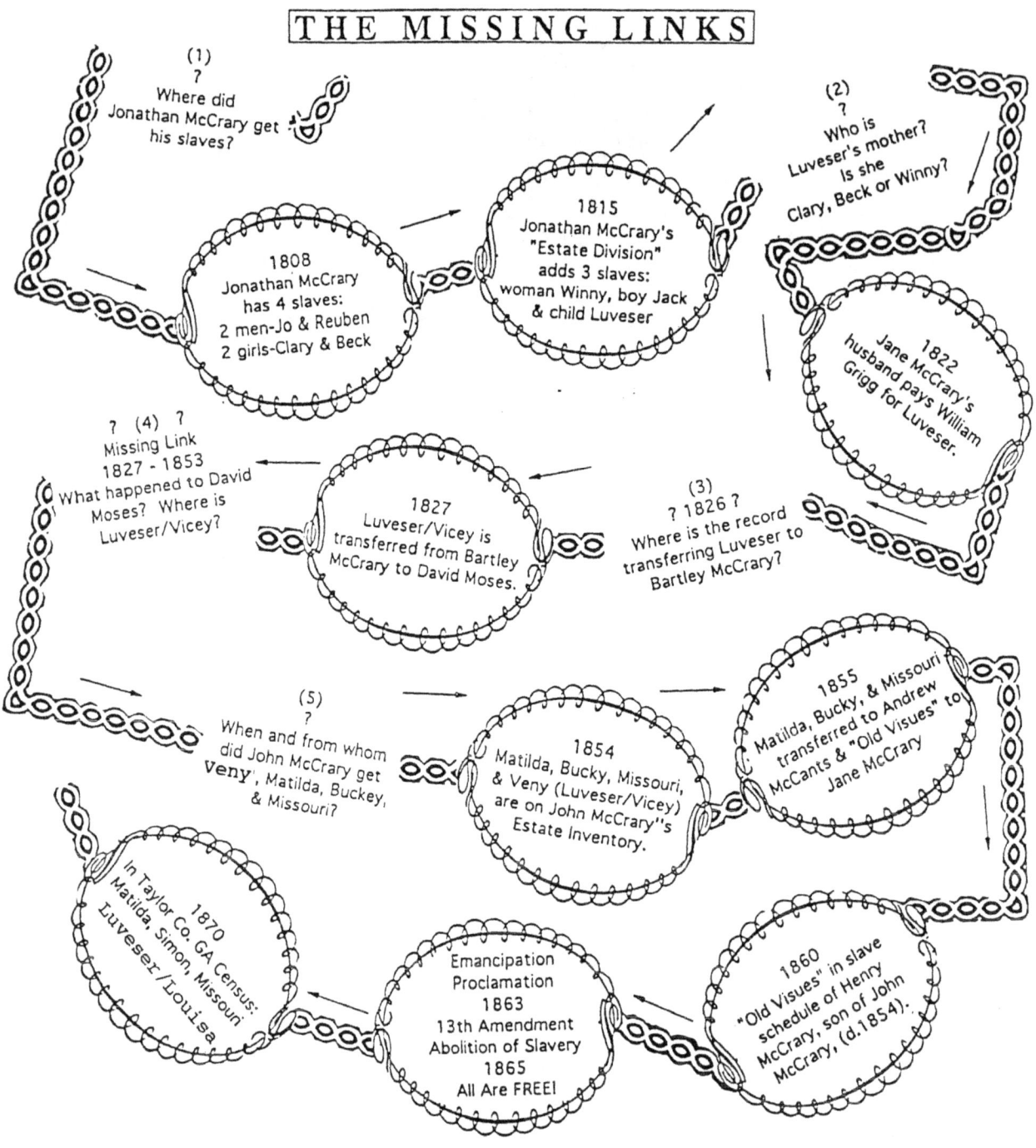

Chart 3. Five Missing Links in my ancestral trail of Luveser and her family.

Chapter Eighteen

MISSING LINKS, DIVINE GUIDANCE AND JOHN McCRARY

After fourteen years of research, spanning the period from the Revolutionary War to the freedom of the slaves in 1865 and on to the 1870 Census--there are still five missing links in the chain of my ancestors' trail. (See Chart 3.)

At times, slave ancestral research was like the story of my neighbor's little boy, Darryl, in the shopping mall who ran to see Santa Claus, found his chair empty and Santa Claus missing. He returned to his mother in a mood of disappointment. "Momma, I found where Santa Claus is, but he ain't there." Likewise, numerous records were discovered bearing the given names of my slave ancestors, but where they originally came from and some records showing their transfer to new owners were missing. I also sensed disappointment as descriptions (like ages and family relationships) needed for positive identification were not there.

Missing links need clues to be found. To find the five missing links in my research would greatly enhance the completion of this writing. However, I feel that success has already been reached through what I describe as "Divine Guidance." To me, my Divine Guidance was provided through patience for probing into the past and potential for interpreting vague clues from inferences lurking in illegible handwriting.

As I studied the documents I found it necessary to make changes in some assumptions. John McCrary, who died in 1854, was listed in the Baldwin County Tax Digest in 1818 as "John McCrary, Jr." with two slaves. (See Revelations). Since his name appeared in the Estate

Division of Jonathan McCrary (See Record Group No. 3), I assumed "John McCrary, Jr." to be Jonathan McCrary's son. The record below from the Baldwin County Book of Returns, 1813-1839, submitted by "Bartley McCrary, Administrator of the Estate of John & Johnathan McCrary dec'd" for the year 1817 included a statement *disproving* my assumption:

1817   Cash pd. John McCrary Jr. for John McCrary, Senior, as per

     Voucher No. 4 $190.00

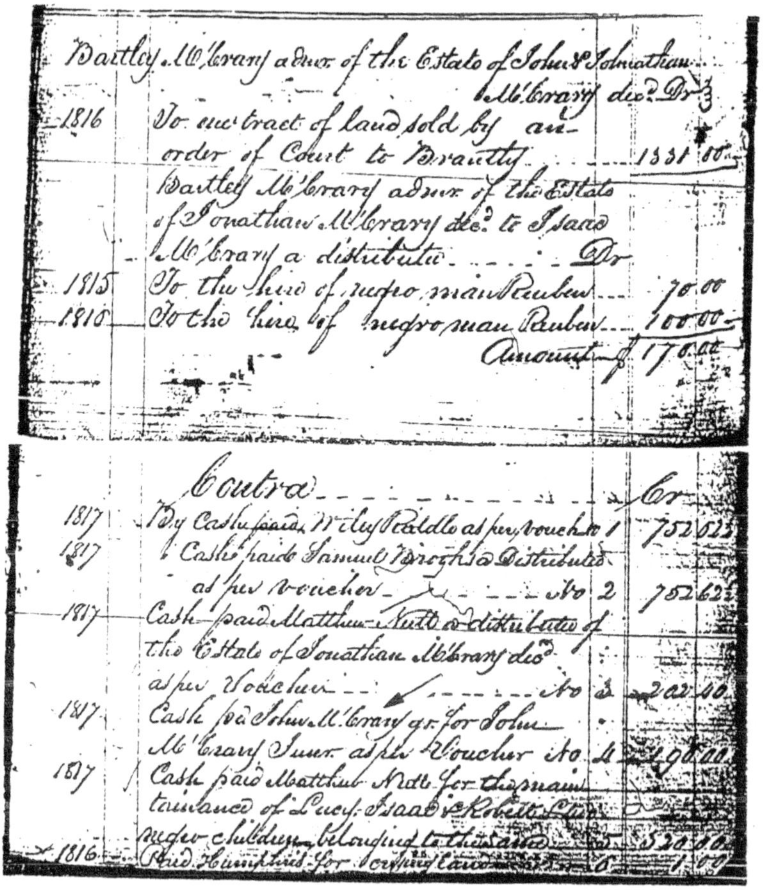

Fig. 7-50B. Return filed by Bartley McCrary, Administrator of the Estates of John and Johnathan McCrary. Baldwin Co. GA Court Records, Book of Returns, 1813-1839, p. 25.

Fig. 7-50B. Return for John and Johnathan McCrary.

Slave Ancestral Research

The following question was asked by my friend, Irene Johnson, "Will you have to trace the slave owner's family too?" I did not have the complete answer then. My answer now is, "to some extent." When there were people, as the slave owners, who had complete control over every aspect of your ancestors' lives, there is a natural instinct to want to know them. How I learned about them is what made this story.

Efforts to locate a McCrary family history or genealogy had been unsuccessful. Data gathered during my visit to the DAR Library in Washington, DC was the beginning. However, prior to the DAR Library visit, I had seen at the Georgia Archives in Atlanta, in their "Name File" references to a McCrary family included in a book by Lewis W. Rigsby, *Historic Georgia Families* (Baltimore, Genealogical Pub. Co., 1969). A copy of this book was not available in my local area. Requests through inter-library loans were unsuccessful. I formed a habit, to visit libraries in whatever places I happened to be. So when my son's doctor's appointment was scheduled near the University of Florida in Gainesville, I arrived early. My footsteps led directly to the University Library. The library not only had Rigsby's book, but the early tax digests of Hancock and Baldwin Counties. I had only a day before learned that the McCrarys were in Hancock County in 1796.

Things just seemed to fall in place in the right sequence. I called it Divine Guidance. When I listed the McCrary Baldwin County marriages earlier in this text, I wrote Missouri H. McCrary's marriage to John Chapman simply because her name was Missouri. My ancestor, Matilda McCants, (Luveser's daughter) had a daughter named Missouri (see 1870 Taylor County Census, Fig. 7-2). When I read in Rigsby book, page 145, about Jane Bartley McCrary and her marriage to James McCrary, I saw that Missouri Holliman McCrary who married John Chapman, was the *daughter* of Jane Bartley and James McCrary. It was this Jane who received Luveser from her father, Jonathan McCrary's Estate in 1815. This find made me wonder if Jane gave Matilda, Luveser's child, to serve, Missouri Chapman and Matilda named her daughter after Missouri Chapman. This was only speculation because it was a practice to give newly married daughters Negro slaves as servants.

I did not attempt to record a McCrary genealogy. From Rigsby, page 145; the Data File on John McCrary, Sr. at the DAR Library; from census and probate records; I compiled information on the family background of John McCrary, Jr. He owned my slave ancestors when he died in Taylor County in 1854.

John McCrary, Jr. was listed in the Talbot County 1850 Census, age 61. He was born in South Carolina about 1789. He was the son of John McCrary, Sr., a Revolutionary War soldier, whose wife Jane died in South Carolina. Jonathan McCrary and Bartley McCrary, a Revolutionary War soldier and John McCrary, Jr. were brothers. Jonathan McCrary married Anna Taliaferro (b. ca.1768-1864) in Virginia and moved to Baldwin County, Ga. to be near his brother, Bartley. John McCrary, Sr. had a daughter, Lettice who married Matthew McCrary, son of Col. Robert McCrary, a Revolutionary War soldier. Lettice and another brother, Matthew, lived in Warren County, Ga. Lettice's brother, Matthew died in 1816 and Lettice in 1825, (All dates are circa.) in Warren County.

A marriage record of John McCrary to Jenny McCrary 12 March 1813 in Baldwin County is believed to be John McCrary, Jr. After the death of Bartley McCrary in 1826 in Baldwin County, John McCrary, Jr. moved to Talbot County, Ga. about 1830 residing in the Carsonville District which became a part of Taylor County in 1852. The first Tax Digest of Taylor Co. (1852) listed John McCrary as "Sr." since he had a son, John Jr. Other sons were Bartley and Henry; and two daughters, Jane who married Lucious Q. C. McCrary, 4 January 1855; and Elizabeth, who married Andrew McCants 14 January 1844.

John McCrary had the fourth largest number of Negro slaves in 1852 in Taylor County, which numbered 33. His land holdings were vast, 4,059 acres, valued at $16,500. His total estate value was $46,000.

John McCrary's Estate Records revealed his death date as c.1854. His son-in-law, Andrew McCants, served as administrator of his Estate.

In the early pages of this text when I listed all of the slaveholders with the names McCrary and McCants from the 1850 and 1860 Talbot and Taylor County Georgia Slave Schedules, I had not the slightest feeling that John McCrary and his son-in-law Andrew McCants were the last owners of my slave ancestors, Luveser, Matilda, Bucky (Simon) and Missouri. I had unknowingly written the names of the slave owners of my kinfolks right at the beginning of this project. Slave ancestral research, is truly "something else."

GEORGIA

County Map For The State Of GEORGIA
TRACKS AND TRAILS

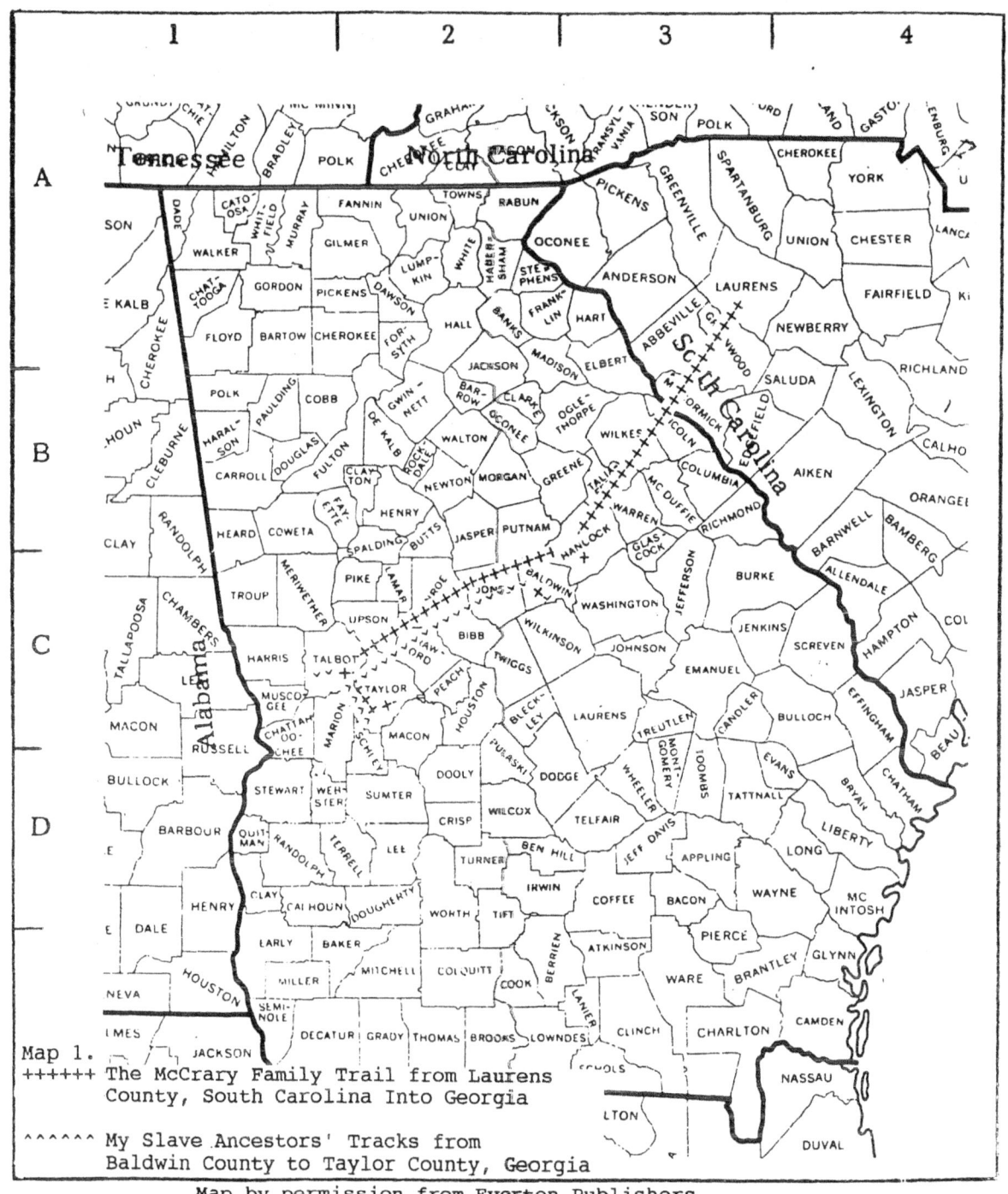

Map 1.
++++++ The McCrary Family Trail from Laurens County, South Carolina Into Georgia

^^^^^^ My Slave Ancestors' Tracks from Baldwin County to Taylor County, Georgia

Map by permission from Everton Publishers.

The Handy Book for Genealogist, 6th ed. rev.
Logan, Utah: Everton Publishers, 1971, p. 47.

Chapter Nineteen

SO LITTLE TO GO ON
REFLECTIONS

In the records, there was so little to go on: no surnames no references to fathers of children, nor recognition of family relationships, frequent omission of ages and even their names. Records unearthed questions with no places to go for answers. Were they house slaves or field hands? Nothing recorded to help me get a feel for their character and temperament. How did they cope?

Conditions set my mind wondering, inquiring, as my mother, said, "How it was way back there then," for Veny, Tildy, Simon, Abram and Missoury. They were her ancestors too, but she knew nothing about them. Each lived from childhood through slavery. If field hands, they slept on mattresses made of cotton or dried grasses, sewn or thrown together by rough-textured hands. They lived in unpainted cabins with hinged door-like windows, wooden or earthen floors, a table, a bench, a chair or two.

Veny and Tilda, as historians described their day, rose before sunrise to fix the food and feed the family, then rushed to the field, no time to clear away things. A bell sounded at noon for the mid-day meal, prepared by the Negro cook, under the watchful eye of the mistress in the Big House. A Negro woman was assigned the chore of keeping the children too young for work under the lash in the fields. Babies slept, tied to bent backs, drenched in sweat. At the muffled sound of the first cry, suckling babes were swung around to the mother's breast to feed.

Children, men, women, young, old, weak, feeble, sunscorched; labored from sun-up to sundown, plowing, digging, hoeing, planting, picking, plucking, peeling, shelling, shucking, packing, whatever grew in the fields. Darkness dragged weary bodies to fill crowded shacks, the evening meal, hushed singing, whispered prayers; dreaded male late-night visits from the Big House or overseer; a few hours sleep, the crack of dawn, a bell rings, time to rise again.

Were Veny and Tildy house slaves? Did they want life in the outside cabins with the rest of their kindred? Were they resigned to the duties of cook, housekeeper and mammy to the fair-skinned babies and children whose status in life surpassed their own? The records held no answers.

As for Simon and Abram, my male slave ancestors, likewise, there was so little to go on: no listing of surnames, infrequent references to age as "a Negro boy" or "a Negro man." And most importantly, no recorded listing with their wives, Matilda (Tildy) and Simon; Emily and Abram. Who fathered Veny's children? How many did she have and how many were sold away? There were no complete family units with their children.

Simon was born in Virginia. However, a record of his entry into Georgia was not found. Were they skilled laborers? Simon may have worked at a mill and Abram as a "boot and shoemaker," their occupations listed in the 1880 Taylor Co. Census. Neither Simon, Abram, Veny, Tildy, nor Missoury learned to read or write. The records on my ancestors included fees paid for midwifry, doctor visits, purchased clothing and shoes.

How did it feel searching for my slave ancestors? I felt a broad spectrum of emotions. The saddest was the reality of seeing very young children at the age of three or four sold away from their mothers. I sensed their unsettled feeling of being shifted from place to place among uncaring people who valued only their work and not their welfare; who split families apart, as if they did not feel love, nor pain nor any human emotion. I often felt knotted frustration, feeling their struggle to simply live and hope for the day when they could be with their families and no longer feel the pains of endless work, endless separations, strife and suffering.

Freedom did come. For many, it was too late. But Veny, Matilda (Tildy), Simon, Abram, Emily and Missoury survived. If they had not, I would not be here.

From this experience, I learned first-hand how the chains of slavery crippled their lives. I learned their names which appeared with many variations for Luveser, including: Lovenia, Veny, Vicey, and Visues. Matilda was recorded as Tilda and Tildy. I learned the names of their masters and overseers. I learned how my kinfolks were involved in common slave practices recorded at that time in records that I did not know existed.

At the first sight of my folks in the records, fresh smiles flashed, then quickly vanished, provoking the thought, "Oh, my God, these are my kinfoks and this is what happened to them!"

Fine penmanship sprawled across pages of giant size court record books like exquisite works of art, recording with meticulous care their gender, "Negro woman, Negro man, boy, girl, child and their dollar value." The contents of the writers' script with its graceful curves, jerked my thoughts from quiet admiration to verbally admonish: "What a beautiful handwriting, why didn't he write their names?" The beautiful penmanship meshed with the illegible and both fell into my pile of "seeing and not wanting to believe" records. Conflicting emotions pushed my search deeper into the past with an eerie feeling of satisfaction. An intense feeling of compassion for the life imposed on my ancestors touched a tender place in my heart.

I cannot imagine the depth of anguish they felt by living day by day, year after year, in such a way. But the fact that they survived meant that they found ways to cope and perhaps, times to laugh and scrape pleasure from something out of their meager existence. Admiration and love evolved from the search. Knowledge of my ancestors: Luveser McCrary, Simon and Matilda McCants, Abram and Missouri Johnson, Abram and Emily Holton and Mary Riley, came only after years of research and study. Their physical features are a mystery as no photographs are known to exist. However, their lives, once hidden from history, have now become alive due to my discovery. That fact brings to me a great measure of comfort.

I met Matilda's granddaughter, Emma Davis, my great grandmother once (See Frontispiece.) when I was a junior in high school. She was not born a slave. Great Grandma Emma was born about 1866 or 1867, but her mother, Emily and father, Abram Holton were slaves. How I wish that I had gathered the courage to ask the questions smoldering inside about slavery, but I was afraid. As my mother said, "That's the way it was back there then," children were not encouraged to ask grownups many questions. But now, I have found my slave ancestors, and some of the answers.

Chapter Twenty

THE DESCENDANTS OF LUVESER McCRARY

Descendants of Luveser McCrary

GENERATION NAME
1 Luveser McCrary b: ABT 1780 in Baldwin Co., GA d: in Taylor Co., GA
.... 2 Matilda McCants b: ABT 1825 in Baldwin Co., Ga.
.... +Simon McCants b: ABT 1815 in VA m: December 22, 1866
.... 3 Emily McCants b: ABT 1835 in GA
.... +Abram Holton b: ABT 1827 in KY
.... 4 Dorcas Emma Holton b: ABT 1866 in Butler (Taylor), GA d: November 18, 1947 in Pelham (Mitchell), GA
.... -Charlton Ray b: February 1874 in Taylor Co., GA m: May 20, 1888 in Taylor Co. GA
.... 5 Irene Ray b: May 1890 in Taylor Co., Ga. d: September 15, 1969 in Sanford (Seminole), FL
.... -Lucious Moore b: March 15, 1892 in Rhines (Dodge), Ga. m: May 01, 1910 in Mitchell Co., Ga. d: February 25, 1942 in Pehlam (Mitchell), Ga.
.... 6 Jewell Moore b: February 21, 1911 in Mitchell Co., Ga. d: May 05, 1992 in Sanford (Seminole), FL
.... -Sylvester Jackson b: May 25, 1908 in Washington Co. or Worth m: September 09, 1929 in Mitchell Co., Ga. d: December 23, 1980 in Sanford (Seminole), FL
.... 7 Mary Louvenia Jackson b: April 03, 1930 in Cotton (Mitchell), Ga.
.... -John Henry Anderson, Sr. b: December 13, 1927 in Tallahassee (Leon), FL m: August 01, 1953 in Sanford, (Seminole), FL d: January 14, 1986 in Orlando (Orange), FL
.... 8 John Henry Anderson, Jr. b: June 26, 1955 in Hammond(Lake), Ind
.... -Mary Joyce Edge m: August 19, 1981
.... 9 John Henry Anderson III b: August 19, 1980
.... 8 Julie LaVera Anderson b: August 02, 1957 in Columbus(Muscogee), Ga. d: October 02, 1993 in Atlanta (Fulton), Ga.
.... *2nd spouse of Mary Louvenia Jackson:
.... -Joel Van Fears, Sr. b: August 10, 1938 in Lufkin (Angelina), Tx. m: July 21, 1967 in Sanford (Seminole), Fl.
.... 8 Joel Van Fears, Jr. b: August 05, 1973 in Daytona Beach (Volusia), Fl.
.... 7 Annie Doris Jackson b: February 21, 1932 in Pelham(Mitchell), GA
.... +Edward Ellis Goins b: September 17, 1927 in New Orleans, LA m: May 25, 1955 in New Orleans, LA
.... 8 Irene Katrinka Goins b: November 02, 1948 in Sanford(Seminole), FL
.... -Jeffrey Lane Bradley b: November 06, 1951 in Jamaica(Queens), NY m: May 15, 1976 in Rochester, NY
.... 9 Tara Amani Bradley b: September 30, 1977 in Rochester(Monroe), NY
.... 9 Ashley Dionne Bradley b: December 09, 1985 in Rochester(Monroe), NY
.... 8 Krystal Renel Goins b: December 25, 1961 in New Orleans, LA m:2 May 1992 p:New Orleans, LA
.... -Darryl Anthony Bush b: 5 Mar. 1963 Melrose Park (Cook) ILL
.... 9 Kristian Goins b: July 05, 1985 in Los Angeles, CA
.... 9 Kai Imani Bush b: December 30, 1993 in Chicago (Cook), IL
.... 8 Katrice Ancel Goins b: May 27, 1963 in New Orleans, LA
.... -Glenn Haisley
.... 9 Kirby Haisley b: in New Orleans, LA
.... 9 Glenn Haisley, Jr. b: August 16, 1993 in New Orleans, LA
.... 8 Edward Ellis Goins, Jr. b: December 25, 1964 in New Orleans, LA
.... -Ramona Elinor Olguin b: May 08, 1967 in Stockton, CA m: May 22, 1987
.... 9 Christopher Caleb Goins b: July 17, 1985 in San Joaquin, CA
.... 9 Kadesha Shantay Goins b: July 26, 1988 in Upper Heyford, Oxfordshire, England
.... 9 Ellis Josiah Goins b: September 05, 1989 in Oxfordshire, England

.... 7 Christine Jackson b: December 31, 1937 in Sanford(Seminole), Fl
.... +Theodore Collins b: ABT 1930 m: February 10, 1956 in Miami(Dade), FL
.... 8 Venita Patrice Collins b: October 06, 1959 in New Brunswick, NJ
.... +Danny McKinney b: November 11, 1958 in Sanford(Seminole), FL m: June 29, 1980 in Sanford(Seminole), FL
.... 9 William Joseph McKinney b: May 15, 1981 in Mid-West City, OK
.... 9 Kia Marie McKinney b: July 11, 1983 in Wert, Holland
.... *2nd spouse of Christine Jackson:
.... +Marvin Richard Johnson b: May 20, 1938 in Kissimmee (Osceola), FL m: March 13, 1964 in Carton CO, GA
.... 8 Marvin Richard Johnson, Jr. b: August 05, 1968 in Sanford(Seminole), FL
.... +Tracey Michelle Turner m: October 15, 1994 in Orlando(Orange), FL
.... 8 Damon Sylvan Johnson b: October 10, 1972 in Tampa(Hillsborough), FL
.... 7 Jimmie Dean Jackson b: December 20, 1943 in Sanford(Seminole), FL
.... +Paulette LeBlanc b: April 30, 1950 in New Orleans, LA m: October 15, 1970 in New Orleans, LA
.... 8 Christopher Patrick Jackson b: February 18, 1971 in Ne Orleans, LA
.... 8 Dena Semone Jackson b: March 11, 1973 in New Orleans, LA
.... 8 Steven Girard Jackson b: May 27, 1976 in New Orleans, LA
.... *2nd spouse of Jimmie Dean Jackson:
.... +Antoinette Briggs b: April 04, 1958 in New Orleans, LA m: September 25, 1988 in Las Vegas, NV
.... 8 Courtney Jackson b: August 01, 1986 in New Orleans, LA
.... 8 Christy Briggs Jackson b: July 05, 1992 in New Orleans, LA
.... 7 Sheralyn Darnell Jackson b: June 08, 1945 in Sanford(Seminole), FL
.... +Jacob Ponder Brinson, Sr. b: June 23, 1944 in Monticello, FL
.... 8 Jacob Ponder Brinson, Jr. b: March 04, 1964 in Seminole Co., FL
.... Dawna Felecia Pursley
.... 9 Shannon Corey Brinson b: May 04, 1983 in Rochester(Monroe), NY
.... 8 Kimberly Dionne Brinson b: December 13, 1969 in Rochester, NY
.... *2nd spouse of Sheralyn Darnell Jackson:
.... +John Wright m: May 27, 1989 in Sanford (Seminole), FL
.... 7 Sandra Jackson b: December 01, 1946 in Sanford(Seminole), FL
.... 6 A.C. Jay Ray/Charles Mansfield b:21 Oct.1906 p: Ga.; d:1 Mar. 1978 p: Hudson Co. N.J.;
.... 6 Julius Moore b:21 Feb. 1911 p:Pelham (Mitchell)Ga. d:1962 p:Hoboken,N.J.
.... 6 Emma Lee Moore b:2 May 1913 p:Pelham, Ga.; d:25 May 1979; Altamonte (Seminole) FL.
.... 6 Farma Moore b:13 Oct. 1915 p:Pelham (Mitchell)GA. d:27 Sept.1983 p:Altamonte Spgs. (Seminole)FL.
.... 6 Louise Moore b: July 1917 in Pelham (Mitchell) Ga., d. July 1, 1980 in East Orange (Essex) N.J.
.... 5 Susie Ray b:11 Sept.1891 p:Berrien Co.GA; d:1969 p:Pelham (Mitchell)GA.m:1902 p:Pelham, GA Jessie Singleton
.... 4 Bailey Holton b:1862 p:Taylor Co. GA m:Lizzie Mumfort
.... 4 Peter Holton b:1867 p:Taylor Co. GA; d:9 Dec.1937 p: Crisp Co. GA; m:Add Johnson
.... 4 Abraham Holton b:1868
.... 3 Missouri McCants b: ABT 1853 in Taylor Co. GA
.... 3 Isabella McCants b: ABT 1860 in Taylor Co. GA
.... 3 Matilda McCants b: ABT 1862 in Taylor Co. GA
...... 2 Josh McCrary
...... 2 Ned McCrary
...... 2 Sendy(Lucinda) McCrary

Chart 4

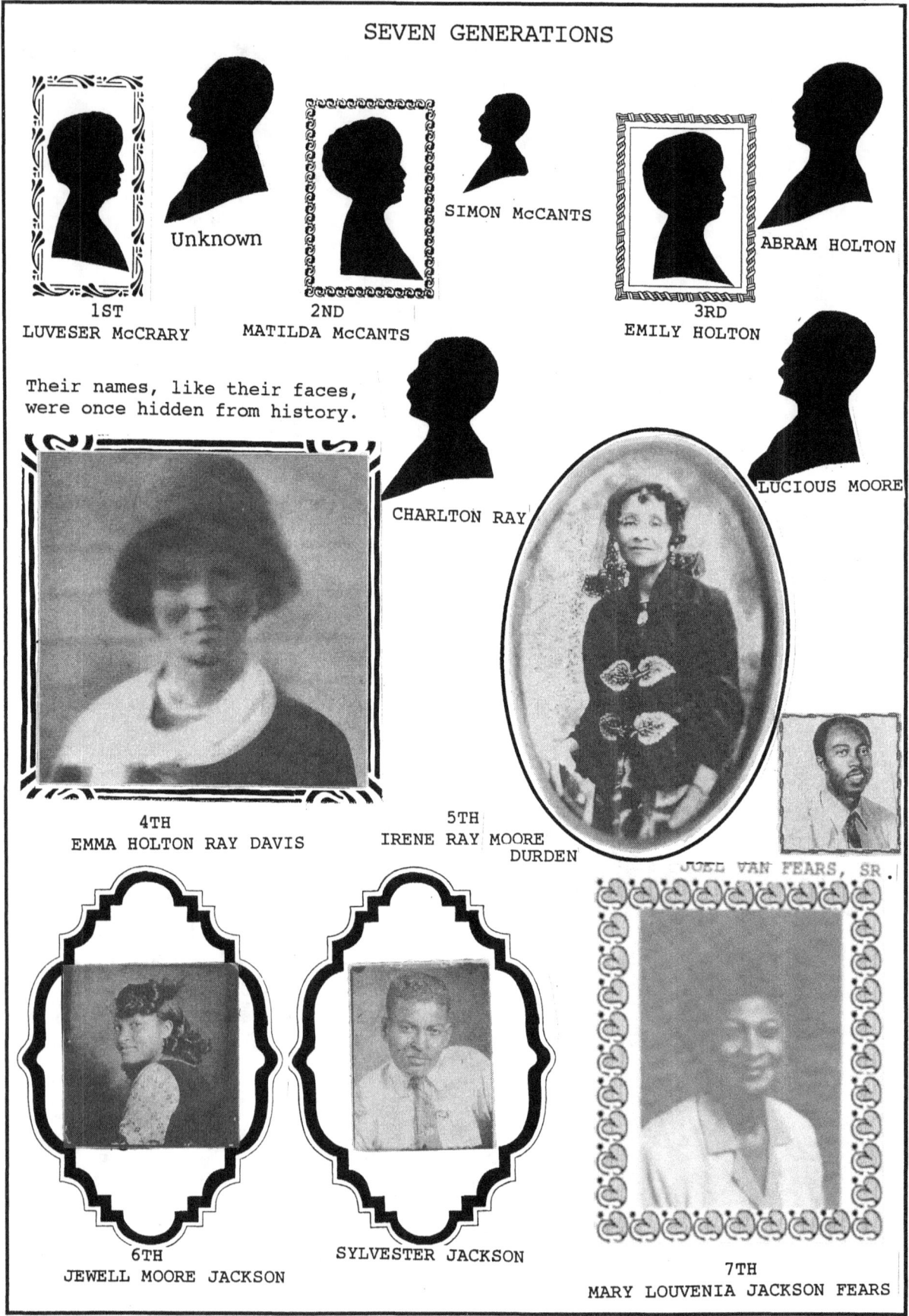

SEVEN GENERATIONS

Their names, like their faces, were once hidden from history.

1ST LUVESER McCRARY — Unknown

2ND MATILDA McCANTS — SIMON McCANTS

3RD EMILY HOLTON — ABRAM HOLTON

4TH EMMA HOLTON RAY DAVIS — CHARLTON RAY

5TH IRENE RAY MOORE DURDEN — LUCIOUS MOORE

6TH JEWELL MOORE JACKSON — SYLVESTER JACKSON

7TH MARY LOUVENIA JACKSON FEARS — JOEL VAN FEARS, SR.

"Daddy"

(6) San

(1) Mary L.

"Momma"

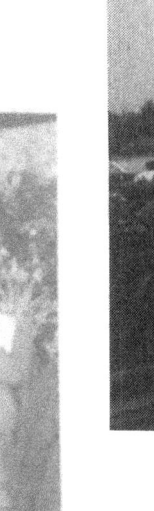
(4) Jimmy (5) Darnie (3) Christine

(1) Mary L. (2) Doris (5) Darnie

OUR FAMILY

Father, Sylvester Jackson
Mother, Jewell Moore Jackson

"Five girls and a boy"

1. Mary L. Jackson Fears
2. Doris Jackson Goins
3. Christine Jackson Johnson
4. Jimmy Dean Jackson
5. Sheralyn D. Jackson Brinson
6. Sandra Jackson

(Listed in order of birth.)

PHOTOGRAPHS OF THE
DESCENDANTS OF LUVESER McCRARY

    The photographs on the next few pages are of the 7th, 8th and 9th Generations of Luveser McCrary. These descendants are the vessels to pass on to future generations the knowledge of their ancestors who are no longer hidden from history, but alive, for their names have been recorded and they will forever remain a living part of American history.

John H. ANDERSON, Jr.   John H. ANDERSON, III

DR. JOHN ANDERSON
1927 • 1986

Mary Edge Anderson

Julie L. ANDERSON

Katrice Krystel

Ellis

Doris JACKSON GOINS   Edward Ellis GOINS, Sr.

Glenn Haisley, Sr.
Kirby
Katrice Ancel GOINS Haisley

Kirby, Glenn, Jr.

Jeffrey BRADLEY   Katrinka G. Bradley

Ashley   Tara

Ramona Elinor Goins   Edward Ellis GOINS, Jr.

Christopher Caleb   Ellis Josiah   Kadesha Shantay

Darryl Bush   Kristian

Krystel Renel GOINS BUSH

Kai Amani

Marvin R. JOHNSON, Sr.
Christine JACKSON JOHNSON

Damon Sylvan JOHNSON

Venita Patrice McKINNEY
Danny McKinney   William Joseph
Kia Marie

Marvin R. JOHNSON, Jr.
Tracey Michelle Turner Johnson

248

Jimmie Dean JACKSON Antoinette Briggs Jackson

Courtney Christy

Paulette LaBlanc Stephen Dena Christopher

Jacob   Kimberly
Sheralyn D. JACKSON BRINSON

Jacob P. BRINSON, Sr.
Kimberly

Jacob P. BRINSON, Jr.
Shannon Corey

Sandra JACKSON

A more precious expression of love for my kinfolks cannot be found than this written account of my family for future generations.

Mary L. Jackson Fears

Photograph Indentification Numbers for the
Descendants of Luveser McCrary

```
GENERATION        NAME
ID NO.
     1 Luveser McCrary b: ABT 1780 in Baldwin Co., GA  d: in Taylor Co., GA
        2 Matilda McCants b: ABT 1825 in Baldwin Co., Ga.
           +Simon McCants b: ABT 1815 in VA  m: December 22, 1866
        3 Emily McCants b: ABT 1835 in GA
           +Abram Holton b: ABT 1827 in KY
           4 Dorcas/Emma Holton b: ABT 1866 in Butler (Taylor), GA  d: November 18, 1947 in Pelham (Mitchell), GA
              +Charlton Ray b: February 1874 in GA  m: May 20, 1888 in Taylor Co., GA
              5 Irene Ray b: May 1890 in Taylor Co., Ga  d: September 15, 1969 in Sanford (Seminole), Fl
              +Lucious Moore b: March 15, 1892 in Rhines (Dodge), Ga.  m: May 01, 1910 in Mitchell Co., Ga.  d: February 25, 1942 in Pelham (Mitchell), Ga.
                 6 Jewell Moore b: February 21, 1911 in Mitchell Co., Ga.  d: May 05, 1992 in Sanford (Seminole), Fl.
                 +Sylvester Jackson b: May 25, 1908 in Washington Co. or Worth  m: September 09, 1929 in Mitchell Co., Ga.  d: December 23, 1980 in Sanford (Seminole), Fl.
(3)                  7 Mary Louvenia Jackson b: April 03, 1930 in Cotton (Mitchell), Ga.
                        +John Henry Anderson, Sr. b: December 13, 1927 in Tallahassee (Leon), Fl.  m: August 01, 1953 in Sanford, (Seminole), Fl.  d: January 14, 1986 in Orlando (Orange), Fl.
   (7)                 8 John Henry Anderson, Jr. b: June 26, 1955 in Hammond(Lake), Ind.
                        +Mary Joyce Edge m: August 19, 1981
    (4)                   9 John Henry Anderson III b: August 19, 1980
      (5)              8 Julie LaVera Anderson b: August 02, 1957 in Columbus(Muscogee), Ga.  d: October 02, 1993 in Atlanta (Fulton), Ga.
       (8)             *2nd spouse of Mary Louvenia Jackson:
(1)                     +Joel Van Fears, Sr. b: August 10, 1938 in Lufkin (Angelina), Tx.  m: July 21, 1967 in Sanford (Seminole), Fl.
 (2)                    8 Joel Van Fears, Jr. b: August 05, 1973 in Daytona Beach (Volusia), Fl.
 (9)                 7 Annie Doris Jackson b: February 21, 1932 in Pelham(Mitchell), GA
                        +Edward Ellis Goins b: September 17, 1927 in New Orleans, LA  m: May 25, 1955 in New Orleans, LA
  (10)                  8 Irene Katrinka Goins b: November 02, 1948 in Sanford(Seminole), Fl.
 (17)                   +Jeffrey Lane Bradley b: November 06, 1951 in Jamaica(Queens), NY m: May 15, 1976 in Rochester, NY
 (18)                      9 Tara Amani Bradley b: September 30, 1977 in Rochester(Monroe), NY
 (20)                      9 Ashley Dionne Bradley b: December 09, 1985 in Rochester(Monroe), NY
 (19)                   8 Krystall Renel Goins b: December 25, 1961 in New Orleans, LA
                        +Darryl Bush
      (25)              9 Kristian Goins b: July 05, 1985 in Los Angeles, CA
      (26)              9 Kai Imani Bush b: December 30, 1993 in Chicago (Cook), IL
      (27)           8 Katrice Ancel Goins b: May 27, 1963 in New Orleans, LA
 (11)                   +Glenn Haisley
 (14)                   9 Kirby Haisley b: in New Orleans, LA
      (15)              9 Glenn Haisley, Jr. b: August 16, 1993 in New Orleans, LA
      (16)           8 Edward Ellis Goins, Jr. b: December 25, 1964 in New Orleans, LA
 (12)                   +Ramona Elinor Olguin b: May 08, 1967 in Stockton, CA  m: May 22, 1987
 (22)                   9 Christopher Caleb Goins b: July 17, 1985 in San Joaquin, CA
      (21)              9 Kadesha Shantay Goins b: July 26, 1988 in Upper Heyford, Oxfordshire, England
      (24)              9 Ellis Josiah Goins b: September 05, 1989 in Oxfordshire, England
      (23)
```

251

ID No.

(29) 7 Christine Jackson b: December 31, 1937 in Sanford(Seminole), FL
(31) +Theodore Collins b: ABT 1930 m: February 10, 1956 in Miami(Dade), FL
(32) 8VenitaPatrice Collins b: October 06, 1959 in New Brunswick, NJ
(33) +Danny McKinney b: November 11, 1958 in Sanford(Seminole), FL m: June 29, 1980 in Sanford(Seminole), FL
        9 William Joseph McKinney b: May 15, 1981 in Mid-West City, OK
(34)   9 Kia Marie McKinney b: July 11, 1983 in Wert, Holland
(29) *2nd spouse of Christine Jackson:
(28) +Marvin Richard Johnson b: May 20, 1938 in Kissimmee (Osceola), FL m: March 13, 1964 in Carton CO., GA
(36) 8 Marvin Richard Johnson, Jr. b: August 05, 1968 in Sanford(Seminole), FL
(35) +Tracey Michelle Turner m: October 15, 1994 in Orlando(Orange), FL
(30) 8 Damon Sylvan Johnson b: October 10, 1972 in Tampa(Hillsborough), FL
(37) 7 Jimmie Dean Jackson b: December 20, 1943 in Sanford(Seminole), FL
(41) +Paulette LeBlanc b: April 30, 1950 in New Orleans, LA m: October 15, 1970 in New Orleans, LA
(44) 8 Christopher Patrick Jackson b: February 18, 1971 in Ne Orleans, LA
(43) 8 Dena Semone Jackson b: March 11, 1973 in New Orleans, LA
(42) 8 Steven Girard Jackson b: May 27, 1976 in New Orleans, LA
(37) *2nd spouse of Jimmie Dean Jackson:
(39) +Antoinette Briggs b: April 04, 1958 in New Orleans, LA m: September 25, 1988 in Las Vegas, NV
(38) 8 Courtney Jackson b: August 01, 1986 in New Orleans, LA
(40) 8 Christy Briggs Jackson b: July 05, 1992 in New Orleans, LA
(46) 7 Sheralyn Darnell Jackson b: June 08, 1945 in Sanford(Seminole), FL
(48) +Jacob Ponder Brinson, Sr. b: June 23, 1944 in Monticello, FL
(45) 8 Jacob Ponder Brinson, Jr. b: March 04, 1964 in Seminole Co., FL
      -Dawna Felecia Pursley
(49) 9 Shannon Corey Brinson b: May 04, 1983 in Rochester(Monroe), NY
(47) 8 Kimberly Dionne Brinson b: December 13, 1969 in Rochester, NY
(46) *2nd spouse of Sheralyn Darnell Jackson:
     +John Wright m: May 27, 1989 in Sanford (Seminole), FL
(50) 7 Sandra Jackson b: December 01, 1946 in Sanford(Seminole), FL
     6 A.C. Jay Ray
     6 Julious Moore
     6 Emma Lee Moore
     6 Earma Moore
     6 Louise Moore
    5 Susie Ray
   4 Bailey Holton
   4 Peter Holton
   4 Abraham Holton
  3 Missouri McCants b: ABT 1853 in Taylor Co., GA
  3 Isabella McCants b: ABT 1860 in Taylor Co., GA
  3 Matilda McCants b: ABT 1862 in Taylor Co., GA
 2 Josh McCrary
 2 Ned McCrary
 2 Sendy(Lucinda) McCrary

Photograph Indentification Numbers for the
Descendants of Luveser McCrary
Chart 4

NOTES

Page 14.
1. For an excellent treatise on slave family life, see Herbert G. Gutman, *The Black Family in Slavery and Freedom, 1750-1925*. (New York: Vintage Books, 1976). Gutman "examines different aspects of the development of the slave family and enlarged slave kin group." Chapter One deals with the slaves and ex-slaves during and just after the Civil War." Gutman's research proved that "Despite a high rate of earlier involuntary marital breakup, large numbers of slave couples lived in long marriages and most slaves lived in double-headed households." p.xxii.

Page 47.
2. Gutman, Black Family in Slavery and Freedom, Chapter 6, "Somebody Knew my Name," pp.230-256. Gutman quotes many sources revealing that a large percentage of slaves adopted surnames different from their last owners. In Table 31, "Surnames of Slaves and Their Last Owners After Emancipation as Reportd by South Carolina and Texas Blacks Interviewed in 1937," 73% of South Carolina and 66% of Texas slaves interviewed took a different surname from the owner. p.245.

Ibid. p.245. "Men and women freed in 1865, selected, retained or changed surnames..." The only clue that I had to finding the owners of my slave ancestors was their surnames, McCants, McCrary and Riley. Since, according to Gutman, slaves did not always take the surname of the last owner, I strongly hoped that the owners had the same name as my ancestors.

Ibid. p. 238. "A few unusual plantation documents and scattered other evidence also show that Nineteenth Century slaves had different surnames from their owners."

Page 51.
3. Three groups of Talbot County Returns with names of the guardians were considered as having the names of my slaves ancestors. They were the Fanning family, the Gray and Snelling families. Research revealed marriage connections between the families and guardians of their minor children.

A daughter from the first wife of Matthew McCrary, (Jane Foster McCrary) had married Eddie McCrary Greene. Anna Greene married John McCriff/Moncrief in Baldwin County, 27 Feb. 1803. William Moncrief became guardian of the Fanning minors after Thomas Greene. Felix Greene also served as a guardian of Fanning minor children. Bryan Fanning married Elizabeth Greene in Wilkes County in 1822. Brown Fannin (sic) married Matilda Davis in Fayette County, Ga. David Moses, (name may have been recorded in reverse in some records) may be Moses Davis related to Matilda Davis who married Brown Fannin. A David Moses or Moses Davis is in the Fayette County 1830 Census. David Moses received "Vicey and child and Sindy," in Bartley McCrary's Inventory. (The child is believed to be Matilda McCants)

NOTES

See Record Group 1, page 80. Due to these McCrary-Greene-Fanning-Moncrief-Davis marriage connections and the appearance of the names Matilda and Missouri in the Fanning Returns, I considered the Fanning family as probable owners of my ancestors before John McCrary.

Robert Snelling's will listed my ancestors' names. Legatees (heirs) in the Division of William Snellings, Robert's father, included Jonathan Gray and Archibald Gray's two sons, John T. and James J. John T. purchased some of John McCrary's property in 1854. (J. T. Gray purchased "1000 sheep oats" and "5 bushels of peas," as shown on text pages, 137 and 138.) Robert Snellings was a guardian for Ariana Gray, a minor child. Robert Snelling's will, recorded in Talbot Co. Will Book A, pp.160-163, included this stipulation about the slaves, "Immediately after my death, my Exor. to dispose at public or private sale all of my Negro property: **Simon**, Harry, Bob, Jack & Jill, Betty, Mary, Henny, Eliza and Infant child, Andrew, **Matilda**, Jim, Molly, **Jane**..." I did not find the "Sale" for Robert Snelling's Negro property. The executor of the will was Robert's brother, John Snellings. The Snelling and Gray families were considered possible owners before John McCrary.

Page 77.
4. I consulted DAR records on descendants of four McCrary Revolutionary War soldiers who were applying for membership in the DAR. The four-page applications listed the names of the soldiers, their approximate birth and death dates, places of birth and death, names of wives and children. The applications also listed sources used by the applicants to prove their relationship to the four Revolutionary War soldiers. These records included documents I had accumulated on the McCrary family. With the repetition of so many names, I was anxious to see family relationships because my records showed the same slave names on several McCrary family records. The National Numbers for the records I consulted were: 724444-A719, 656131, 481134, 656131, 653-472, 574801, 746234, 737717, 513674, and 679318. Only one record was copied for inclusion in the text, the Pay Bill of Capt. James Dillard printed on text pages 203-206. From the records, I learned about the Revolutionary War service of John, Bartley, Thomas and Robert McCrary, their family marriages, land dealings, appearance in Georgia tax records and further places to search. Most importantly, I learned that they came from Laurens, County, South Carolina and went to Georgia after the war. I learned about their family relationships and *name* confusion was clarified.

In Bobby Gilmer Moss, *Roster of South Carolina Patriots in the American Revolution,* (Baltimore, Genealogical Publishing Co., 1985) the McCrary family service record is listed. John McCrary, Sr. served 83 days in the Militia during 1781. Matthew McCrary, Sr. served in the Militia before and after the fall of Charleston. Bartley McCrary served in the Militia after the fall of Charleston. Robert McCrary, was a Captain in the Militia in 1775 and was in the Florida Expedition under General Andrew Williamson. Robert became a Lieutenant Colonel under Col. James Williams, pp.609-610. McCrary fathers and sons served in the Revolution.

NOTES

Page 81.
5. The DAR records helped to solve the mystery about Albert G. Beckham after 1840 when his name no longer appeared in Georgia Federal Census Schedules. He left the state for Alabama and died in Elmore County. I went to libraries during family vacations in whatever places I happened to visit. A good habit formed was to search as many Georgia genealogical publications and family histories as time would allow. I learned about the Beckham family and discovered Georgia genealogical journals to be an excellent source for information on early Georgia settlers.

Page 84.
6. For a discussion relative to the most inhumane of common slave practices, that of dividing families, see Frederick Bancroft, *Slave-Trading in the Old South*, (New York: Frederick Ungar Publishing Co., 1959). "Where slaves and more slaves were regarded as the highest form and the most respected evidence of wealth, they were seldom reared expressly for the market ten or fifteen years off; yet the rearing of them was deemed most important and because the sale of at least some of them was likely either to pay debts, to obtain money or for division between heirs or legatees, that contingency was rarely lost sight of...If only part of a gang was to be disposed of, it was the young slaves." p.67.

Bancroft devotes chapters in his book to "Early Domestic Slave Trading," "Dividing Families," "Selling Children Separately," "Restrictions," and "Hiring Practices." Hiring practices was of special interest to this writer because, before the research, I was unaware of its frequency. "Hiring records" appeared most often in McCrary family records called "Returns." The "hiring records," enabled my research to follow more closely the footpaths of the McCrary slaves.

Ibid. p.145. Bancroft stated, "Slave-hiring was a restricted kind of slave-trading and was most common in all Southern States. It concerned not the title to the slave, but only his or her labor for a definite period or purpose and usually at a specific price...Prestige of some degree went with the ownership and the hiring of slaves...Self-interest prompted the owner to try to prevent his human property from suffering any physical injury...

Ibid. p. 145. Bancroft quoted a spokesman, Chancellor Johnston in 1839:

"Hired slaves are commonly treated more harshly, or with less care and attention, than those in possession of their owner. Their health is less attended to; they are less likely to increase, and their moral qualities are almost always deteriorated." Bancroft exprssed the view of the slaves to the practice. "To the slave, the hiring was less objectionble than sale to a bad master, but more objectionable than sale to a good master, for this brought a comfortable home and lasting associations."

NOTES

Slave hiring was one of scores of wrongs during slavery. However, sometimes a master hired a slave to a white artisan to be taught a skill, like carpentry, or shoemaking. A skill acquired in this manner helped many freedmen to support their families after emancipation.

Pages 121-122.
7. For a greater understanding of the true feelings of slaves, see Marion Wilson Starling, *The Slave Narrative, Its Place in American History*, (Washington, D.C.: Howard University Press, 1988). Starling includes a comprehensive list of research centers where copies of slave narratives are available for researchers. In their own words, slaves recorded the dreadful experiences of their lives.

While trying to identify my slave ancestors, ages were almost always omitted. I tried to guess the age of my female ancestors by observing the number of children. Their child-bearing years may have begun by the age of fifteen.

A "chief plague" in the lives of many slave girls was described in the narrative of Linda Brent, *Incidents in the Life of a Slave Girl, Written by Herself*, (Boston: Lydia Maria Child, 1861).

"I now entered my fifteenth year--a sad epoch in my life of a slave girl. My master began to whisper foul words in my ear. Young as I was, I could not remain ignorant of their import, I tried to treat them with indifference or contempt...I turned from him with disgust and hatred. But he was my master...He told me I was his property; that I must subject to his will in all things. My soul revolted against the mean tyranny. But where could I turn for protection? No matter whether the slave girl be as black as ebony or as fair as her mistress. In either case, there is no shadow of law to protect her from insult, from violence, or even from death; all these are inflicted by fiends who bear the shape of men...I know that some are too brutalized by slavery to feel the humiliation shrink from the memory of it." p.4.

Page 173.
8. This record showed the first appearance of the slave girl Emoline in the McCrary records. Was Emoline, Matilda McCants' daughter, Emily who married Abram Holton?

If Emoline is accepted as Matilda's daughter, Emily, then questions about the "Emily" listed in Catharine Daniel's Estate must be considered. Since the death of Catharine occurred *after* the decease of John McCrary, it is possible that Emily was purchased *from* John McCrary *before* his death. I found no record of that. Limitations always existed in the research.

After I saw Voucher #13 concerning medical attention given to the girl Emoline in John McCrary's records, I reviewed Catharine Daniel's Inventory and Sale and looked for Riley records.

NOTES

I discovered that Joseph Riley's Talbot County Inventory of 1850 listed an Emily, a woman. She was transferred to Joseph's minor son, John W. S. Riley, and Joseph's older son, Alexander Riley was appointed guardian of John. Another son, Thomas Riley served as administrator of Catharine Daniel's Estate.

In Pike County, Ga., 23 November 1837, William Riley married Susan Kilgo. Emily from Catharine Daniel's Estate is sold to S. W. Kilgore in 1859. However, S. W. Kilgore is not listed as a slave owner in Taylor nor Talbot County in 1860. The implication was that Negro property passed between the Riley, Daniel and Kilgore families. I continued to search for an Emily connected with the McCrary family.

Larkin Colbert had an Emily who was hired from his Talbot County Estate in 1849 to John McBryde in Talbot County. It was interesting to find that Wright Riley married Amanda McBride in Talbot County Marriage Book v. B. The Colbert surname was recorded in several McCrary records of Baldwin County. Wiley McCrary married Polly Colbert and William Colbert Married Lettice McCrary. William Colbert was a legatee in the final division of Bartley McCrary's Estate and received part of his Negro property, Ben, Joicey, Jim and Little Ben. (See Record Group No. 1) Andrew Colbert was one of the appraisers of John McCrary's property.

With all of these Colbert connections to the McCrary family, the "Emily" in the estate of Larkin Colbert could have been my ancestor Emily, daughter of Matilda and the mother of Peter, my great granduncle. Emily is listed with her son Peter in both 1870 and 1880 Taylor County Census Schedules. I was very sure of her identity; it was the search for her *owner* that boggled my research efforts. Frequent references to the Talbot County records were made because the district where the McCrary's lived in Talbot became Taylor County in 1852. My kinfolks were in Talbot County until the county boundary lines changed in 1852.

My ancestor, Emily, could have been owned by Larkin Colbert, Catharine Daniel and John McCrary, either or all of them. When slave families are separated, surnames and ages are omitted, given names varied in spelling, and the owners unknown, possibilities are limitless. My efforts to trail my ancestors through McCrary family connections was a good course to follow, but it held no definite assurances for identifying my folks with unquestionable certainty. My strongest belief is that the Emily, Abram and Mary on Catharine Daniel's Inventory were my kinfolks. Further research is needed for positive assurance.

Since a marriage record of Emily and her husband, Abram Holton was not found in Taylor County, I was further convinced that they were taken from the county after they were sold during the settlement of Catharine Daniel's Estate.

GLOSSARY

Below are legal terms used in Georgia County records which were compiled by personnel at the Georgia Archives.

Annual Return. A yearly report on the disposition of a deceased person's goods or property made to the court by an administrator or executor. Returns filed by guardians of minor children recorded income and expenditures for the support of the minor children.

Appraisements. Estimated value of articles of property of deceased persons.

Deed. A conveyance passing a present interest (as opposed to a will which passes no interest until after the death of the maker).

Deed of Gift. A conveyance passing a present interest prior to death.

Dismission. Discharge by the court of an executor or administrator who has completed his duties in regard to an estate's administration.

Division. Apportionment among heirs of an estate.

Intestate. Without making a will. The word is often used to identify the person himself, the one who died without making a will.

Guardian. One who legally has the care and management of the person or estate or both of a child during its minority, or of another adult who for some peculiarity of status, defect of age, self-control or understanding, is considered incapable of administering his own affairs.

Inventory. A detailed list of articles of property of a deceased person.

Letters of Administration. The instrument of appointment issued by a court by which an administrator is authorized to take charge and administer the goods and property of an intestate.

Minor. A person under the age of legal competence.

Personality. Personal property or chattles; ie. things which are movable in point of law as opposed to realty or real property.

Sale. Absolute transfer of property or goods in which title passes to the buyer.

Tax Digest. A list of taxable landowners in a county and the amount of tax paid or owed and the location of the land.

Probate. Proof of a will; i.e., act or process of proving a will in a court of law having jurisdiction over estate matters.

Voucher. A receipt or release which may serve as evidence of payment or discharge of a debt or certify to the correctness of an account.

Will. The legal declaration of a person's intention as to the disposition of his property after death.

SELECT BIBLIOGRAPHY

I list here the sources that I used in the writing of this book. This bibliography is not a complete record of all the works that I consulted. I have included the most relevant research sources with the purpose of guiding readers with interest in slave ancestral research. For further study in Afro-American history, a detail list of sources are cited in John Hope Franklin's "*From Slavery to Freedom: A History of Negro Americans*. New York: Alfred A. Knopf, 1980. For a Directory of Resources by states, see Charles L. Blockson, *Black Genealogy*, Baltimore: Black Classic Press, 1991.

BOOKS

Austin, Jeannette Holland. *Georgia Intestate Records*. Baltimore: Genealogical Publishing Co., Inc. 1986.

_____. *Index to Georgia Wills*. Baltimore: Genealogical Publishing Co., 1985.

_____. *Georgia Bible Records*. Baltimore: Genealogical Publishing Co., 1985.

Bancroft, Frederick. *Slave-Trading In The Old South*. New York: Frederic Ungar Publishing Co., 1959.

Biographical Souvenirs of the States of Georgia and Florida, 1889, Reprint. Easley, SC: Southern Historical Press, 1976.

Blair, Ruth. *Some Early Tax Digests of Georgia (1790-1818), Vidalia, Ga.:* Genealogical Reprints, 1971.

Breeden, James O., ed. *Advice Among Masters, The Ideal in Slave Management in the Old South*. Westport, Conn.: Greenwood Press, 1980.

Brent, Linda. *Incidents in the Life of a Slave Girl, Written By Herself. Boston:* Lydia Maria Child, 1861.

Brooks, Ted O., and Robert S. Davis, Jr. *Georgia Genealogical Work-book*. Atlanta: Genealogical Society, 1987.

Carter, Mary. *A Century of Warren County Georgia Wills, 1790-1890*. Albany, Ga.: .Georgia Pioneers, 1966.

Cook, Anna Maria Green. *History of Baldwin County, Georgia*. Spartanburg, SC: Reprint Co., 1878.

Davis, Robert Scott, Jr., *Research in Georgia*. Easley, SC: Southern Historical Press, 1981.

Davidson, William H. *A Rockaway in Talbot: Travels In An Old Georgia County*. 4 vols. West Point, Ga: Hester Printing Co. 1983-

Douglass, Frederick. *My Bondage and My Freedom*. 1855, reprint, with a Foreword by Larone Bennett, Jr., Chicago: Johnson Publishing Co., 1970.

Eakle, Arlene, and Johni Cerny. *The Source: A Guidebook of American Genealogy*. Salt Lake City, Utah: Ancestry Publishing, 1984.

Everton, George B., Sr., ed. *The Handy Book for Genealogists*. 7th ed. Logan, Utah: Everton Publishers, Inc., 1981.

Franklin, John Hope. *From Slavery to Freedom: A History Of Negro Americans*. New York: Alfred A. Knopf, 1980.

Government Printing Office. *Where to Write for Birth and Death Records*. Washington, DC: Government Printing Office.

Genovese, Eugene D. *Roll Jordan Roll: The World the Slaves Made*. New York: Vinage Books, 1976.

Green, Robert L. Mrs., "Baldwin County 1810 Tax List." *Georgia Genealogical Magazine, No.71-2 (1979): 11-20.*

Gutman, Herbert G. *The Black Family in Slavery and Freedom, 1750-1925.* New York: Pantheon Books, 1976.

Handy Book for Genealogists. 6th ed. Edited by George B. Everton, Sr. Logan, Utah: Everton Publishers, Inc., 1981.

Jones, Jacqueline. *Labor of Love, Labor of Sorrow: Black Women, Work, and the Family From Slavery to the Present.* New York: Basic Books, Inc., 1985.

Kirkham, E. Kay. *The Handwriting of American Records For a Period of 300 Years.* Logan, Utah: Everton Publishers, Inc., 1973.

_____. *How To Read the Handwriting and Records of Early America.* Logan, Utah: Everton Publishers, Inc., 1965.

An Index to Georgia Tax Digests. 5 vols. Spartanburg, SC: The Reprint Co., 1986.

Lest We Forget, A Guide to Genealogical Research In The Nation's Capitol. 8th ed. Annandale, VA: The Annandale Stake of The Church of Jesus Christ of Latter-Day Saints, 1992.

Lucas, Silas Emmett, Jr. *Some Georgia County Records, Being Some of the Legal Records of Columbia, Hancock, Jefferson, and Warren County, Ga.* Easley, SC:. Southern Historical Press. 1977.

Maddox, Joseph, and Mary Carter. *37,000 Early Georgia Marriages.* N.P., 1975. Covers 29 counties; names are from *Georgia Pioneer Magazine.*

_____. *40,000 Early Georgia Marriages.* Rev. ed. N.P., 1977. Covers 29 counties.

Moss, Bobby Gilmer. *Roster of South Carolina Patriots in the American Revolution.* Baltimore: Genealogical Publishing Co., Inc., 1985.

Reynolds, Harriet Dickson. *Colonel Robert McCrary (1732-1809) of North Carolina and Some of His Descendants.* Typescript. at the National Society, Daughters of the American Revolution, Washington, DC.

Rigsby, Lewis W. *Historic Georgia Families.* Baltimore: Genealogical Publishing Co., 1969.

Starling, Marion Wilson. *The Slave Narrative, Its Place In American History.* 2nd ed. Washington, DC: Howard University Press, 1988.

Wood, Virginia S., and Ralph V. Wood. *The 1805 Georgia Land Lottery.* Cambridge: The Greenwood Press, 1964.

GENEALOGY

Blockson, Charles L., and Ron Fry. *Black Genealogy.* Baltimore: Black Classic Press, 1991.

Doane, Gilbert Harry, and James B. Bell. *Searching For Your Ancestors, The How and Why of Genealogy.* Minneapolis: University of Minnesota Press, 1973

Streets, David H. *Slave Genealogy: A Research Guide with Case Studies.* Bowie, MD.: Heritage Books, Inc., 1986

Rose, James, and Alice Eichholz. *Black Genesis.* Detroit: Gale Research Co., 1978.

Walker, James D. *Black Genealogy: How to Begin.* Athens, Ga.: University of Georgia Center for Continuing Education, 1977.

Westin, Jeane. *Finding Your Roots*: How Every American Can Trace His Ancestors at Home and Abroad. Los Angeles: St. Martins Press, 1977.

FEDERAL CENSUS SCHEDULES

National Archives. Washington, DC. United States Department of Commerce, Bureau of the Census, *Manuscript Population Schedules for the Fourth, Fifth, Sixth, Seventh, Eighth, Ninth, Tenth, Eleventh, Twelfth, Thirteenth and Fourteenth Censuses (1820, 1830, 1840, 1850, 1860, 1870, 1880, 1900, 1910 and 1920,* for Hancock, Baldwin, Talbot, Taylor, Pike, Warren and Bibb Counties in Georgia) Available on microfilm.

_____. Manuscript Slave Schedules for the Seventh and Eighth Censuses. (1850 and 1860) for Talbot County, Georgia.

_____. Manuscript Slave Schedule for the Eighth Census for Taylor County, Georgia.

_____. Manuscript Manufactures Schedule for the Eleventh Census, Taylor County, Georgia (1880).

PERIODICALS

Georgia Journal and Messenger Newspaper, 22 November 1854.

Taylor County News, Special Edition, 1952, Butler, Georgia

The Georgia Genealogical Magazine
Southern Historical Press
P.O..Box 738
Easley, SC 29641-0738

Georgia
Genealogical Society Quarterly
Georgia Genealogical Society
P.O. Box 38066
Atlanta, GA 30334

Georgia Pioneers Magazine
Georgia Pioneers
P.O. Box 1028
Albany, GA 31702

Journal of Negro History
Association For The Study of
Afro-American Life and History
Morehouse College
Box 20
Atlanta, GA 30314

Journal of the
Afro-American Historical and
Genealogical Society
P.O. Box 73086
Washington, DC 20056-3086

BIBLIOGRAPHY

PROBATE RECORDS

Microfilm available from the Family History Center, Church of Jesus Christ of Latter-Day Saints, Salt Lake City, Utah.

Georgia. Court of Ordinary, Baldwin County Probate Record
Number			
	0415171	Inventories and Appraisements	
	0423186	Court Minutes	1808-1854
	0423187	Court Minutes	1806-1814
	0423188	Court Minutes	1827-1844
	0423189	Court Minutes	1844-1868
	0423190	Court Minutes, Trial of Slaves	1812-1838, 1837-1841
	0415173	Returns	1813-1839
	0414174	Returns	1831-1852, 1855-1856

Georgia. Court of Ordinary, Hancock County
	0847837	Tax Digest	1796, 1804, 1837, 1853, 1864
	0222008	Index, Deeds and Mortgages, v. A-C	1794-1887
	0222010	Deeds & Mortgages, v. AB-C	1794-1800

Georgia. Vital Records, Taylor County
	0321087	Marriages v.Z.	1865-1871
	0321088	Marriages v.4.	1872-1897, 1897-1910
		Court of Ordinary	
	0321089	Index to Probate Records	
	0321090	Wills	1853-1917
	0321098	Inventories and Appraisements	1852-1952
	0321099	Distribution of Estates	1858-1887
	0321100	Estate Sales	1852-1909
	0321101	Vouchers	1852-1858
	0321102	Returns and Vouchers	1858-1864
	0321107	Index, Deeds & Mortgages	1852-1932
	0321110	Deeds & Mortgages v.A-B	1852-1866

Georgia. Court of Ordinary, Talbot County
	0249371	Wills	1828-1928
	0249382	Inventories and Appraisements	1829-1855
	0249383	Inventories and Appraisements	1855-1877
	0249385	Annual Returns v.A-B	1828-1848
	0249386	Annual Returns v.C	1848-1853
	0249387	Annual Returns v.D	1853-1859
	0249388	Annual Returns v.E	
	0249409	Sales Books v.A-B-C	1856-1875
	0249410	Probate Records	

LIBRARIES AND ARCHIVES

Family History Lbrary
Church of Jesus Christ of Latter-Day Saints
Salt Lake City, Utah 84321

Georgia Department of Archives and History
330 Capitol Avenue, SE
Atlanta, GA 30334

LaGrange Archives
Troup County Regional Library
500 Broome St.
LaGrange, GA 30240

Library of Congress
Jefferson Building
1st Street and Independence Avenue
Washington, DC 20540

National Archives
Pennsylvania Ave. and 9th Street NW
Washington, DC 20036

National Archives, Atlanta Branch
1557 St. Joseph Avenue
East Point, GA 30344

National Society
Daughters of the American Revolution Library (DAR)
1776 "D" Street, NW
Washington, DC 20006-5392

Vital Records Service
State Department of Human Resources
47 Trinity Avenue, SW
Atlanta, GA 30334

RESEARCH CENTER

Schomburg Center for Research in Black Culture
515 Malcolm X Blvd (Harlem)
New York, New York 10037

NAME INDEX

This index lists names with different spellings together, example, **Jonathan/Johnathan**, etc. Females are listed by both maiden and married names. Slave documents omitted surnames and gave only given or first names. Slave names are printed under the names of their slaveowners. The slaveowner's name appears with the text page for his or her **slave list**. A series of page numbers following a slave's name are for that individual slave. Slave names appeared in documents with a variety of spellings. The names are placed together for the same individual slave as follows: Zussre/Missouri/Missoury.

Anderson
    John Henry, Jr. 236; John Henry, Sr. 236; John Henry, III 236, Julie L. 148, 152; Julie LaVera 236, Mary Joyce Edge 236
Andrews, Dr. 159

Barrow 210
Bateman
    Bryant 79, 111, 145; Charity 79, 145
Becham
    A. G. 69, 115; Albert G. 73, 74, 79, 81, 111, 145; Mary 73, 79, 81, 111, 145
Beall
    Amelia Milly 211, J. D. 173
Bells, Dr. 159
Berry/Falkenberry
    James F. 145, 179, 199; Mary 179
Bivins, S. 115
Black, A. 115
Bradley
    Ashley 236, Irene Katrinka 236, Jeffrey Lane 236, Tara Amani 236
Briggs, Antoinette 237
Brinson
    Jacob Ponder, Jr. 237, Jacob Ponder, Sr. 237, Shannon Corey 237, Sheralyn Darnell 237
Buck 23
Bucks, Wyatt 34
Bush
    Darryl 236, Kai Amani 236, Kristian 236
Butt, Eldrige C. 181

Calton, Sary 97, 145
Chambers, David 210
Chapman
    John 145, 227; Missouri H. 145
Colbert
    Andrew J. 181, Jonathan/Johnathan 105; Lettice 111, William 81, 111, 115, 117, 145
Coleman, Jane 47, 193
Collins
    Theodore 237, Venita Patrice 237
Cosby, Ardna 146
Crane, A. 103

Culpepper
    Benjamin 109
        Slaves: Austin 109, Edy 109, James 109

Daniel
    Caroline 43, Catharne, 40, Catharine 39, 40, 43, 46, 47, 48; Emily 39, 47; Jenny 39, 40, 47; Lovynia 39, 40; Lucinda 40; Mary 39, 40
Darryl 225
Davis, Emma 234
Dean, William 107
Deloach, Christopher Columbus 148
Dickson, C. B. 173
Dillard, Capt. James 207, 209, 211
Drane
    Dr. 159; Matthews 167, 169; William 167, 169, 175
Duncan
    Ann 36; Ben 33, 34, 35; Charlotte 34; Delcy 34; Emeline 34; Emily 33, 34, 35, 36; Emoline 33, 34; Green 33, 34, 35; Hannah 33, 34, 35; Harrey 35; Harrison 35; James 33, 34, 35; James M. 34, 36; Lucretia 34, 35, 36; Mary 36; Matilda 33, 34, 35; Moses 33, 34, 35; Penny 33, 34, 35; Silva 36; Susan, 34, 36; Thadeus F. 35, 36; Warren 33, 35; Wiley 36; William 35
Durden/Durding/Durdon
    William 109, 115, 117, 145

Eason, Nancy 146
Echols, Arlene 21
Edge, Mary Joyce 236

Fanning 51, 56, 58
    Elizabeth 57; John 57; Mary 57
Fanning, James G. 57
    Slaves: Annis 57; Basen 57; Charlotte 57; Ciller 57; Dennis 57; Dinah 57; Lucy 57; Martha 57; Matilda 57; 58; Nancy 57; Patience 57; Peter 57; Simon 57; Simon 57; Peter 57;
Feagan, Aaron 105

INDEX

Fears
Bedie, 62; Caroline 62; Gus 62; Joel 59, 62; Joel Van, Jr. 236; Joel Van, Sr. 236; Mary Louvenia Jackson 236; Sarah Battle Long 62

Ficklin, C. F. 181, 193
Freeney, Gillah 210

Goins
Christopher Caleb 236; Doris Jackson 236; Edward Ellis, Jr. 236; Edward Ellis, Sr. 236; Ellis Josiah 236; Irene Katrinka 236; Kadesha Shantay 236; Katrice Ancel 236; Kristian 236; Krystel Renel 236; Ramona Elinor 236

Goode, William 210

Gray
Albert 51; John T. 175

Griffeth, James 5
Grigg, Wm. 101, 103

Hall, D. M. 115

Haisley
Glenn, Jr. 236; Glenn, Sr. 236; Kirby 236

Hamilton, J. A. 159, 165; W. J. 159, 165
Hansel, Wiliam 115
Harris, Thomas 83
Hay, James C. 117,
Herrington, Able 145
Hillsman, Josiah 175
Holbon, Abe 8
Holcomb, F. P. 148
Holliman, Missouri 227

Holton
Abe 4, 7, 59, 60; Abraham 8, 237; Abram 9, 22, 39, 40, 43, 46, 47, 60, 73, 232, 233, 234, 236; Add 1; Annie 1; Baley/Bailey 8, 9, 237; Dorcus/Dorceus 7, 8, 9, 14, 36, 236; Emily 7, 8, 9, 22, 39, 40, 46, 47, 59, 73, 232, 233, 234; Emma (Ray Bay Davis) 1, 14, 36, 234, 236; Marcelee 70; Peter 1, 2, 7, 8, 9, 73, 237; Peter, Jr. 1

Howe
Catharine 47; Harriet 48

Hubbard, John 83
Huff, J.J. 193,
Hutchings, Charles 209

Jackson
Annie Doris 236; Antoinette Briggs 237; Christine 237; Christopher Patrick 236; Christy Briggs 237; Courtney 237; Dena 237; Doris 236; Jewell Moore 153, 236; Jimmie Dean 237; Mary Louvenia 70, 236; John S. 40, 43, 47; Sandra 237; Sheralyn Darnell 237; Steven Girard 237; Sylvester 153, 236

Jameson, Geo. 109
Jamieson, Catherine L. 146

Johnson
Abel 4, 5, 7; Abraham 4, 7, 8, 231, 232; Christine 237; Damon Sylvan 237; Irene 227; Marvin Richard, Jr. 237; Marvin Richard, Sr. 237; Tracey Michelle 237; Missouri/Missoury 7, 8, 14, 47, 134

Jones
Bernard, 219; Henry 105; LaVerne 219

Jourdan, Matthew 145

Kilgore
Ann 43; S. W. 40, 47; Simon 43; Solomon 43

Lamar, Thomas 210
LeBlanc, Paulette 237
Lee, Thos. 117
Lincoln 4, 121
Lloyd, A. 161
Long, Henry 62; Sarah Battle 62

MaGriff, Richard 210
Mary 23

McCants
A., 131; Andrew 15, 17, 61, 145, 154, 157, 159, 179, 183, 185, 191, 193, 201; Andrew J. 17; Bartley 157, 179; Bartley L. 185; Becky 51, 52, 69, 89, 129; Charles 134; Eddy 193; Eliza 4, 9; Emily 236; G. 179; George R. 193; Hampton 134; Henry 15; 157; Henry G. B. 185; Isabella 4, 7, 9, 141, 237; Issac 134; J. B. 193; J. M. 60; Jane 157, 193; James 17; Jeremiah C. 17,193; Jeremiah H. 193; John 157; John A. 17; John L. B. 185; Margaret 17; Mahaley 193; Mary 134; Mary C. E. 193; Matilda/Matildy 1, 4, 5, 7, 8, 15, 18, 22, 39, 46, 47, 48, 51, 52, 58, 59, 62, 69, 70, 73, 89, 129, 133, 134, 141, 219, 237; Missouri/Missoury 4, 5, 22, 46, 47, 48, 62, 69, 89, 133, 134, 141 237; Phillis/Philice 134; Sarah Jane 185, Sarah L. 193; Sillie 134; Simon 1, 4, 5, 7, 8, 9, 14, 15, 22, 39, 46, 47, 48, 56, 58, 59, 70, 73, 134, 154, 229, 231, 232, 233, 236; Sylvia 134; Tildy 1, 9, 14, 51, 56; Wash; 193;

William G. 157; Wright 134; Zussre 51, 52, 69, 129
Mccants, Andrew (d.1862) 191
  Slaves: Lewis 191; Luisa 191; Hannah 191; Eliza 191; James 191; Charles 191; Curtis 191; Rubin 191
McCrary
  Albert 134; Amelia Milly 211; Andrew 145; Ardna 146; B. 185; Bartley, Sr. 17, 62, 67, 68, 69, 70, 73, 75, 77, 81, 83, 89, 91, 107, 117, 118, 122, 123, 143, 145, 148, 152, 153, 161, 163, 170, 173, 175, 176, 179, 197, 201, 207, 210, 211, 212, 216, 219, 220, 226, 228; Bartley, Jr. 17, 68, 79, 111, 113, 115, 117, 118, 121, 129, 131, 212; Catherine, L. 146; Charity 79; Colon 17; Elizabeth 145, 191; Flurnoy 134; G. 131; G. F. 159; Gillah/Gilliah 17; Gilly 179, 193; Gilly F. 197; Gracey 145; H. B. 131; Hampton 134; Harriet 134; Henry 17, 123, 129, 131, 159, 179, 189, 190, 228; Henty B. 201; Isaac 68, 91, 105, 107, 109, 145, 146, 210, 211, 212, 216; J. C. 181; J. P. 159; James 68, 79, 81, 103, 111, 115, 145, 212, 227; James B. 211; Jane 79, 91, 103, 129, 145, 183, 209, 211, 212, 213, 216, 220, 228; Jane G. 179, 189, 199; Jenny 145, 228; John 17, 18, 51, 52, 55, 56, 58, 60, 61, 62, 68, 69, 73, 79, 81, 89, 99, 105, 107, 109, 111, 115, 117, 129, 131, 133, 141, 143, 145, 146, 147, 148, 152, 153, 157, 159-171, 173, 175, 176, 183, 189, 190, 191, 193, 197, 207, 209, 210, 212, 220, 225, 228, 229; John A. 17; John A. I/J. 179, 199; John B. 17, 18; John, Jr. 68, 207, 211, 212, 213, 225, 226, 228; John, Sr. 68, 93, 209, 210, 211, 212, 213, 215, 216, 226, 228; Jonathan/Johnathan 68, 91, 101, 103, 121, 129, 179, 209, 210, 211, 212, 216, 220, 226, 228; Jonathan B. 146; Jonathan P. 199; Joseph 134; Josh 237; Kinian 121; L. Q. C. 60, 159; Lucious Q. C. 189, 199, 213; Lettice 145, 228; Letty/Letitia 91, 93, 211, 212, 216; Louisa/Louiser 4, 5, 7, 14, 15, 22, 59, 70, 143, 219, 220; Lovenia 69, 70, 73, 79; Lovinia 4, 5, 7, 8, 14, 15, 22, 59, 70, 73, 129, 133, 141, 219, 220; Lucy 134; Martha 121, 145; Mary 73, 79, 111, 145, 179; Matthew/Mathew 91, 93, 109, 115, 117, 118, 121, 123, 146, 207, 209, 210, 211, 212, 216, 220, 228; Matthew, Jr. 210; Matthew, Sr. 210; Missouri H. 145, 227; Nancy 146; Ned 134, 237; Patsey 145; Peter 134; Prudence 134; Rachel 212; Rheuben 134, Robert 79, 93, 111, 134, 207, 209, 210, 211, 216, 220, 228; Sallie 134, Sarah 145, Sendy/Lucinda 237; Susan 134; Tabitha 121, 145; Thomas 207, 220; Veny, 51, 73, 99, 129, 131, 232; W. M. 79; Wiley, 79, 145; Willie 111, 115; William 17, 68, 79, 105, 107, 115, 117, 118, 121, 123, 134, 210, 212, 216; William, Jr. 121

SLAVE OWNERS

McCrary, Bartley (d.1826) 79 (Slave List 217)
  Slaves: Alfred 79, 81; Balkus 79, Ben 79, 81, 84; Bird 79, 81; Cesar 79, 93; Charity 79; Clark 79; Dick 79, 93; Ellick 79, George 79, Jim 79, 81, 84; Joicey 79, 81, 84, 133; Joshua/Josh 79, 83, 122; Hampton/ Hamp 79, 81, 84, 133; Hardy 79, John 79, London 79, 93, 113; Lovenia 79, 107, 122, 123; Mary 79, 81, 83, 122; Ned 79, 122, 133; Orrange, 79, 143, 144; Patience 79, 81, 111, 133; Patrick 79, 83; Patsey 79; Peter 79, 81, 133; Sam 79, Sindy 79, 122; Vicey 79, 83, 122, 133;
McCrary, Issac (d.1817) 105 (Slave List 217)
  Slaves: Betsy 105, 107, 109; Dick 107, 109; Dicy 105, 107, 109; Jude 105, 107; lucy 105. 107; Luvis/Lewis 105, 107, 109; Peter 105, 107; Saml 105, 107; Stephen 105, 107, 109
McCrary, John (d.1854) 134 (Slave List 217)
  Slaves: Allen, 134, 181; Bill 134, 181; Bucky/Becky 134, 152, 154, 181, 191, 212, 229; Caroline 134, 154, 181, 189; Cassa 134, 181, 189; Cresy 134, 181; Dick 134, 181; Eddy 134, 181; Emoline 134, 173; Flousury 134, 181; Frances 134, 181; Gus 134, 181; Hamp 134, 181; Issac 134, 181; Joe 134, 181; Litty 134, 181; Madison 134, 181; Mallissa 134, 181; Margaret 134, 181; Matilda/Tildy 134, 152, 153,

154, 176, 181, 191, 193, 212, 227, 229, 231, 233, 236; Ned, 154, 181, 189; Peter 134, 154, 181, 189; Phillis 134, 181; Ralia 134, 154, 181; Robert 134, 154, 181, 189; Rueben/ Ruben 134, 181; Sally/Sal 134, 154, 181, 189; Sarah 134, 181; Stephen 134, 181; Tom 134, 181; Touns 134, 181; Viny/Veny/ Vinus/Visues/ Lueser/Luveser 134, 152, 153, 154, 176, 181, 212, 220; Will, 134, 181, 189, 221, 227, 229, 231, 233, 236 Zussre/ Missoury/ Missouri 134, 152, 154, 176, 181, 191, 193, 212, 227, 229, 231, 232, 233
McCrary, John, Sr. (d.1814) 91 (Slave List 217)
    Slaves: Betty, Bill, Cassey/Cass 91, 93; Ceaser 91, Dick 91, Dycea/Dicey 91, Eden/Eaden 91, 93; John 91, London 91, 113; Rachel 91, Wynney/Winny 91, 97
McCrary, Jonathan (d.1808) 97 (Slave List 217)
    Slaves: Beck 97, 99; Clary 97, 99, 211, 212; Jack 97, 99; Jo/Joe 99, Luveser/Louesa 97, 99, 103, 211; Reuben/Rubin 97, 99; Winny 99
McCrary, Matthew (d.1816)
    Slaves: Bill 217, Chapman 217, Chaney 217, Cloe 217, Eden 217, George 217, Hagar 217, Hannah 217, Joe 217, Jude 217, Maria 217, Nancy 217, Patsy 217, Peter 217, Tom 217
McCrary, Matthew (d.1846) 123 (Slave List 217)
    Slaves: Daniel 123, Fanny 123
McCrary, Robert (d.1827) 111 (Slave List 217)
    Slaves: Alfred 123, Bird 123, Hardy 123, London 113
McCrary, William (d. 1819) 115 (Slave List 217)
    Slaves: Bazel 115, 117, 121; Ben115, 117, 121; John 115, 118, 121; Jude 115, 117, 121; Lucy 115, Ned 115, 117, 121; Patience 115, 117, 121; Peter 115, 117, 118, 121; Old Sam 115, 117, 121; Henry 115
McKinney
    Danny 237, Kia Marie 237, Venita Patrice 237, William Joseph 237
McLendon, Jan 75
Miller, Ezekiel 115
Missouri 133

Montgomery
    James 209, Samuel 115
Moore
    Earma 237, Emma Lee 237; Fanny 219, Irene 236; Jewell 236, Julious 237, Louise 237, Lucious 236
Morand/Moreman
    A. W. 43; Anna 43; D. W. 40; 43, 47; E. W. 43; J. D. 43; James 43
Moreman, Ann 40, 43
Morgan, Isaac 210
Moses, David 79, 111, 122, 145
Mote, Daniel 209
Mukey/Murkey Issac 181, 183

Nicholes, H. J. 148
Nicholson, Nathaniel 177

Olguin, Ramona Elinor 236
Owens, A. F. 43

Parker, John 105
Poindexter, Jenny/Jane 79, 81, 83, 111, 122, 143, 145, 216
    Slaves: Mary 83, 84; Harriet 83, Hampton 83, 84; Roady/Rhoda 83
Pursley, Dawna Felecia 237

Ragland
    E. 40, 43; Eve 40, 43, 47; G. 161; Hudson 40; Thomas 159
Rankin, Maurine 219
Ray
    A. C. Jay 237, Charley/Charlton 8, 9, 36, 236; Emma 9, Irene 9, 236; Susie 9, 237
Rease, Benjamin F. 175
Riddle, Wiley 145
Riley
    Harriet Howe 48, Joseph 17, Joseph, Jr. 17, M. L. 60, Mary 8, 15, 18, 39, 40, 47, 59, 233; Nancy 17, 18; Peter E. 60; T. J. 60 Thomas J. 17, 39, 47, 48; Thomas Jefferson 48, William 17
Roper, James E. 171, 173
Ross, George 209
Rubin 23
Rucker
    F. S. 159, J. A. 159

Salter, Richard 145
Sarah 23
Scurlock, John 145
Smead, Elijah 210
Steel, Eve 40
Sturdivant
    John 157, 159, 163, 181, 183, 185, 201 Susie 23 Sylvia 133

Thomas, Jessie 83
Tilly 210
Townsend, Henry 209
Turner
    John 58, Tracey Michelle 237

Visage, Sam/Samuel W. 159, 167

Wadsworth 209
Wallace, John H. 171
Weldon, Sarah J. 179
White
    Charles David 34, James 34

Wilder, Tilman Buckner 210
william, John 115, 117,
Willis, Britton 115
Woods
    Abel 210; Martha E. 35
Woolsey, William 83
Wright, John 237

The Author

Mary L. JACKSON FEARS

Mary Louvenia Jackson Fears is a retired public school media specialist. Aside from her interest in genealogical research and lecturing, she is a professional storyteller. She is the author of the companion book to this publication, The Jackson-Moore Family History and Genealogy.

She is a graduate of Bethune-Cookman College, Daytona Beach, Florida and holds a master's degree in Library and Information Science from Florida State University, Tallahassee, Florida.

The author resides in Daytona Beach, Florida with her husband, Joel V. Fears, Sr. and Joel, Jr. Another son and grandson, John H. Anderson, Jr. and John III, live in Tallahassee, Florida.

www.ingramcontent.com/pod-product-compliance
Lightning Source LLC
Chambersburg PA
CBHW081417230426
43668CB00016B/2267